JUST MAKING MOVIES

Just Making
Movies

Company Directors on the Studio System

Ronald L. Davis

University Press of Mississippi   Jackson

www.upress.state.ms.us

The University Press of Mississippi is a member
of the Association of American University Presses.

Illustration credits: Pages 2, 138, 154, and 204, courtesy of Jerry
Ohlinger's Movie Material Store; pages 26, 40, 60, 82, 102, 124,
172, 190, courtesy of Photofest

12 11 10 09 08 07 06 05 04   4 3 2 1

♾

Library of Congress Cataloging-in-Publication Data

Davis, Ronald L.
 Just making movies : company directors on the studio system /
Ronald L. Davis.
    p. cm.
 Includes index.
 ISBN 1-57806-690-5 (cloth : alk. paper) — ISBN 1-57806-691-3
(pbk. : alk. paper)
   1. Motion picture producers and directors—United States—
Interviews. 2. Motion picture industry—United States.
3. Motion pictures—Production and direction. I. Title.
PN1998.2.D38   2005
791.43002'33'092273—dc22   2004005495

British Library Cataloging-in-Publication Data available

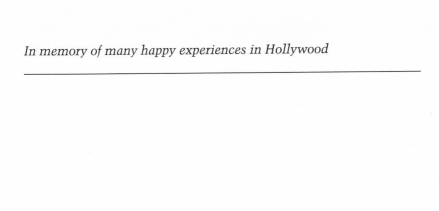

In memory of many happy experiences in Hollywood

CONTENTS

INTRODUCTION

Motion pictures have often been called the director's medium, since a director puts his or her stamp on the finished film far more than with plays in the live theater. Most of the classic movie directors insisted on full control over their projects and assumed a dictatorial position. "Every picture has a certain rhythm which only one man can give it," director Fritz Lang maintained. "That man is the director. He has to be like the captain of a ship." Stories abound about strong Hollywood directors—John Ford, Frank Capra, Alfred Hitchcock, among others—refusing to work so long as a producer or a meddlesome studio executive was present on the set. "Don't you have an office?" Ford barked at a prying producer, who meekly accepted that the authoritarian director was in command and retreated, convinced that the quality of the finished film would justify Ford's autocratic attitude. After all, the legendary director eventually won six Academy Awards, four for feature films and two for documentaries. No slouch in the Oscar's race, Frank Capra earned three Academy Awards within a five-year period, which seemed to validate his motto of "one man, one film." That is, that one person, the director, makes the film. Alfred Hitchcock never won an Oscar for his direction, although he was nominated and his film *Rebecca* earned the Best Picture award in 1940, yet his work was recognized as technically superb and Hitchcock himself probably became better known to the general public than any of Hollywood's Golden Age directors since Cecil B. DeMille.

The old studios could afford to pamper their prestige directors and grant them the autonomy to become *auteurs*, a term originating with French director Francois Truffaut, who argued that the director is the true author of a completed film, since the director is the force that blends the component arts and techniques into a harmonious whole. But Hollywood's big studio system operated like factories, turning out product—ideally fifty-two movies a year, one to supply showcase theaters across the country with a new bill each week—with profit the overriding goal. The old studio heads were expert showmen but equally shrewd businessmen, whose business was entertainment. While the moguls did not expect to make money on every picture their assembly line produced, studio executives made sure that the company's prestige films were balanced by movies calculated for quick commercial results. Hollywood's major studios in the late 1930s, 1940s, and early 1950s—Metro-Goldwyn-Mayer, Paramount, Warner Bros., Twentieth Century-Fox, and RKO—all owned or controlled a chain of theaters, and those theaters needed a weekly product and in turn assured producers of a ready market. The studios' assembly lines therefore ground out motion pictures much as Henry Ford's plants manufactured automobiles and General Electric's factories assembled home appliances. "It was not called the motion picture industry for nothing," said veteran screenwriter Julius Epstein, who with his twin brother, Philip, was part of the team responsible for the final script of *Casablanca* (1942). Churning out screenplays for Warner Bros. in those days, Epstein said, "was like working at belts in a factory. The studio produced a picture a week."

Although the budget-minded moguls were willing to risk big money on important productions directed by their top filmmakers, they were far less openhanded with routine pictures that were assigned to lesser directors the company had under long-term contract. Each of the big studios maintained a group of company directors that shot the scripts handed to them and rarely initiated and developed their own projects. They were workmanlike in their craft and could be relied on to finish pictures on time and within the designated budget. These company directors were highly competent yet in most cases added fewer distinctive touches to the final film than the special value the great directors could be expected to deliver.

Most of the secondary directors came up through the ranks of the studios. Some began as office boys or messenger boys and graduated to assistant directors or dialogue coaches before being assigned their own pictures. Like the prestige directors, they approached their work with double vision—one eye toward artistic merit, the other toward box office success. "We knew that if the pictures did no business," director Vincent Sherman said, "there would be no studio." When option time came around, when studio executives determined whether or not the services of talent under contract would be continued, Warner Bros.' production head, Jack Warner, would inquire what pictures the director in question had made during the past year and whether or not that person's films had made money. If they had, the option was likely picked up.

Attuned to a profit-oriented system, the company directors gave as much attention to detail as time and budget would permit. They recognized that many of the pictures they were assigned were not of high quality yet remained hopeful that a better project would follow. Whereas the so-called *auteur* directors could command top designers, the best cinematographers, and the most illustrious of the studio's stars, lesser directors frequently had to settle for young contract players and second best, although most studio craftspeople were of proficient quality. Sometimes a director was consigned to a budget picture, often a revision of a script the studio had filmed profitably a few years earlier, with the express purpose of putting certain personnel the studio had under contract to work. Vincent Sherman agreed to that makeshift arrangement on Warner Bros.' *Backfire* and as a reward was soon given *The Hasty Heart*, a truly fine picture which he made in England in 1949 to take advantage of the studio's frozen assets abroad.

From time to time company directors who yearned for a continuous stretch of their talent grew frustrated with the scripts assigned to them. What the studios offered them as appeasement was a constant supply of properties to film, the equipment and facilities to do acceptable work, a guaranteed substantial income, and the hope of making an occasional film that was superior. Seasoned studio craftsmen knew how to keep within a modest budget and produce movies that looked more important than they were. Bryan Foy, who headed budget pictures at Warner Bros., advised directors working on an inexpensive production: "Keep it moving. You can't see the teeth on a buzzsaw." Filmmakers at all studios agreed that no picture was better than its script. "If you've got a good script," veteran director Andrew Stone said, "let the office boy direct it. With good actors and a good script, anybody can direct." Most directors would consider Stone's comment an overstatement and contend that if they couldn't add value even to a good script, they weren't much of a director. But certainly working with an outright bad screenplay doomed the project to failure.

What sold most Hollywood films in the Golden Era were its stars, and the publicity departments of the big studios were clever and aggressive in amplifying the glamour of contract players. Yet the director remained the major creator after the script was written and the leader that shaped a project into a cinematic achievement. Even those filmmakers incapable of putting much of a distinct trademark on their work had acquired an understanding of what were the key scenes in a script, skill at motivating actors, and a keen sense of the visual.

The director's first obligation upon receiving a script was to confer with the writer or writers who developed the screenplay in conjunction with the producer. Changes in the script might be suggested, and while those alterations were being made the director probably would spend time scouting locations, any exteriors needed away from the studio. Discussions were also held with the set and costume designers to make sure that the proper mood would be projected in each scene to develop the characters and further the underlying concept of the film. Conferences might also be scheduled with the musician who was to compose the score for the movie, since the texture of the music must serve the drama. In advance of these meetings the director had probably spent time researching and studying the period, the place, and the society involved in the story to be filmed. No matter what their prior experience might be, skilled filmmakers agreed that careful preparation was an essential part—at least half—of a director's job, since only through detailed planning could the shooting of a picture be expected to go smoothly.

Before a project went before the cameras, an assistant director prepared a breakdown of the script that listed, for each set, the scenes to be shot there, the actors needed, and the wardrobe and props that would be required. From that breakdown the assistant director, working with the director and the unit manager, would prepare a daily shooting schedule. It was the assistant director's job to see that the director had everything needed for each day's work, including whatever extras would be required for the day's shoot. No matter how thorough the planning, improvisations occasionally, sometimes frequently, had to be made on the set, including last-minute modifications in the dialogue to make it play better. Although the less prestigious directors lacked the power to make unilateral changes and dictate the way director-producers did, they nonetheless were the acknowledged force in command of the set. The consensus among virtually all classic filmmakers was that as much of the story as possible should be told with the camera.

For dramatic stories most of the old directors favored working in black and white. Filming in color was far more expensive and was largely reserved for musicals, Westerns, and outdoor adventure pictures. Even the lesser contract directors felt privileged to have at their disposal the studio's stable of experienced character actors, who added cohesion and depth to pictures. With the studio's storehouse of props and expert special effects department available for use, little was impossible for a director with imagination and taste, and the company's capacity to market the completed movie stretched to global proportions.

On most days when a production was being filmed, the directors and camera crew arrived at the studio by 8 A.M. While the director looked in on the picture's stars as they made up for the day's work, the camera crew arranged the first setup, having been instructed the evening before on what it would be. By 9:00 the set would normally be lighted properly, with stand-ins going through the action for the technicians. Once the actors arrived on the set and the full company had assembled, it was the director's job to convey assurance, inspire confidence, and encourage performers to take chances that might add nuances to their interpretation. More than anything the atmosphere of a set was a reflection of the director's personality. Henry Hathaway's bad temper and blistering tongue were notorious and often created tension on his sets, whereas Henry Koster's gentle disposition encouraged a relaxed mood that erupted into laughter and fun between takes. Astute directors recognized the importance of keeping a set alive during the lengthy lulls while the electricians, camera crew, and sound technicians prepared the next setup. It was desirable not to let the actors' energy level drop, and some directors handled the problem by talking to their actors or encouraging conversation among them.

Every director had a personal approach to guiding performances. Some were essentially ushers, telling actors where to move. Others acted out what they wanted from players, and still others inspired actors to perform on a higher level through quiet talks out of earshot from the rest of the cast. Arthur Lubin discovered early in his career that yelling at actors was the worst thing he could do. He got much better results by taking them aside and saying "Do this or do that." A few directors, particularly in filming comedy scenes, served as an appreciative audience during takes, spacing laughter so that it could be edited out and not interfere with the recorded dialogue. Seasoned stage actors particularly often needed to be reminded to hold down their performance and not overdo for the camera, which captured the slightest movement. In close-ups, actors learned, it was better to think the part rather than act it.

Like the great filmmakers, each of the company directors was skilled enough to devise his own method of handling actors and problems that arose in their work. Joseph Newman recognized that "we're all human beings and we all have doubts and phobias," and he developed a reassuring way of easing those during production difficulties. Charles Walters realized that he lacked the stature to demand the script revisions that he thought were necessary on *Easter Parade*, since the expensive musical was only his second time to direct. He solved the problem by getting his stars behind the changes he wanted and letting them make the demands. Vincent Sherman, who had been a writer before becoming a director, had a sense for taut structure in drama and proved himself valuable enough to his studio to be allowed to adjust scenes until he felt the balance was right.

Above all, the successful director had to be a problem solver. It was essential for the filmmaker to know the rudiments of photography and film editing. To not give the cutters the coverage they needed for the edited film could cost the studio money if retakes later became necessary. Yet company directors particularly were ever mindful of costs, and the wise ones knew that by giving the cutters too much film they ran the risk of having their concept of the movie distorted. Through the entire shoot the director had to maintain a preconceived notion of what the film was about and how it should look on the screen. As in a chess game, the filmmaker had to anticipate a multitude of moves in advance, yet maintain a degree of flexibility. In time the veteran director developed instincts, automatically viewed the day's work in terms of camera setups, became adept at logistics, and knew how to shape the material at hand so that the pieces fit together with the right dramatic punch and whatever mood the filmmaker thought was needed.

Moving a company unnecessarily from one set to another wasted time and cost the studio money. At the end of each day's work on a shoot an assistant director made out a production report, logging the scenes that had been completed, the number of setups used, the amount of film exposed, and any other pertinent information. Every morning the producer knew precisely how much the picture had cost up to that point from the report delivered to him.

Most moviemakers today are products of film schools, but in the big studio era directors learned their craft mainly from observation and practice. Even experienced directors who came to Hollywood from the stage had to learn motion picture technique. Female directors in the Golden Era were extremely rare. Dorothy Arzner, a former film editor, was the only notable woman director in Hollywood until actress Ida Lupino began directing in 1950.

Of the twelve interviewees included in this volume, Joseph Newman, Henry Hathaway, Gordon Douglas, and Budd Boetticher served as assistant directors before being elevated to a directorial position. Irving Rapper, Michael Gordon, and Frederick De Cordova, all from the stage, worked as dialogue directors in Hollywood before they were given their own pictures to direct. Vincent Sherman, also with stage experience, started in the film business as an actor, then became a screenwriter, and ended his long career as a sought-after director of A pictures. George Sidney did second unit directing, made scores of screen tests, and won two Oscars for shorts before directing his first feature film. Arthur Lubin spent years making budget movies before directing more important pictures. Charles Walters had been a talented choreographer on the Broadway stage and at MGM before he graduated to directing big screen musicals. Henry Koster had made films in Germany and Hungary before coming to the United States, where he launched his American career in 1936 with a successful Deanna Durbin picture at Universal, then the largest of Hollywood's minor studios. Although half of these directors attended college, none of them had the benefit of the film courses that would be available on university campuses a generation later.

Of these twelve directors only Henry Hathaway (for *Lives of the Bengal Lancer* in 1935), Henry Koster (for *The Bishop's Wife* in 1947), and Charles Walters (for *Lili* in 1953) were nominated for an Academy Award for best direction of a feature film. None of them won. Yet all twelve were sensitive to production standards and the flow and rhythm of the pictures they made. None were extravagant with their studios' money, and all kept to a tight budget. None achieved the renown they perhaps deserved, although each revealed distinguishing features in his work and developed a personal style. Henry Hathaway and Joseph Newman believed in reality, whereas Henry Koster and Arthur Lubin leaned toward whimsy and Charles Walters worked in a glossier mode. All twelve essentially directed the pictures their studios wanted made and earned a reputation for working fast and efficiently. Each did the best he could with the resources available to him, and while some were better filmmakers than others, all twelve were valued by the studios that employed them and came to be respected by their peers. All of them made films that were box office successes and some that are still considered classics. Although John Ford, Frank Capra, and William Wyler repeatedly won Hollywood's most coveted awards and brought the greatest esteem to their studios, it was these company directors and the utility directors of less stature—the ones who made "quickie" films for provincial audiences—that kept the Golden Age movie companies solvent.

By the mid-1950s, with the migration of the American middle class to the suburbs, rapid changes in postwar social patterns, and television threatening to become the nation's predominant entertainment form, the big studios began to break up. Their power had been on the wane since 1948 when a government decree mandated that the studios had five years to divest themselves of their theater chains. In 1956 the Metro-Goldwyn-Mayer lot was so reduced in activity that it reminded actress Carolyn Jones "of an ancient dowager that was divesting herself of her jewels before going to bed at night, and she was about halfway through." A year later there were only a handful of movies in production at Twentieth Century-Fox and Warner Bros., both of which had been a beehive of activity only a short time before. The old directors and producers had started to drift away as the number of feature films dwindled. Many of the former utility directors, who were noted for their economy and competence, moved into television production. More and more empty sound stages at the surviving studios were rented out to television companies and independent film producers.

In the late 1960s the once powerful motion picture studios were being taken over by conglomerates—Paramount by Gulf and Western,

Universal by Music Corporation of America, United Artists by the Transamerica Corporation—and had become little more than real estate operations and distributing organizations for independent producers. By then the contract rosters of the old studios were no more, and the function of the moguls who had shaped the American movie industry had been usurped by agents, bankers, and lawyers. Much of the glamour and magic of Hollywood vanished as the great stars grew older and supporting players in films became increasingly unfamiliar to audiences. "All of us in the business were somewhat nostalgic about the demise of old Hollywood," said producer Walter Seltzer, "because something we knew and cherished was gone and would never come back." With the studios no longer turning out a steady, balanced stream of movies to fill their theaters, the once-valuable company directors were no longer consistent with current production methods, and in most cases they had been among the first to retire or seek opportunities elsewhere. But their role in the operation of the big studio system was vital, for they were the filmmakers that kept the assembly lines cost-efficient and moving and movie theaters across the nation filled with a constant flow of marketable entertainment.

The twelve interviews collected in this volume were conducted by the author between 1980 and 1988 and are part of the Ronald L. Davis Oral History Collection at Southern Methodist University. These interviews, published here for the first time, have been edited for publication and are arranged in the order in which they were taped. The tapes and complete transcripts may be found in the DeGolyer Library on the SMU campus.

JUST MAKING MOVIES

HENRY KOSTER

More Lovable than Tough

Henry Koster, born in Berlin, Germany, in 1905, gained fame during the late 1930s as director of the first Deanna Durbin musicals. Later he made successful comedies for Metro-Goldwyn-Mayer, Samuel Goldwyn, and Twentieth Century-Fox. A loyal contract director until 1966, Koster directed more than one hundred films and added to his respect as a craftsman, as well as gaining wide popular acclaim, with *The Robe* (1953), the first motion picture released in CinemaScope. Married to former actress Peggy Moran, the screen director and his wife moved shortly after this interview to a retirement community in Camarillo, California, where Koster died in 1988.

The following interview was taped in the director's home in Pacific Palisades, California, on August 13, 1980.

D: Mr. Koster, how did you become interested in motion pictures?
K: I was in high school in Germany; I used to go to movies very often when I was a teenager. I admired Ernst Lubitsch, and I visited him on the set in Berlin. I watched him shoot *Anne Boleyn* in Germany and finally was introduced to him. I was studying to be a painter, and of course getting into the movies wasn't easy. So I made a living painting posters and signs for show windows. Then I got a job drawing animated cartoons, which were quite new at the time. I had my own ideas for animated cartoons. In Germany they had the cartoons not as short subjects, but as commercials on the screen during intermissions. Theaters usually had two features, and after the first feature the lights came on and the people who had seen the show walked out and others came in. I noticed that people didn't pay much

3

attention to my animated cartoons while the audience was coming and going, so I tried to get additional ideas and make the commercials more interesting. I was only nineteen years old at the time.

One day a director called me and said, "Who writes the gags for your commercials?" I said, "I do." And he said, "Could you come over and help me? I have to do a comedy." So I helped him on that, and that was my first step into the movies. Then I wrote scripts and I dropped the painting altogether, because I noticed that I could make more money in the movies. I wrote my first script in 1925. I sold it and got a lot of money and began writing for pictures, but I always wanted to be a director.

D: Didn't you write several of the scripts that Kurt Bernhardt shot?

K: Yes, I wrote most of his stories when he was in Germany. Then Hitler came in, and I went to France and Bernhardt went to France. By that time I was a director myself in Germany. I had already directed two or three pictures. But when Hitler came in, I had to flee the country. I went to France and later got a job in Budapest, where I directed several pictures for Universal. My friend [producer] Joe Pasternak gave me a job as his director, and I directed a Hungarian movie star by the name of Franciska Gaal, who was very famous at the time. I directed a few of her pictures, and in 1936 I got my contract with Universal in Hollywood through Mr. Pasternak.

I got the contract to come to Hollywood when Mr. Pasternak was asked to come to America. He said he would only come if he could bring this young director—that was me. The people at Universal said they were up to their hips in foreign directors and that they didn't want any more. Pasternak said if they didn't want me, he wouldn't come either. So they agreed to take me and gave me a contract with a very low salary, the lowest they could give at that time. I couldn't speak English when I arrived in this country. Carl Laemmle, the head of Universal, was from Germany, too, and could speak German. Pasternak and I told him that we'd look around the studio a couple of days. Laemmle said, "You look around a couple of days and come back and we'll discuss what you can do here." After three days we came back, and Mr. Laemmle wasn't at the studio anymore. He had sold the company, and the new owners refused to accept our contract. We threatened to sue them, and they finally said, "All right, you make one picture and then get the hell out of here." We agreed to that, but I knew that if the picture was any good, I could stay. In 1936 I made a picture with Deanna Durbin called *Three Smart Girls*, and it was a success. So they kept me.

D: Was Durbin already an established performer?

K: She had never made a movie before. She was a singer on the Eddie Cantor radio show. She was thirteen years old at the time, a child singer. I didn't want anybody unknown to star in my picture; I wanted somebody who had experience. But her agent said, "Oh, she's absolutely lovely and she made a test at Metro with another young girl, Judy Garland, and I can show you the test." I looked at the test, and she looked good. I went to the Eddie Cantor show to meet Durbin, and she said she wasn't interested in pictures. Her agent, Jack Sherrill, tired to talk her into doing the picture, and I tried to talk her into it. The studio had already told me that my picture had to be done cheaply and that I couldn't have an experienced actress.

Finally I talked Durbin into a test, and the test was fine when she stood quiet and didn't move. She told me she didn't know how to act. So every night while we were making the picture I went to her house and taught her how to smile. I said, "The mouth goes up in the corners when you smile and goes down when you cry." That's the way we started. The picture was quite a hit. After the preview at the Pantages Theater in Hollywood, Mr. Lubitsch came to me and shook my hand and said, "You did a very fine job and I'm proud to know you." A photographer took a picture of us in the lobby, and my career went on from there.

D: What was Deanna Durbin like as a person?

K: Delightful. She was wholesome, quite beautiful; she could sing but she was scared to act and scared of people. She was just at the age when most girls are scared of everything. She was just starting to become a young lady, but she was really more of a child.

I had written *Three Smart Girls* myself, the story. I wrote most of my early pictures myself, although I had to have the assistance of experienced American writers because I couldn't write dialogue, nor could I write English. But the basic idea was always mine and so was the story structure. After my first picture in Hollywood I think I made $300 a week.

D: Universal obviously recognized that you had talent.

K: Well, the president of the company, whose name was Charles Rogers, thought *Three Smart Girls* was just a flash in the pan. He asked me what I'd like to do next, and I told him I'd like to make a picture with a symphony orchestra. An assistant producer was sitting next to Rogers, and they said, "People in America don't want to hear symphonic music." I said, "That's funny, because I was at the Hollywood Bowl last night, and there were 18,000 people listening to Beethoven's Fifth Symphony."

Universal turned the idea of making a picture with a symphony orchestra down at first. They said, "If you'd use Benny Goodman or Tommy Dorsey, we might consider doing the picture." I said, "No, I want a big symphony orchestra with a big conductor. There are too many pictures made with dance bands. I want to try to get Leopold Stokowski. If I get him, would you make the picture?" The people at Universal said, "You can't get him. He's with the Philadelphia Orchestra." So I contacted Stokowski's agent and went to Philadelphia. I told Stokowski the story, and he agreed to play the part. He insisted on recording the music in Philadelphia because he had all the accommodations there.

They made things very difficult for me at Universal. They called me in and said, "Do you know that you are three days behind schedule?" One of the big scenes in the picture was when the orchestra goes to Stokowski's house and plays for him to convince him that they are professional. Studio executives said, "We'll have to cut that scene out because we have to stick to the schedule." I said, "How will you explain the story? How will the audience know why Stokowski decides to conduct the orchestra?" They said, "We do that very simply in Hollywood. We just put a newspaper in that says, 'Stokowski decides to conduct orchestra.' That's all you have to do." So I had a hysterical fit. Somebody said, "Why don't you let him have his way and if the picture loses money, he's out and he can go back to Vienna or wherever he came from." I made the picture, and it was another hit. Then I wanted another raise, and Universal didn't want to give it to me. I threatened, and I got it. I ended up making a lot of money.

D: Adolphe Menjou was featured opposite Durbin in *One Hundred Men and a Girl*, the picture you're talking about. Was he pleasant to work with?

K: Very pleasant, a nice gentleman. I've always doubted the success of my work, and he said, "Look, I tell you, this picture is a smash. I know it, and don't you worry." He comforted me. I helped him as an actor, and he certainly helped me as a worrier.

D: Altogether you made six films with Deanna Durbin.

K: Six or seven, I'd have to count. But quite a few. Always with Joe Pasternak.

D: Did you have a musical background yourself?

K: No, but I come from a family of musicians. My grandfather was an opera singer, my grandmother was a pianist, my mother studied piano but never did anything about it except play at home for us. I had to go twice a week to the opera in Berlin. First I hated it and I suffered. Finally I loved it. I had to go to the symphonies of course, too. We had great conductors in Germany at the time.

I'd heard Leopold Stokowski conduct on records in Berlin. That's why I suggested to Universal that we make a picture with him. He was a perfectionist. I had to do a close-up of him in a scene, and we lit the scene with his stand-in. When it came time to do the scene, we couldn't find Stokowski. Finally we found him in the corner, and a boy was polishing his shoes. I said, "Mr. Stokowski, would you please come? We don't need your shoes shined; it's only a close-up. For all I care you can wear slippers." He said, "I won't risk that. My shoes have to look perfect even if you only photograph my face." And he came in with polished shoes and did the close-up for me.

D: Do you have pleasant memories of making *The Rage of Paris*?

K: That was a difficult film, and another good one. Danielle Darrieux, the star, came to this country with her husband. I had known her in Paris. Bernhardt had directed her in a picture, and I had written the screenplay. But when she and her husband arrived in Hollywood, the script for the picture we were to make was wrong, and they threatened to leave. We had to shoot although the script wasn't ready. Things like that happen in the life of every director and every producer. We have memories that are pleasant and those we'd rather put in the drawer or burn in the fireplace.

D: After your success with the first Deanna Durbin film, did the other Durbin pictures have a fairly substantial budget?

K: Well, certainly higher than the first one. I remember that *Three Smart Girls* cost $250,000 to produce, and *One Hundred Men and a Girl* cost $580,000. That sounds terribly low today, but it was low even for those days. The average A production cost anywhere from $700,000 to $1,000,000, unless it was a Cecil B. DeMille epic. Then the budget went way up to $2,000,000. I had to make pictures cheaper and faster, and my experience of making so many quickies in Germany helped me to keep within the allotted budget. I think *Three Smart Girls* was shot in about twenty days, maybe twenty-two days. *One Hundred Men and a Girl* probably took thirty-five days.

D: I know that Deanna Durbin got her first screen kiss in *First Love*.

K: Yes, by Robert Stack. I found him at the university, he was a student. Somebody told me, "There's such a handsome young man who would like to be an actor." I met Stack, and he was then twenty or something. I tested him, and we took him for Durbin's first lover. I had a brilliant writer at the time by the name of Bruce Manning. He was the funniest man I ever met and the best comedy writer I ever met. Some incidents with him I cannot quote because they contain too many dirty words.

D: Do you have fond memories of *Spring Parade*?

K: That was a lovely picture, I liked that. It was a Viennese musical. The music was by Robert Stolz. He was a great composer in Vienna. He was considered by many the new Strauss. Deanna Durbin was in that, and for the first time she was playing a grown-up young lady. The picture had a few difficulties. Miss Durbin was getting a little more demanding. I remember one scene, which we had to shoot at night on the back lot. She had to walk down a street with Robert Cummings holding hands and speaking love dialogue. I was sitting on a camera crane with my cameraman, Joe Valentine, and we were setting up the scene with stand-ins. It got to be after midnight, and I finally called my assistant and said, "Get Miss Durbin and Mr. Cummings, we are ready to shoot." He came back and said, "Mr. Cummings is here but Miss Durbin left." I said, "She left!" I was fifty feet above the ground on that crane. So I went down, and I said, "Where is she?" "Well, she told her wardrobe girl that she doesn't work this late and went home." So I got pretty mad, and I resigned from the picture. The next morning the big men got me in and got her in. I said, "If this young lady wants to work with me, fine. If she doesn't want to work with me, just as fine. I have other opportunities in this town." So we made up and I came back. Later she did little things like that once in a while, but they were always straightened out by the producers.

D: What was Robert Cummings like?

K: Oh, brilliant, wonderful. I made five pictures with him. I thought he was the best leading man I ever worked with. He had that marvelous comedy talent and also a romantic quality.

D: Weren't those Durbin pictures the biggest money-makers for Universal during the late 1930s?

K: They were considered the pictures that saved Universal. I think they made millions at the time.

D: *It Started with Eve* was another Durbin picture. Didn't you work with Charles Laughton on that one?

K: Yes. We were very close friends. I painted him once. I paint portraits. He played in *It Started with Eve,* and just when we were doing that picture the war started. I had not become a citizen yet. You have to be in this country five years, and in 1941 I hadn't been here quite five years. I had to stay home after eight o'clock at night because of the curfew. I was not only a foreigner, I was an enemy alien—a German. Every night at eight o'clock Charles Laughton came to see my wife and me, and he sat with us all evening and read to us. It was part of what he was rehearsing for his one-man show. He read things that were unknown to me, which I found delightful. But he also read Shakespeare and the Bible. Peggy [Moran] and I got engaged at Laughton's house. We've been married now for nearly forty years.

D: On *It Started with Eve* your cameraman was Rudy Maté.

K: He was a wonderful cameraman. I knew him from Paris. I thought he was one of the best, if not the best European cameramen.

D: What was Maté's special talent?

K: The shots he did were absolutely brilliantly elegant, and the close-ups of women were unbelievably fascinating. He photographed that beautiful picture, *Gilda,* with Rita Hayworth that Charles Vidor directed. I think she never looked so beautiful. He photographed two of my pictures, and Durbin looked prettier than ever. Women were crazy to have him on their pictures. He was such a gentle, pleasant person, full of charm and humor. I never heard him use a dirty word, or say anything bad about anybody. He used to tell funny stories on the set, but always very decent.

D: On *Between Us Girls* weren't you also producing as well as directing?

K: That was one of those experiences like *Rage of Paris.* Diana Barrymore, John Barrymore's daughter, played in it, along with Bob Cummings and John Boles and Kay Francis. Diana Barrymore was a hard person to cope with. She meant well, but I think she had some of the mental difficulties that her father had. She was always busy with other things when we wanted to shoot her scenes. Also it was not a good picture. That was a remake of a European picture that was made in Budapest, with Pasternak producing but one I did not direct. They wanted to have a showcase for Diana Barrymore, thinking that she might become a great actress. I don't think she had any of the Barrymore talent, but she had the Madame Sans-Gene attitude on the set and in her private life. She was, well, may I say the poor man's Tallulah Bankhead.

D: Why did you leave Universal?

K: To join Pasternak again. He had left before me. He had a contract at Metro-Goldwyn-Mayer, and my seven-year contract with Universal was up. So I joined Metro in 1943.

D: Did you find things at Metro done on a more lavish scale than what you'd known at Universal?

K: Not more lavish but more business-like and more organized. Not that Universal was not organized. I thought Universal was the most pleasant studio I ever worked in. But Metro-Goldwyn-Mayer was such a huge undertaking, almost a mechanism of production, which does not easily apply to the making of motion pictures. There was nothing unpleasant there; we had a good time working with Pasternak.

D: Was *Music for Millions* your first film at Metro?

K: I think so, yes. That was also a story of an orchestra. José Iturbi was in it, and Jimmy Durante, who was such a great entertainer and perhaps the nicest man in show business who ever lived.

D: Was June Allyson, the picture's star, good to work with?

K: Very much so. I did several pictures with her. She had that marvelous gravel voice, and I thought she was a great talent. We were very close for a while. She was in *Music for Millions*, *Two Sisters from Boston*, and *My Man Godfrey*. I made a remake of *My Man Godfrey* with a German actor who misbehaved. It's pretty tough to direct pictures. It's not so tough to direct, but it's tough to cope with the personalities who are temperamental.

D: Did you find working with child stars, Margaret O'Brien in the case of *Music for Millions*, difficult?

K: She was very easy. It was her mother sitting behind me on the set who caused problems. I'd say, "That was good, print it." I'd see Margaret O'Brien look at me, but look a little over my head. Sometimes she'd shake her head and say, "Mr. Koster, could we do that once more." Her mother behind me had made a sign that she wanted it done again, but the child had to tell me. So I asked the higher-ups if it would be possible to keep her mother off the set. "No, no," they said, "Margaret doesn't feel secure if her mother isn't there, and we agreed that she could be on the set." So when you direct pictures, you have these little incidents to cope with.

When you start to direct a picture, you have something in mind that you want to do, and you are darn lucky if you get approximately what you had in mind. You never get it quite the way you imagined it would turn out to be, because there are so many difficulties. The up-hill fight destroys so many good intentions. Maybe I wasn't the right chemistry to direct. I did my best to make good pictures; I did a few that I'm proud of. But I could not become completely brutal with actors, as I know some directors did. For instance, Elia Kazan once beat up Marlon Brando on the set. Otto Preminger threw Lana Turner off the set when he was making *Anatomy of a Murder*. He threw her out and got Lee Remick instead, a darling actress. I never threw anybody out, I just resigned when it got too much for me. I did that two or three times. Maybe I should have hit people more, or spit at them, or whatever was the tough thing to do.

D: Did you find that you had to be a psychologist on the set?

K: Yes, of course. Since I mostly did comedies, I always tried to create a relaxed and happy atmosphere on the set, and that's not always possible. I have worked with actors and actresses who seemed to be out to destroy the pleasant atmosphere in the studio. I don't know if I did the right thing in trying to cope with those situations. I've had actresses who suddenly refused to turn their left cheek to the camera. I made a picture for Sam Goldwyn, who was a great man and absolutely the best producer who was ever in this industry, if only for the simple reason that he always hired the best people he could possibly get. He had Robert Sherwood write for him and William Wyler direct for him. But in the picture I did for him I had to do this love scene with Cary Grant and Loretta Young.

D: You're talking about *The Bishop's Wife*.

K: Yes, that was in 1947. Miss Young refused to show her right cheek to the camera, and Mr. Grant didn't want that side to the camera either. Now how do you do a love scene when both people look to the right? So I finally decided to have them both look out the window. He puts his hands on her shoulders and they say their dialogue.

Then he leans his cheek to her head. The next morning Mr. Goldwyn called me into his office and said, "What's the matter with you? Are you crazy? Is that supposed to be a love scene?" I said, "Mr. Goldwyn, they refused to turn their faces to each other. Neither wants their right face to the camera." He said, "They did!" And he came down to the set with me, and there was Mr. Grant and Miss Young. He said, "I saw the rushes, Loretta and Cary. From now on you draw only half your salary because you only let me use half of your faces." And he walked out.

Every actor has a good side and a bad side, or they think so. I know that most of them think so, even though some of them have a perfect face. I worked in the time of handsome and beautiful people. Today that isn't too important. We have wonderful stars that are not too handsome at all. Dustin Hoffman is a brilliant actor, but he's not particularly handsome and he's short. Yet he's a greater actor than any of those he-men heroes we had with the beautiful faces.

D: Did you like *The Unfinished Dance*?

K: Fairly well, yes. That was a ballet picture. David Lichine choreographed the dances. That was also with Margaret O'Brien. She played a little dancer who makes a ballerina break her legs. The picture was not financially successful, I know that. This was also a remake of a French picture. Remakes are no good, you cannot create. You have to recreate and recreate something that was brilliant before. It never comes out and is rarely successful.

D: My rule is not to see remakes. For example, I refused to see the remake of *All Quiet on the Western Front* that was made for television.

K: Seeing *All Quiet on the Western Front* was one of my last experiences in Germany. The picture was released just before Hitler came to power in 1932. I was at the opening, and the Nazi troopers of Adolf Hitler brought mice and let them run in the aisles because they didn't want this picture, which they claimed was a disgrace to the German army, shown. There was a scene in it where one of the German soldiers during an attack in the trenches does his business in his pants because he's so afraid. That was something that happened with young soldiers. But the Nazi troopers threw eggs and tomatoes at the screen and made them stop the picture. That scene had to be cut out because the Nazis said that no German soldier would do that; he would fight.

D: Later you directed a number of films at Twentieth Century-Fox.

K: I got a contract with Twentieth Century-Fox and spent seventeen years there.

D: How did you find the atmosphere at Fox compared with Metro?

K: Very pleasant. I had a good position there. I became very friendly with Darryl Zanuck, who was the executive producer. But I never made a picture with Zanuck producing, I always had other producers. I was very fortunate to get Sam Engel, who I think was the best producer we ever had there. And Charles Brackett, who was a writer-producer with whom I worked at Twentieth Century-Fox. Although I was close to Zanuck and I admired him as a man, I had the feeling that he didn't like to pay too much attention to the pictures that he hadn't personally produced. I think he had some sort of ambition to make his own personal productions stand out in comparison with other pictures.

I was making a picture in London for Twentieth Century-Fox called *No Highway in the Sky,* an aircraft story based on a novel by Nevil Shute. James Stewart, Marlene Dietrich, and Glynis Johns were the stars, and I consider it one of my finest pictures. I thought it was a marvelous story and a marvelous script by very fine writers. And to work in England was a true pleasure. I finished the picture and I had to go back to Hollywood to start another one. When I went back to Hollywood, there were still two or three scenes left to be done on *No Highway in the Sky* in London. One was only a close-up of Miss Dietrich, and one was a shot of the plane taking off from the airfield in London. Since we couldn't use any of the existing aircraft, we had to build our own plane. Since we couldn't build a whole plane, we camouflaged a British plane and then had a model built with a wing spread of about eight feet, which we used for the long shots. I needed one shot of that plane taking off from the airport, and it was a very important shot. I left my instructions with the cameraman and the man who made the miniature, and I waited in Hollywood for the shot to arrive at the studio.

The shot came, and the aircraft took off but suddenly started vibrating. The shot was unusable. I went to Zanuck and said, "Darryl, that shot came from London and we can't use it." He said, "What's wrong with it?" I said, "Well, there's a vibration in the plane; it bumps in the air as it goes up. Would you please send a wire to London telling them that they need to make the shot again?" He said, "Let me see it."

He came to the projection room, and he saw the shot with me and said, "That's good enough." I said, "Darryl, you can't leave that in." He said, "Why not? So the plane bumps a little in the air." I said, "But a plane must take off smoothly." He said, "Look, this stays in. This picture has already gone over its schedule and over the budget.

To do that shot over again would cost a few thousand dollars. I won't permit it." And he walked out. The shot is still in the picture. I was very upset, but somebody explained to me that Zanuck didn't want perfection in the pictures he didn't personally produce.

D: Did you find Marlene Dietrich good to work with on *No Highway in the Sky*?

K: There was a little friction because she didn't care for the part. It wasn't big enough. She played a movie actress in it who is just a passenger on the plane. She has beautiful scenes with Jimmy Stewart, but I don't think she was too happy on that picture. Jimmy Stewart, as always, was grand and wonderful to work with.

D: Was *The Luck of the Irish* an interesting film for you?

K: Very. That was my first picture at Twentieth Century-Fox, and I had Tyrone Power and Anne Baxter as my stars. I enjoyed that very much. The screenplay by Philip Dunne was good, and I was very happy doing the picture. Tyrone Power was a perfect gentleman, and we got along just fine and became friends. While I was shooting in London on my next picture, *No Highway in the Sky*, he was on the stage in London doing *Mister Roberts*. We spent many evenings together there, with my wife and his beautiful wife, Linda Christian.

D: Was Anne Baxter a solid actress?

K: Oh, yes. If anything she was sometimes too much Anne Baxter and not quite the character she played. There are so many shadings in acting talent. There are two kinds of truly great actors. One kind really becomes the part and you don't even know that the person is an actor. Then there is the kind that is always an actor but is so great that no matter what the actor does, you admire it and believe every line the person says. Spencer Tracy was Spencer Tracy all right, but he sank into a part in a picture and became completely the person. It was the complete enactment of another character, although he was always still Spencer Tracy. I think Anne Baxter was always Anne Baxter, but she was wonderful in her performances.

D: Did you enjoy making *The Inspector General*?

K: Yes. I was directing Danny Kaye. I am not too fond of having someone behind me controlling what I'm doing, and in Danny Kaye's pictures his wife, Sylvia Fine, who was a brilliant woman and lyric writer, had to okay everything. I sometimes became a footman on the set—just doing the scenes with him, not with the other actors. I always used Charles Laughton's wife, Elsa Lanchester, whenever I could. She was in *The Inspector General* and in *Come to the Stable*. I painted her about a half year ago, and the portrait was exhibited in a gallery that Francis Lederer owns. Somebody bought the picture. It's the only painting I ever sold. But Elsa is a great character.

D: Did you enjoy making the Betty Grable films?

K: Oh, Betty Grable was a wonderful character, too, and witty. Betty was not a great dancer, not a great singer, and not a great actress, but altogether she was a very likable personality. We made two or three pictures together, and the things that took place were so funny. Some were dirty, because she didn't mind using that kind of language. For instance, we were shooting a picture on a set at Twentieth Century-Fox, and next door they were making a Western. I was shooting a love scene with Grable and Dan Dailey, and suddenly there was a terrific report from a gun next door. Grable turned around and yelled, "I don't even know your husband!" That was the only clean remark she ever made. But her wit was so fast.

D: What memories do you have of making *Harvey*?

K: That was my favorite picture. I loved the play, and I loved making the picture. That was one of the few pictures where there was no difficulty with anybody. We all got along fine, and somebody said that it was Harvey [an invisible rabbit] who did that. He gave us the spirit of friendship that made for a good collaboration. Jimmy Stewart, who also did *Harvey* on the stage, is a brilliant actor, very cooperative, very friendly, very intelligent, very witty. I don't think I've ever worked with a better actor than James Stewart in my life, and we made four or five pictures together.

D: Was it difficult when you made *Mr. Belvedere Rings the Bell* to come into a series already established?

K: It was only difficult to top the success of the first one, *Sitting Pretty*. I made three or four pictures with Clifton Webb, but I never had a scene as funny as when he put the bowl of cereal over the baby's head in *Sitting Pretty*. *Mr. Belvedre Rings the Bell* was taken from a stage play called *The Silver Bell*, and the part wasn't too probable for Clifton. José Ferrer played it on the stage. But Clifton did very well with the part.

D: How did you feel about *Stars and Stripes Forever*?

K: I love march music, and I've always loved Sousa. So that was fun to do. That was, I think, the first picture I had my son in. He was only a child and played the son of Sousa. Later he played Richard Burton as a child in *My Cousin Rachel,* he played the little boy on a donkey in *The Robe,* and he played a schoolboy in *Good Morning, Miss Dove.* Now he is a well known doctor in San Francisco. I wanted him to be a pianist. He studied piano for many years and is a brilliant pianist. But he wanted to be a doctor.

D: I know that you directed a segment of *O. Henry's Full House.*

K: That was one of the finest pictures I ever made. I did that with Charles Laughton, Marilyn Monroe, and David Wayne. The picture was a series of short stories by O. Henry, and my episode, "The Cop and the Anthem," is the story of a man who wants to go to jail and can't get in.

D: That was an unusual film for Fox to make.

K: Yes. We were five directors who did five short films. Jean Negulesco, Henry King, Howard Hawks, and Henry Hathaway directed the other four episodes. Howard Hawks's segment, "The Ransom of Redchief," was later cut out. That was the one with Oscar Levant and Fred Allen, who played two kidnappers. But I got a lot of comments on my part of the film. When you are making motion pictures, there are few things that you're proud of.

D: Was Marilyn Monroe difficult to work with?

K: This was only a short picture for me, only about twenty or twenty-five minutes, but she was just marvelous. Marilyn Monroe had been an artist's model. My wife's father, Earl Moran, is an artist who paints nudes on calendars. He's an old gentleman now, but he used to be well known. He told me about Marilyn, and we talked about that on the set. She liked him very much, because when she had nothing to eat, she posed for him and he gave her money to eat. Jayne Mansfield was also one of his models.

D: You mentioned *My Cousin Rachel* a moment ago. Was that a good experience?

K: It was Richard Burton's first picture in America. Yes, it was a very good experience, and I was working with a marvelous producer, Nunnally Johnson, who also wrote the screenplay. Nunnally was a brilliant man. Burton was a young child-man when he came over from England, and we got along just fine. He had a temper but I never saw that temper, because he didn't use it on me or Olivia de Havilland or anybody else on the set.

There was a scene where Burton had to climb outside a house to reach Olivia's balcony. He ran toward the house and started to climb

up and slipped. I said, "Let's shoot it again, Dick," and he slipped again
and fell. He got up and ran his head into a stone wall several times,
until I thought he was going to kill himself. We had to go and pull him
back. He said, "I can't do it! What's the matter with me?" He wanted
to hit his head again, and we had to stop him.

D: Was there a great deal of location work involved in making *The
Robe*?

K: No, none. We built Jerusalem on the back lot of Twentieth
Century-Fox. The studio had one lot in the [San Fernando] Valley,
where some of the scenes were shot. But usually we built everything
on the back lot.

The Robe was difficult because that was the first CinemaScope picture. At that time it was very complicated to shoot in CinemaScope.
The film is the same size, but the image is squeezed. Then in the projection it is spread out on the screen so that the images become the
normal size. That gives you the wide screen. But the camera we had
on *The Robe* was one of the first specimens of that particular camera,
and it had two focusing devices. One assistant had to focus the camera and one had to focus the squeezing device, and very seldom was
that in focus. We were always going with bated breath to the projection room in the morning to see the rushes, and usually we had to
do two or three of the five scenes we had shot over, because the people
were out of focus. That was especially the case when the camera
approached the actors or pulled back, and the focus had to be adjusted.
There were two men running with the camera to hold it in the proper
focus. It's quite annoying when you have a scene that is hard to do
and you finally get it, and then the next day they say you have to
do it over because the focus is not sharp.

D: Was there also difficulty in simply filling up the additional space
CinemaScope provided?

K: No. I always liked that. I'd seen the first wide screen in 1925,
when Abel Gance showed the picture *Napoleon*. He had three screens
and three cameras and three projectors. I was at the opening in Berlin
at the Palace Theater, and he showed the Battle of Marengo on three
screens, with huge masses of soldiers. Only the screens didn't quite
work in sync, I mean the projectors, so there was a wiggling and
trembling between the three screens. Besides, there was a distortion
of image. The man who later did Cinerama found the solution for
that by shooting with the right camera to the left side, with the left

coming to the right side and the center coming to the center. That's why the screen had to be in a half circle. That's the way they got it together. But Cinerama was very expensive.

D: Was cinematographer Leon Shamroy helpful to you in learning to shoot in the CinemaScope process?

K: Oh, yes. He'd get so mad when it was out of focus. He was a great cameraman, and he did beautiful photography. When we got in the projection room he threw things when he saw a beautiful love scene he had done out of focus. If we kept the actors in the same spot, the focus was all right.

D: Was Victor Mature a good actor to work with?

K: Yes, he was nice to work with, amusing. He very much looked out for his money always. Betty Grable and I decided we'd have a party at the end of *Wabash Avenue*. Betty said she'd bring the food if I'd bring the drinks. We asked, "Vic, what are you going to bring?" He said, "Well, I'll bring the dessert." The next day we had a big party on the set for all the employees and bit players. Betty had ordered food from Chasen's, and I had ordered a hundred bottles of scotch and vodka so everybody could drink as much as they wanted to. Vic came in with a bag of jelly beans. I said, "What is that?" He said, "That's dessert." I said, "Vic, I thought you'd bring some cakes or something!" He said, "Not me. Jelly beans are delicious, that's all I ate when I was a boy." We had to send for cake.

D: Did you enjoy making *Desiree*?

K: Sort of. Working with Marlon Brando wasn't too easy. He had to play this part because he had walked off of *The Egyptian*. He didn't want to play Napoleon, and he was right because Marlon is an introvert and Napoleon was a blasting extrovert. And Marlon Brando is a mumbler. He had to play this part to settle the lawsuit over his having walked out during the production of *The Egyptian* that Michael Curtiz directed at Twentieth Century-Fox. Marlon didn't like that part either, and they sued him for millions. The suit was settled if he'd agree to play any part they gave him, and that any part was Napoleon.

Personally Marlon Brando is a fascinating man, probably one of the greatest actors this country has produced, or the world for that matter. But that wasn't his part. We had some little discussions about how Napoleon should be played, because I had a different opinion of the way it should be acted. He'd always say, "I have to play it, and that's

the best I can do." That was about it. I couldn't hit Marlon Brando
like Kazan did once on *A Streetcar Named Desire* when he did something awful to Kim Hunter.

D: Would you research an historical film like *Desiree*?

K: Very much. It so happened that my father was a Napoleon buff,
and he had a big collection of books on Napoleon in his library. So I
knew quite a bit about Napoleon, but of course I did more research in
preparation for the picture.

D: Was Merle Oberon an interesting actress to work with?

K: Oh, what a lovely girl she was! The most beautiful woman. I
don't know if you know, she had something wrong with her skin on
one cheek, because just before we made *Desiree* she had been left
under a lamp too long and it had burned her. She went to a doctor,
and he had treated the burn with sandpaper she told me, and her
cheek was somewhat inflamed. Later it got better. But there again
she couldn't show one side of her face, or she didn't want to. It was
just a little spot of skin on her face, which could easily be covered up
by makeup. It didn't bother anybody but her. So in the picture I was
very limited in directing her scenes. I ought to write an autobiogra-
phy about my difficulties.

D: Did you enjoy making *The Virgin Queen* with Bette Davis?

K: Yes. I was signed to do the picture by Charlie Brackett. I had
worked with Richard Todd, who played Sir Walter Raleigh, in a wonderful picture called *A Man Called Peter*, in which he played Peter
Marshall, the pastor of the Senate. And I was very happy to work
with Bette Davis, who was just great. Before we started the picture a
fellow director called me and said, "Have you met her?" I said, "No,
not yet, but we'll get together next week." This director said to me,
"If you want to keep your health and your mind, don't do the picture,
because she is impossible. I couldn't get along with her. There was
nothing but fights. I went home crying every night."

Well, that was something to worry about. I had enough troubles
without having to deal with an impossible actress. So I called Bette
Davis and asked if I could see her. She said, "Come right over." I
went to her home, and we had tea. I told her what I'd heard and said,
"I am too old to go through so much trouble. I couldn't stand it. Are
you that impossible with every director?" She said, "No, only the
ones who don't know what they're talking about. I fought the man

you talked to all the way through. I know it was tough for him, but it was tough for me, too. I don't want to give a bad performance. Do you know your business?" I said, "Well, I'd like to flatter myself by saying yes." She said, "Well, if you know what you're talking about, we'll be friends." She and I never had the slightest friction.

The script was originally called *Sir Walter Raleigh*, but I made it as *The Virgin Queen*. Zanuck liked to change titles of pictures. For instance, *The Luck of the Irish* was initially called *The Shamrock Touch*, which I liked better. I fought against the change. I thought *The Luck of the Irish* was a bad title for that picture, because everybody would think they were going to see a football picture. This was a story about an American reporter who finds a leprechaun in the woods, and from then on the leprechaun protects his career as a newspaperman. But Zanuck thought *The Luck of the Irish* was a better business title.

D: Was *Good Morning, Miss Dove* a favorite picture of yours?

K: One of my favorites. I have about five favorites, and that's one of them. *Harvey*, *A Man Called Peter*, *One Hundred Men and a Girl*, and *Come to the Stable* are some of my favorites. I loved doing those pictures. *Good Morning, Miss Dove* was marvelous with Jennifer Jones, who is such a lovable lady and such a fine actress. She went through all the stages of aging in that picture. She was a young school teacher who grows older and finally is an old lady in the hospital. That's not easy to do, but it was a beautifully-written script. Jennifer Jones was wonderful.

Jennifer was a nervous lady, like all good actresses, like Bette Davis and Audrey Hepburn. They are nervous but always trying to improve on what they're doing, trying to do the very best they can do. It is not only the fear of ruining their careers, but it is also their ambition to do their best. I have encountered that so many times because I was fortunate enough to work with the finest stars in the industry.

I've been fortunate in my life. A newspaperman in Rome interviewed me once and asked, "How do you like your job?" I said, "I have a job which I love so much, and for which they pay me so much, but I would be glad to pay them to let me do it. And I have a wife and I like her so much that if she weren't my wife, and I was married to somebody else, I'd cheat on my wife to be with Peggy." (Both laugh.)

D: Were there logistical problems on *D-Day, the Sixth of June*?

K: In a way. The problem was that the picture wasn't supposed to cost too much money, and I didn't have enough soldiers to invade the beaches of Normandy. So I had to do everything with eighty soldiers that Eisenhower did with twenty thousand.

D: You worked with Robert Taylor on that film.

K: Robert Taylor I guess was the handsomest actor there ever was. But he always said, "I'm not an actor. I don't know what I'm doing." I'd say, "Robert, you did *Camille* with Greta Garbo." He said, "Believe me, I didn't know what the hell I was doing. But a beautiful director, George Cukor, told me what to do. He acted it and I just copied him, and out came a good performance. You show me what to do and I'll do it." He had a complex that he couldn't do the work, that he wasn't born to be an actor. I think Robert Taylor had talent. Maybe he was not a genius like the other great actors, but he grew into a talent. I think you can learn by learning how to relax and not being afraid of the camera.

D: Did you find problems transferring *Flower Drum Song*, a Broadway musical, to the screen?

K: No. I loved the show, and I loved the music, which was so lovely. I worked with all Chinese and Japanese actors on that. There was not one Caucasian actor in it. Rodgers and Hammerstein kept a close eye on the production. They had in their contract that nothing could be changed without their okay. They always protected their properties. They had had the experience of someone fooling around with the plot of their shows and with their songs. We directors like to do that to give the show our personal stamp. But that wasn't allowed on a Rodgers and Hammerstein show. I gladly went along with their design because the show was so interesting and fun to do.

D: Did you find *The Story of Ruth* an interesting film?

K: Yes. The actress who played in it was not who I wanted to have. I wanted Susan Strasberg, the daughter of Lee Strasberg, for that, and I even tested her. But the studio wanted someone else. We got this actress from Israel, her name was Elana Eden. She came from Tel Aviv, and she was on the stage there. She was completely inexperienced in pictures. I don't think she was quite adequate, although she was very attractive and a good actress, but too much from the stage.

D: Do you have fond memories of *The Singing Nun*?

K: I have no fond memories of it. That probably was the most difficult thing I ever did. Not the picture, but the procedure of the production. On that picture there was absolutely nothing but friction. I decided this was the last thing I'd ever do. I never did another picture.

It was too difficult. It wasn't easy to work with some of the people, but it was impossible to work with the producer [John Beck], who by the way had been the producer of *Harvey*. But on this picture we just couldn't get along because he had constant friction with the star, Debbie Reynolds, who didn't want him to come on the set. The producer insisted that he be on the set, and she walked out. I was in between. We finally finished the picture, and I never saw it. I didn't want to see it.

D: Had filmmaking in Hollywood changed a great deal by that time?

K: No, it was the same, except that some of the collaborators and performers had become more careful and more fearful of doing the wrong thing. That's why it became so difficult for the people who tried to produce something good and penetrate with new ideas. That was really very difficult. I do not blame anybody but my own personality, of not being able to be really tough. The truly great directors are very strong in mind and fist. I wish I could have been stronger and insisted on firing more people, or hit more people, or not accepted a story. I believed in security of production and security of my job. I was under contract to studios. It would have been better if I had been independent and just done the pictures I wanted to do. Many of these pictures I did not care to make. But since I was under contract—seven years to Universal, three years to Metro-Goldwyn-Mayer, one year to Goldwyn, seventeen years to Twentieth Century-Fox—I had to do what I was told to do. Later it occurred to me that if I hadn't been under contract and sat at home and waited until something came along that I liked, it would have been better. But I didn't do that. I liked the idea of being paid all year around and paying for the college education of my children and the mink coats of my wife.

D: Did you develop an overall philosophy of filmmaking?

K: Well, if you want to call it a philosophy. I believed in complete relaxation before I started to build a scene, because you come on the set and everybody is tense, especially the actors, with few exceptions. I don't know why. Orry-Kelly, who designed costumes for one of my pictures, told me, "There are only two times when I like actors and actresses—the first three months of their career and the last three months of their career. In between they're impossible to handle." And he was right, because the constant fear in a performer becomes overwhelming. They're afraid of doing something wrong and that their career will be finished.

D: Don't you think there's a fear in many fields, once a person has established a level of success, that one can't equal or go beyond what's already been accomplished?

K: That's it.

D: It seems that anybody, a writer or a composer, whose career is constantly on the line for appraisal, is bound to face insecurity.

K: Of course, but there's a great difference. A writer or a composer doesn't have anybody to face but himself when he works. An actor faces the director, the producer, the writer, and the cameraman, and that becomes difficult.

D: Not to mention public approval.

K: A screen actor doesn't face the public until later, not while he creates. Only the stage actor faces the public during a performance.

D: Do you feel that you put your signature on the films you made?

K: I tried to. I couldn't always penetrate, I couldn't get through, but I tried to reflect my personality, which today would probably be too gentle and too sentimental and too coy. I wouldn't want to make any more pictures. I'm too old anyway. But I don't want to go to the trouble of going home and not being able to sleep, and getting up at six o'clock in the morning to see rushes.

Filmmaking is much better now. The writers are going much deeper into characterization. When I was a young man, I went to an opening of an American picture called *The Gay Divorcee* with Fred Astaire and Ginger Rogers, and I was delighted. Not only was I delighted that they were such marvelous dancers, but with the story, the jokes, and the fun. Last year I saw the picture on television, and I don't know how I could have like it. The picture had no depth whatsoever, it was completely two-dimensional. Today writers go to the widest extent to show the inside of a human being. I went through that, too, but only when we had truly great writers. I worked with Robert Sherwood, who was great, and Mary Chase, who did *Harvey*. They both penetrated the skin of people.

D: Do you think that your professional life contributed to your personal development?

K: Of course, your work can't help leaving some impression on you. Directing makes your life entirely different from the life of a bookkeeper or a jockey or what-have-you. It leaves a mark. I consider myself very fortunate, because I know that my talents were limited and my personality not quite what a director's should be. I tried hard to create a comedy atmosphere, a leisurely pace, and a beautiful spark of humor on my sets, but I could never deal with difficulties easily. Darryl Zanuck told me once, "You have to be the head and impress upon your actors that there is no resistance possible." I said, "But Darryl, sometimes I may be wrong and the actor might be right." He said, "You have to put your fist on the table, even if you think you are wrong, because that's the only language actors know." And he was right.

Henry Koster's Feature Films

1932   *Das Abenteuer der Thea Roland* (in Germany)
1933   *Das Hassliche Madchen* (in Germany)
1934   *Peter* (in Hungary)
          Kleine Mutti (in Hungary)
1935   *Katharina die Letzte* (in Austria)
1936   *Das Tagebuch der Geliebten* (in Austria)
          Three Smart Girls
1937   *100 Men and a Girl*
1938   *The Rage of Paris*
1939   *Three Smart Girls Grow Up*
          First Love
1940   *Spring Parade*
1941   *It Started with Eve*
1942   *Between Us Girls*
1944   *Music for Millions*
1946   *Two Sisters from Boston*
1947   *The Unfinished Dance*
          The Bishop's Wife
1948   *The Luck of the Irish*
1949   *Come to the Stable*
          The Inspector General
1950   *Wabash Avenue*
          My Blue Heaven
          Harvey

1951   *No Highway in the Sky*

Mr. Belvedere Rings the Bell

Elopement

1952   *O. Henry's Full House* ("The Cop and the Anthem" episode)

Stars and Strips Forever

1953   *My Cousin Rachel*

The Robe

1954   *Desiree*

1955   *A Man Called Peter*

The Virgin Queen

Good Morning, Miss Dove

1956   *D-Day, the Sixth of June*

The Power and the Prize

1957   *My Man Godfrey*

1958   *Fraulein*

1959   *The Naked Maja*

1960   *The Story of Ruth*

1961   *Flower Drum Song*

1963   *Mr. Hobbs Takes a Vacation*

Take Her, She's Mine

1965   *Dear Brigitte*

1966   *The Singing Nun*

IRVING RAPPER

From the Dramatic Stage

Director Irving Rapper was born in London in 1898 and at the age of eight moved with his family to the United States. He joined the Washington Square Players while a student at New York University and later directed plays in London and on Broadway. Under contract to Warner Bros. for nearly two decades, he worked at the studio first as a dialogue coach and subsequently directed some of the company's most important films, including three classic Bette Davis pictures: *Now, Voyager*, *The Corn Is Green*, and *Deception*. Retired since 1978, Rapper died in Woodland Hills, California, in 1999.

The following interview was taped in the director's home in Los Angeles on August 13, 1980.

D: Mr. Rapper, could we start with your telling me how a New York boy from London first became interested in theater?

R: Having been born in England, when I arrived in this country I was conscious of the fact that I wasn't speaking Americanese, and I was made fun of. The British accent, more or less, stuck with me. As I was growing up, I knew that I'd have something to do with the English language. First it was going to be law, but when I was studying law I knew that it wouldn't be law, that I was trying to satisfy my mother. I was the only son in the family. While I was in college, I started to direct varsity shows. Even in high school, when somebody got up to recite a poem, the teacher would say, "Oh, sit down, let Rapper come up and recite that." It all started in school.

D: Did you study theater at New York University?

R: Never, but I directed their first varsity show and continued to do so for a few years. That's how I got through school. And I directed some of Columbia's, too.

D: Didn't you direct a production of *The Late Christopher Bean*?

R: Yes, for producer Gilbert Miller, but that was later in my career. The first play I ever directed was *Five Star Final* in London. I had gotten sentimental about England. I received a special curtain call on opening night, and I met the then Prince of Wales and Noel Coward and really got off to a good start over there. I was very lucky in the beginning.

D: How did the New York stage compare with the London theater at that time?

R: Well, in those days my wits weren't too sharp about plays, but I always felt, even then, that London cared more about the content of a story. There wasn't the flare of showmanship that New York had. And there was no comparison with America's musical plays.

D: I know that you directed a production of *Firebird* on Broadway.

R: Yes, with Judith Anderson and Henry Stephenson. That was a very nice play written by a Hungarian. They always used to say that Gilbert Miller was the greatest importer in the world. He was the greatest producer in the world, because in one year he had three or four of the biggest hits on Broadway. He had under contract Helen Hayes, Jeanne Eagels, Charles Laughton, Leslie Howard. He would wait a year to get the proper second cast from Australia. He was that meticulous. He had great taste.

D: How would you describe Judith Anderson's style of acting?

R: It was rather turn-of-the-century stuff, but she had great stature. When she arrived on the stage, she had a regal bearing. She just swept across the stage.

D: Do you feel that your stage work was good preparation for a film career?

R: It couldn't have been better. I don't know what I would have done without it. When I arrived in Hollywood, all of the directors were hold-overs from the silent days. None of them had an expertise in the theater. Even my great mentor, Michael Curtiz, whom I think was the most versatile director in the Warner Bros. studio, couldn't understand the language too well. Neither did William Dieterle, who was a very scholarly director, or Anatole Litvak, who directed *Mayerling*. I was always cast as dialogue director with these brilliant foreigners, and I learned and tried to unlearn some of their techniques. Michael Curtiz was the most sympathetic man I ever worked with, and I owe a great deal to him.

D: How did your association with Warner Bros. come about?

R: I met an agent who said, "If I sell you to Warner Bros., will you let me be your agent?" I said, "Fine." So I saw Walter MacEwen, who was the head of the studio's story department. He said, "But you've done stage plays; that's too rich for our blood. We have Eddie Robinson and Paul Muni and Jimmy Cagney and Humphrey Bogart, and they make gangster pictures. Haven't you done any of the rough plays?" I walked up and down my room and finally remembered that I'd directed a play in stock called *Crime*. I called MacEwen and said, "I did a play called *Crime* and I'd like to talk to you about it." We met, and he said, "We have a very difficult director, and if you please him we'll give you a long-term contract."

The director was Michael Curtiz, who had a very bad reputation. He was just finishing the editing of *Captain Blood*, and the studio wasn't quite sure whether Errol Flynn was going to be the great star they had groomed him to be. Mike Curtiz came into the office, spoke with a very heavy Hungarian accent, adjusted his tie like George Raft, and said, "Irving, I hear you are a genius from Broadway and Forty-second Street. If you answer me one question right, you have the job." I said, "What's the question?" He said, "Have you ever worked with a Hungarian before?" I said, "I worked with the greatest Hungarian in the world—Ferenc Molnar. We did all of his plays." Curtiz smiled and said, "Here's the script. Tell me what stinks in it and you're my boy."

D: What do you think was Curtiz's special talent as a director?

R: In spite of the fact that he was rather rough and severe, people rarely got angry at him. He murdered the English language and spoke malaprops all the time, which made people hysterical. By the time they deciphered what he meant, they'd lost their anger. Mike had a sharp ear and could tell what sounded right immediately. And his expertise with the camera was terrific. Mike told me, "My big mistake is that I am very heavy-handed and hammy. If I'm hammy, you should tell me."

D: Would you consider Curtiz primarily a visual director?

R: Primarily. I was interested in the visual technique of cinema making. Warner Bros. offered me a picture with Kay Francis at the end of my very first year as a dialogue director. I turned it down because I thought it was terrible. Hal Wallis, the studio's executive producer, took me to task and said, "People have been waiting for years to direct a picture, and here you turn one down. Your feet are pretty much up in the air, aren't they?" I said, "No, Mr. Wallis, my feet are very solid on the ground. I will not start with a B picture."

So I waited a long time. They offered me another picture, a Nazi picture, and I turned that down. I did nothing until I found a script with warmth. I was given rave reviews on my first picture, and in the same year I did *One Foot in Heaven* with Fredric March. That put me seventh on the list in those days; we were numbered at the studio. Right after that came *Now, Voyager*, which is constantly being revived and shown on television.

D: What was the general atmosphere around Warner Bros. in the mid-1930s?

R: It was like a family feud in the Democratic Party. People were always feuding and getting suspensions. I had ten. Bogart said to me, "What's the matter, Skipper, you look down in the mouth?" I said, "Another suspension." He said, "How many does this make?" I said, "It's my tenth." He said, "One more and you'll look like the Golden Gate Bridge."

But the studio was a family. Jack Warner was paying millions of dollars a week on great stars and writers and directors and camera people, so I can understand his point of view. But I wasn't about to submit myself to that kind of system, and Warner knew it very early. One day when I had one of these suspensions and had had a terrible row with Warner himself, he said, "You're going to sit out for four months." That meant I couldn't work anywhere else. I smiled, and Warner said, "What the hell are you smiling about?" I said, "I'm going to go abroad and get something I can't get here." He said, "What's that?" I said, "Culture." He said, "Wait a minute, let's talk this over." So I talked myself out of that suspension.

D: Despite his tumultuous qualities, did you find Jack Warner generally a fair man?

R: Yes. At home he was a brilliant host, and his wife was the most charming woman I've ever met. Once when I was on suspension, Mrs. Warner came rushing over to me at a party and kissed me. I said, "Darling, you're not supposed to do that." She said, "Why not?" I said, "I'm on suspension." And she said, "Irving, sometimes I think Jack doesn't understand either you or me."

D: Would you say that Warner Bros. was a well run studio?

R: Yes. I think it was a great training school for people. We always had about thirty youngsters under contract as performers, and then about ten or fifteen of them would be let go. If Warner liked you, he'd let you do anything you wanted. For instance, I was on suspension when they were about to start *The Corn Is Green*. They called me back, and Warner gave me a $40,000 bonus. That's how he could be kind to you.

I never asked for a picture in my life. They wanted me to do *The Corn Is Green* very much; they had already made fifteen tests. Even though there were big fights between us every day when we worked together, Bette Davis thought I represented the sum total and wanted me to direct this picture. She was a rebellious hellion and very difficult, but we respected each other. I tried to feel as if I was collaborating with her. Suddenly she'd twist around at a certain angle or do something with some volatile move, which she is so dramatically capable of, that would change my entire direction. Often it was to the good, because it was natural.

D: To me one of the strengths of Warner Bros. was the depth of its stock company.

R: Oh, yes. We were surrounded with the most wonderful stable of actors. Max Arnow, who came from New York and was an agent in New York, built up that stock company. MGM had far more glamorous people than we did, far more. But we had the actors.

D: Did you work with Errol Flynn?

R: Only on dialogue. I was supposed to do *Too Much, Too Soon*, where he played John Barrymore. I hadn't seen him for three or four years by then. I never thought he was a great actor, but he was a good funster. He never took life seriously. He was absolutely either drunk or full of jokes. He hated the studio and hated work. He knew he was handsome, and he wore costumes beautifully. But that's all. I don't think Flynn ever qualified as a great actor. He mesmerized audiences with his beauty.

D: Did you know composer Erich Korngold at Warners?

R: He did only one score for me and that was on *Deception*. Because of Ernie Haller's photography the film was beautifully stylized. Korngold's music was heavy, heavy German music, whereas John Collier, who wrote the script, was a light writer. The two clashed. Bette Davis insisted on a melodramatic finish, which I fought. *Deception* was an interesting picture thanks to Claude Rains. I didn't know whether I wanted to do it. I thought the script was good but not good enough. Warner had bought the story for Claude Rains.

D: On *Shining Hour*, your first picture as director, you were fortunate to have a great cameraman, James Wong Howe.

R: Jimmy was great on mood. My reviews were tremendous. I've made a few lousy pictures, but thank God I have a few memorable ones that have played over and over again.

D: *One Foot in Heaven* with Fredric March you mentioned earlier.

R: He was one of my favorite actors. His wife, Florence Eldridge, who was a fine actress herself, said to me in front of Freddie, after she'd seen the first week's rushes, "Irving, you're the first director who has taken the ham out of him." I said, "I wasn't conscious of it." Fredric March was a director's pet. So was Barbara Stanwyck, except that she always did a competent job but never rose to the ultimate heights.

D: *Now, Voyager* is one of the films for which you're best remembered. Was that an easy picture for you to do?

R: No. My mother had just died. I was the only male alive in my family. My father died when I was nine. I told Hal Wallis, "I've got to go back to New York." He said, "Irving, this is the biggest picture I have on my list, and you'll be great for it. Bette Davis is going to play the lead." I said, "Hal, please let me go and I'll come back and do anything you want." He said, "The only way you'll lose your grief is by plunging into work," and that made sense.

Bette Davis and I had been friends while I was a dialogue director. I was the buffer and her advisor. But now I was to direct her. Before production started on the picture I ran into William Wyler in the lunchroom. He was one of my favorite directors and also Bette's. I said, "Willy, I want to ask you a question. What is Bette Davis like to direct?" He said, "I thought you two were best friends." I said, "To direct." He laughed and said, "When she's good, she's an angel out of heaven. When she isn't, don't come to the studio." And I found that out.

The famous cigarette business in *Now, Voyager* was a beautiful gag but it was nothing compared to the great acting in the film. Wallis had cast the picture because I was working on another assignment. I did insist on using Gladys Cooper instead of Dame May Whitty as Bette's mother, because Dame May was a nanny and not capable of dominating and tyrannizing Davis the way the script demanded. It all worked out beautifully. The counterpoint was Claude Rains playing the sympathetic psychiatrist who drew everything out.

We came to the cigarette scene, which was supposed to take place on the coast of South America. We shot it in Laguna, of all places. The scene is in Olive Higgins Prouty's novel. I didn't dream it up. And Casey Robinson transferred it to the screenplay. Paul Henreid later claimed that he thought up the notion of lighting two cigarettes at the same time and passing one over to Davis. Henreid and I were none too friendly.

D: How would Bette Davis work out a characterization?

R: It was not an instant thing at all. She read a script over and over again, and she memorized as much as she could. I hardly ever took a take again because she'd missed a word. It was always an innuendo or some slight thing that wasn't quite right. She's an impulsive worker. If she feels that she's too near or too far from something, or something isn't right, she'll rebel. That's the reason I always had to do my homework and be so flexible. I had to be flexible enough that I could immediately think of something better. Bette is a great technician herself. She doesn't have to look at the camera, she feels where it is. But she double-does something that's good. She punctuates herself tremendously, which is a great attribute and also sometimes a slight weakness. Bette would be far better if she did not read every line as if it were an Academy Award line. That was her trouble.

Once we had a big argument. I said, "Bette, don't give me an argument now. You know what's going to happen. You'll be a hundred per cent right here and you'll be a hundred per cent wrong in the projection room." The more you talked to her, the more she'd resent it and fight you and yell, but she respected you for arguing. You've got to admire the enormous power she projects when she acts. Bette's greatest gift is not only her acting but her visual reaction. She's an overpowering actress, and she uses her eyes to such an advantage. Very often I would rehearse a scene much more than ordinary so that Bette would know what to throw away. Most of the time it didn't help. Sometimes I'd stop her and say, "Bette, you're giving me an elocution lesson. You're spitting your words out." Her own electricity and her determination to be a fine actress were so strong. But she always gave me credit for taste and sensitivity.

D: Why wasn't *Rhapsody in Blue*, a musical, shot in color?

R: The picture would have cost three times as much. My greatest problem on that picture, quite frankly, was in casting George Gershwin. I wanted Tyrone Power, who would have been great because he had those liquid brown eyes and he certainly would have been box-office. But Ty had gone off to war. Jack Warner suggested Cary Grant. Imagine my turning down Cary Grant. I said, "Jack, how can we use Cary Grant? Gershwin's mother and father are peddling pots and pans with a Jewish accent under the elevated in New York. How can the boy talk to his mother and father with an ultra British accent?" Warner said, "Well, what about your friend John Garfield?" I said, "Now you're stabbing me with a knife. Johnny is a marvelous actor and full of heart. He'd be poignant in the part, and he'd be great in the ghetto scenes. But do you see him with a high hat and two beautiful girls later in the picture? Johnny never wore a tie in his life."

D: Did you work well with Robert Alda once he was cast in the Gershwin role?

R: Yes, I did, but I had to teach instead of direct. I surrounded Alda with some great people, although the two girls [Alexis Smith and Joan Leslie] were stock girls. Jesse Lasky, the producer, brought that property to the studio, and he didn't fight as much as I did. Alda tried very hard but he wasn't an experienced actor. When you came on a Bette Davis set, the electricity was charged, and here everything was peaceful and quiet.

D: Was making *The Adventures of Mark Twain* a rewarding experience for you?

R: I thought Freddie March was magnificent, except that his accent was a little too strong in it. He came from the theater and always tended to do a little too much. I wish I'd got him down a little simpler. It would have been better if he'd had a Midwestern, pioneer accent. Alexis Smith was just right for the part of the wife, and Alan Hale was always good for a laugh whenever we worked together. During the shooting of that picture everything was lovely and quiet. To work in a studio and be happy is a rarity.

D: Did you find Alexis Smith a talented actress?

R: She was a hard worker. She was a very pleasant lady, but I don't think she had dramatic greatness. She had great presence. She had a certain style, but there was no fire to her. Having worked with Bette Davis, I must say I've been a little spoiled.

D: How about Joan Leslie, who was one of the female leads in *Rhapsody in Blue*?

R: She wasn't an actress. The last time I was a dialogue director was on *High Sierra*, working with the wonderful Raoul Walsh, who saw more with one eye than I did with two. Leslie was all of seventeen at the time, and I was trying to explain a scene to her. Finally Bogie said, "Irving, let me take over." He said to her, "Do you like ice cream? They're taking the ice cream away from you. Won't you be sad, wouldn't you cry?" She's a lovely girl, but when it came to drama, she wasn't for me.

D: What was Steve Trilling's role at Warners?

R: Steve was a very bad influence on the company, because he got the contract players in great parts and ruined stories. He would always do the dirty work for Jack Warner. Steve himself was a very quiet, polite, nice guy—but not in that job. It took a Hal Wallis to do that job [executive producer] properly.

D: What was Wallis's unique ability?

R: Wallis was an S.O.B. and a tyrant but the most expertised man I ever met. He could tell you the budget on a picture while you were talking to him. He knew a value immediately. His day-to-day judgment was excellent. He was a difficult man to see and really ran the studio. He got the great pictures for Bette and all the other people. It wasn't Jack Warner.

D: Were there problems turning *The Voice of the Turtle*, a successful Broadway play, into a film?

R: No, it gave me greater scope. I wanted Olivia de Havilland for the
girl's part. She was winsome and cute and charming and gullible. But de
Havilland had fought with Jack Warner. "I'd rather close the gates of this
joint than have that so-and-so in this studio," Warner told me. I went to
New York to see the play and came back to the studio, and Eleanor
Parker had the role. She was a lovely lady and gave a good performance,
but she didn't have the star thrust of others. Then I heard the name that
nobody wanted to hear—Ronald Reagan. Reagan came to see me
about playing the male lead, and we began discussing some pertinent
points about the picture. I said, "How do you feel about this story? How
do you like the language? Isn't it the most beautiful you've ever read?
The play is by John van Druten." Reagan said, "Irving, no, I hate this
shit." I said, "One of us will have to leave this picture." And he said,
"I'm doing Warner a favor." I said, "You dare to talk like this to the
director! I'd pay for you to leave right now. You are guilty of being very
ill-mannered and very unprofessional. You are talking about a beautiful
story that lasted two years on Broadway with Margaret Sullavan and
Elliott Nugent in the leads."

Reagan gave a very perfunctory performance in *Voice of the Turtle*.
I hated him; nobody wanted him ever in any picture. I screamed with
laughter when I heard that he'd said in some political speech, "When
I came back from the war. . . . " The only battle he fought was the
battle of Culver City.

D: Why did you leave Warner Bros.?

R: I went to Italy, I did two big biblical pictures there. I had a lot of
money, and I loved to travel. By that time there was a slipping down
of all the studios in Hollywood. I felt that coming, and I didn't see
any good scripts.

D: Had there been financial cut-backs at Warners?

R: Oh, yes, they cut salaries in half. Who the hell wanted half?
Either give me my money or nothing at all. I'd rather enjoy myself.

D: One of your first American films after you left Warner Bros. was
Anna Lucasta. Was that a good picture for you?

R: No. I thought that Susan Hayward was going to do it. But the
playwright, Philip Yordan, who was a little tricky, had promised

Paulette Goddard that she would play the part. I didn't know that. I never would have taken the picture otherwise.

D: Was Goddard an effective actress?

R: Strangely enough, it was like me with Bette Davis—we always seemed to turn out good pictures. Mitch Leisen had turned out one or two good pictures with Goddard. I met Mitch, and he told me, "You'll find Polly lovely." She was straight and frank and always called before we had a meeting to say that she was on her way. She hated lateness.

D: Were you eager to direct *The Glass Menagerie*?

R: No. I'd just finished a big, prestigious picture, which wasn't box office but something I liked very much. Charlie Feldman bought the rights to *The Glass Menagerie*, and they sent me to Italy to talk to Tennessee Williams. He and I turned out to be great friends; he used to come to my house in Malibu all the time. He hated the cast we had in the picture. I always thought we should have cast unknown people. I tested Tallulah Bankhead for the Laurette Taylor role in *Glass Menagerie*. The test was planned to take three days, and it included six scenes. I flew to New York to direct it. The test took place in a low-ceilinged room in a studio in the West 50's during the sweltering summer heat. I went to Tallulah's dressing room to wish her well and noticed a little bottle of whisky on the table. I was frightened to meet her. But she said, "Whatever you suggest, darling, I'll build on. Whatever I say, you'll build on." I thought she was going to be difficult, but she was like a child, so sweet and lovely. I was absolutely floored by her performance. It's the greatest test I've ever made or seen in my life. I couldn't believe I was seeing such reality. Bankhead was absolutely natural, so moving, so touching without even trying. The crew was stunned, too.

After the test was completed I went to Tallulah's dressing room to hug her and thank her. I noticed that some of the drink was gone, but she hadn't touched a drop during the time we worked. Errol Flynn cost Tallulah the part. Jack Warner had suffered because of Flynn's bouts with the bottle and dreaded the same problems with Tallulah. So the studio decided not to sign her.

D: Were you happy about Gertrude Lawrence in the role?

R: Gertrude Lawrence never understood what she was playing. Arthur Kennedy was the only cast member I wanted.

D: When you made *The Brave One*, did you feel that you were taking a risk using a Dalton Trumbo script, since Trumbo had been blacklisted because of his political views?

R: I didn't know for months that the script was by Dalton Trumbo. I gave it to my best friend, and he said, "Irving, it reads like a fairy tale." Of all the Academy Awards, who would ever expect that one would fall on that story?

D: Do you feel that you put your own personality into the films you directed?

R: Oh, very much so. I'm a man of tremendous moods and fanciful imagination. When I work one thing reminds me of another. I just flow with thoughts and ideas all the time.

D: Do you feel that your approach to filmmaking changed over the years?

R: No, I pretty much stuck to what I'd done, because I had a style of my own. As writers are always told by their teachers, "Write what you know." These kids today (and even in my day) think they're making the greatest impression when they move the camera fancifully. No, when you have a camera move, do it gracefully and beautifully. I must say I've been complimented a great deal on the fluidity of my camera. But when people stand still, the camera should stand still.

D: Could you summarize what you feel was the "Rapper style"?

R: No. There's only one answer to that, and it embraces the entire art. Imagination. You go into the realm of fancy. Once you can do that and be convincing, you're a great actor or you're a great artist or you're a great director.

D: Do you feel that your professional life contributed to your personal development?

R: Well, everybody knows that the moment I'm through with a picture I fly off to foreign countries. If I hear English, it's not a vacation. I love to get lost, I purposely get lost. I ask people questions so that I can learn from them. I love that. As a matter of fact, the more successful I am with a picture, I think the more simple I am with people.

D: Do you have a favorite picture?

R: No, because I still think I can do a better job with *Now, Voyager*, even with *The Corn Is Green*, even with *The Brave One*. There's always something that could be done better. If you're a perfectionist at all, you're never really happy with the results.

D: We're always haunted by the things we could have done.

R: Oh, yes. You have nightmares. Sometimes I don't sleep after a preview. That's the reason I run away after I see my films in the projection room. I know some kid in Wisconsin is going to laugh, or some guy in another place is going to snore. Even *The Brave One*, which I knew was a touching story, I never felt the impact of that story until the music by Victor Young was added. I must say, and I'm not being humble, filmmaking is a collaboration. It's not just the director who is responsible for a quality picture. Everything that goes into a film must be right or it's wrong. Filmmaking is an orchestration of beats and stops.

Irving Rapper's Feature Films

1941	*Shining Victory*
	One Foot in Heaven
1942	*The Gay Sisters*
	Now Voyager
1944	*The Adventures of Mark Twain*
1945	*The Corn Is Green*
	Rhapsody in Blue
1946	*Deception*
1947	*The Voice of the Turtle*
1949	*Anna Lucasta*
1950	*The Glass Menagerie*
1952	*Another Man's Poison*
1954	*Bad for Each Other*
	Forever Female
1956	*Strange Intruder*
	The Brave One
1958	*Marjorie Morningstar*
1959	*The Miracle*
1960	*The Story of Joseph and His Brethren*
1962	*Pontius Pilate*
1970	*The Christine Jorgensen Story*
1978	*Born Again*

CHARLES WALTERS

The Dancing Director

Charles Walters was born in Brooklyn, New York, in 1911 but grew up in Anaheim, California. He first gained recognition on the Broadway stage as a dancer in such shows as Cole Porter's *Jubilee* and *Du Barry Was a Lady* and Rodgers and Hart's *I Married an Angel*. He turned to choreography in the early 1940s, was dance director for a number of important Broadway musicals, and joined MGM in that capacity in 1942, becoming a respected member of the Freed unit at the studio. In 1947 Walters directed his first motion picture, *Good News*, and went on to make such classic screen musicals as *Easter Parade*, *The Barkleys of Broadway*, and *High Society*, as well as successful comedies, among them *Three Guys Named Mike* and *The Tender Trap*. He retired from filmmaking in 1966 and died in Malibu, California, from lung cancer in 1982.

The following interview was taped in the director's home in Malibu on August 21, 1980.

D: How did you, a boy from southern California, first become interested in theater and dance?
W: I've danced as long as I can remember. That's all I wanted to do. The family wanted me to be a lawyer, and all I wanted to do was dance. My parents finally insisted that I go to USC after I graduated from Anaheim High School. I danced my way through one year at USC. Even as a pledge in a fraternity I had to dance for my dinner and wait tables every night. I was a freak more or less. A man just didn't dance in those days, at least not in Anaheim. When I was seventeen, some friends of the family came down from Oregon. They said if I would drive them back to Oregon they would send me back by ship.

41

That sounded exciting. On the ship coming home I met a girl named Ada Broadbent, who was the prima ballerina and stager for Fanchon and Marco. I stayed friends with Ada for two or three years, and when I was about nineteen, a unit from Fanchon and Marco was going out on tour and they needed a replacement. I'd never had a dancing lesson, but Ada said, "I think maybe I can coach you enough that you can be the replacement." This was an army unit, and I was on the road with it for six months, making $33.60 a week. I saved $500 and talked the family into letting me go to New York. I didn't know a soul there. All I had was just the blind drive and blind ambition that only youth has.

D: Was *New Faces of 1934* your first Broadway show?

W: Yes. Henry Fonda and Imogene Coca were the two big names in the show. Coca was the first girl I worked with in New York.

D: Did you find her a skillful dancer?

W: Oh, no. Like Judy Garland, Coca was very effective but a faker. She was not a dancer per se. Coca was a hell of an actress and a comedienne and could do the steps and get by. I bought myself a polo coat to go to New York, and this was my first winter there. It was cold in the theater, so Coca would wear my polo coat to rehearse. I did an interlude in the show, and Leonard Sillman, our producer, decided that it would be funny if Coca did the routine with me wearing my coat. Since it was my only coat, I'd wear it to the theater, and her dresser would come over to my dressing room for the coat, and then I'd pick it up on my way out.

D: How was Leonard Sillman to work with?

W: Impossible. He was a big ham and hysterical. They needed a spot in front of the curtain for a scene change, and Leonard said, "I think I'll give Chuck a solo." Here I was a boy out of the chorus and I was getting a solo; it was the thrill of my life. Then Sillman said, "I've got a brilliant idea. I think you should be all in black, with a black curtain behind. We'll illuminate your shoes and put the strobe light on them, and it'll be just feet flying around." I was heartbroken, because I couldn't smile and be charming to sell the number. The first time I did it with an audience the lighting man was drunk and forgot to put on the strobe. So the number was like a five-minute lull. People were coughing and rattling their programs. That was my first solo.

D: How did *Jubilee* come about for you?

W: My dance partner, Dorothy Fox, and I were in a Theater Guild musical called *Parade*. During that year all the scuttlebutt in New York was about the great names that were on a Caribbean cruise writing a new show called *Jubilee*. It was going to be *the* show of the season. Later there were rumors that Moss Hart and Monty Woolley and Sam Harris were out front in the theater to see me. Then three or four weeks after that there were agents at the stage door saying, "Look, if you sign with me I think I can get you an audition for *Jubilee*. One day I was called to the Harris office to read for Monty Woolley. After the reading Woolley nodded to Sam Harris, who said, "Well, we can pay you $350 a week. We'd like you to play the Prince of Wales in *Jubilee*." I introduced "Begin the Beguine" and "Just One of Those Things" and had a part that ran all the way through the show. That really started my career off. I was in almost every important musical for the next ten years. My whole reason for going to New York was to be discovered by Hollywood. I wanted to be at MGM. For me there wasn't any other studio. I couldn't stand the way George Murphy danced; I knew I was better than he was.

D: Was Cole Porter, who wrote the score for *Jubilee*, an easy man to work with?

W: He was very cold. I've done four shows with Cole over the years and still that cold reserve prevailed. Even after the movie *High Society*, the last thing I did with him, I got a very formal note of thanks.

D: What kind of experience was *I Married an Angel* for you?

W: I was pretty well established on Broadway by then. The show opened in the summer, which is not auspicious. So I thought, "What the hell, it's a job, I'll do it." The show was a smash hit, of course, and it ran for over a year. To work with Audrey Christie was a real thrill, and we became close friends. Ballet meant nothing to me at that time. It wasn't until years later that I appreciated who George Balanchine was. My gosh! I was really working with one of the top choreographers. Balanchine was charming, a real delight. I was pure musical comedy, so he didn't give me anything balletic.

D: Was Lorenz Hart, the lyricist, intimately involved with rehearsals?

W: When he was sober enough. I'll never forget our dress rehearsal with the orchestra, which went on and on until about three in the morning. There was snoring in the balcony so loud that we had to stop everything, and people went up to find out who was making so much noise. It was Larry passed out up in the balcony. Richard Rodgers, his partner, was very sober and business-like.

D: Was *Du Barry Was a Lady* an interesting show for you?

W: By that time I was probably twenty-six, and I was beginning to realize that I wasn't crazy about performing. I loved it when we were getting the show together and for the first few weeks when friends were coming to see it. But when we'd settled down to a run, I almost resented it. I disliked the repetition, and there was no air-conditioning in those days. Betty Grable was an absolute joy to work with, just an absolute darling. She was another good faker, but with those legs she didn't have to dance. Believe me, in person she was more doll-like than on the screen. Betty invented the word barrelhouse. She was the dirtiest-mouthed dame I've ever known, but on her it was adorable. Golly, we had fun. But that was my last show as a performer. I'd just kind of had it.

D: Did you learn a great deal from choreographer Robert Alton?

W: Oh, yes. I learned style and fluidity. As a dancer you're always conscious that you must have a style, and style worried me. I finally realized that my style came from simplification. What I did the easiest I did best.

D: Was *Let's Face It* your first Broadway show as a choreographer?

W: Yes, and I found that I loved it. The challenge, of course, was that I had to prove myself. This was my first shot at being a choreographer, and I had to prove to Cole Porter and producer Vinton Freedley that I could do it. *Lets Face It* was Danny Kaye's first starring vehicle, and he was darling to work with. We've remained good friends all these years. Eve Arden was also in the show. I've known Eve for so long, but we've never been friends. She will not break down.

D: How did your MGM contract come about?

W: Between Broadway shows I'd always rush home to California. Usually I drove out because it was relaxing. My friend, John Darrow, and I decided that we should buy some property out here, since it was home for both of us. He had become a big agent in New York, and I was doing very well. John and I bought some property in Hollywood and built a house, and we couldn't wait until my show was over so we could rush out here. Gene Kelly was already at MGM, and John was handling Gene. One day the phone rang and it was Gene. He said, "I'm going to do *Du Barry Was a Lady* as a movie with Lucille Ball and Red Skelton." Seymour Felix apparently was the dance director on the picture, and Gene said, "I can't stand working with him. Where is Bob Alton?" John said, "I just signed him for the new *Ziegfeld Follies*." Gene said, "Well, where's Charlie?" He's the only person that ever called me Charlie. John said, "He's sitting right here." Gene said, "Would he do a number for me? It's my big solo in *Du Barry*." John said, "Chuck, do you want to do a number for Gene in *Du Barry*?" And I said, "Sure, why not."

So I had a four-week contract with the studio to do a number for Gene Kelly in *Du Barry Was a Lady*. Metro liked the number, and they gave me another number in the picture. They liked that and gave me another number. Seymour Felix was getting less and less and less. Finally I did the whole picture. MGM liked the picture and gave me a long-term contract. I was there for twenty-two years.

D: What kind of a man was producer Arthur Freed?

W: Arthur's greatest talent was to surround himself with talent. He could spot talent—Kay Thompson, Roger Edens, Vincente Minnelli, Ralph Blane and Hugh Martin. He could get them. Arthur had ideas, but Roger Edens provided the taste.

D: You did the choreography for the movie *Best Foot Forward*, whereas Gene Kelly had done the choreography for the show in New York. Did you keep any of his material in the film?

W: I never saw the show on Broadway. Metro realized by then that I was better at intimate numbers than big production numbers. By that time I was asking to see scripts; I wanted to know what the characters were. I liked the smoothness of sliding in and out of a number without a bump. I think being conscious of that easy shift helped get me into directing. Freed said to me one day, "Chuck, you think like a director. I think one day you'll be a director." I said, "Oh, Arthur, you've got to be kidding!" I was a rotten actor and never thought I'd be a director. It never entered my mind.

D: Do you have fond memories of working on *Meet Me in St. Louis*?

W: Only working with Judy Garland, which was always pleasant, except for *Summer Stock*. Judy was very comfortable working with me.

D: Did color play a big role in your choreography?

W: I took color for granted. With Minnelli directing, I knew that the picture was going to look beautiful. I was terribly concerned about clothes, about what my dancers would wear, and I worked very closely with the costume designer. I would only get into territories where I felt I could contribute. I never got into the technical areas at all. Freed wanted Judy to be in red and Lucille Bremer in green at the big Christmas dance toward the end of *Meet Me in St. Louis*. Cedric Gibbons, who was the color coordinator and very elegant, said, "Arthur, you can't use red and green in the same scene." Arthur said, "I wonder why nobody ever told God he couldn't have a green stem on a red rose." Cedric shut up.

D: Was Lucille Bremer a talented dancer?

W: She was an excellent dancer, but cold. Cyd Charisse is a beautiful dancer but she's so cold nobody cares. That's why neither of them really became stars. Ginger Rogers couldn't dance, but she had a marvelous style, and she was an actress.

D: What numbers did you choreograph for Metro's *Ziegfeld Follies*?"

W: I did "Madame Crematon," Judy's number. I did "Start Each Day with a Song" for Jimmy Durante, which was cut out. And I choreographed the Sweepstakes sketch with Fanny Brice. Meeting her and getting to know her was such a thrill, because Fanny Brice was history by that time.

D: Do you have fond memories of *Summer Holiday*?

W: That was pretty rough. I loved working with Rouben Mamoulian, because he was so brilliant. But when I say rough, I mean literally some of the terrain we had to work on was rough. Gloria DeHaven and Mickey Rooney had to dance on a hill, and it would have looked too obvious to make holes in it for their feet. That's all I remember; it was a tough number to do.

D: Was the transition from choreographer to director easy for you?

W: I was scared to death! *Good News* was my first picture to direct, and I begged Arthur Freed to let me at least start with a number. So we started with the opening number. When they wheeled the playback machine [which supplied prerecorded music] off the set, I said, "There goes my only friend in the world." I knew that all I had left were words to work with, and the feeling was horrendous. All of a sudden I found that the words and the steps went together. My job was to keep it all fluid and honest. I thought, "Hey, wait, this isn't so bad."

Technically I got myself hung up a few times. If the actors exit right to left and you're going on another set, they've got to come in right to left. Otherwise they would be jumping to the other side of the screen. Those technical things were more difficult for me than the actual playing of scenes.

D: Robert Alton did the choreography on *Good News*.

W: Well, I did some of it. There were so many of us working together harmoniously in the Freed unit. For instance, Bob did "Pass That Peace Pipe," because we could go on with the book while he was rehearsing it. I might do "The Best Things in Life Are Free" or "Just Imagine," the love song June Allyson sings when she's alone. We might be shooting or rehearsing that while Bob was rehearsing "Peace Pipe." So we would all work together, and a number fell to whoever had time to do it. Of course, the director worked mostly with the principals.

D: Was June Allyson good to work with?

W: Oh, excellent, great, a real talent. The first time I met June and worked with her was in the beginning of *Best Foot Forward*. Usually the kids from the theater were very camera-conscious. But the camera didn't bother her, she was marvelous. I said, "June, you've got a hell of a chance in this business, but you've got to do something about that voice. If you have two sentences in a row, you're going to lull everybody to sleep." That shows how wrong a person can be.

D: Were Betty Comden and Adolph Green stimulating to work with?

W: No, no, we didn't get along too well. I don't know why. I had very little to do with them. By the time they did their stuff, it was in Roger Eden's hands. I had very little contact with them. They felt very superior. I was novice Charlie directing my first picture. June went to Arthur Freed before we started shooting *Good News* and said, "Arthur, I know Chuck is a very good dance director and I'm very fond of him, but please, do you think he can direct a whole picture?" And Arthur said, "You got your first picture, June." She didn't say anything more.

D: Had shooting actually begun on *Easter Parade* when Gene Kelly had to bow out?

W: No, the picture was just barely in the rehearsal stage. I was thrilled beyond belief when they got Fred Astaire out of retirement to do the picture. It's an interesting thing about retirement; we're all retired until the phone rings.

D: Did you find working with Astaire a congenial arrangement?

W: He was so nervous and such a worrywart and perfectionist. I can't say that working with him was fun, but it was exciting because I was working with the best. Lots of times he'd whisper, "I don't think I can do that." I'd say, "Fred, what have we got to lose by trying." He'd say, "It feels good, but I don't think I can do it." I'd say, "Let's try it. If you don't like it when we see the rushes tomorrow, we'll redo it." I'd think, "Please, God, I hope I'm right."

D: Was Ann Miller a serious professional?

W: Oh, dear Annie Miller. She was a darling, but kind of a kookie darling. I don't think Annie has ever come off Cloud Nine, wherever that is. She's all over the place.

D: Was Judy Garland having emotional problems at that time?

W: At which time? Name it.

D: During the making of *Easter Parade*.

W: I don't remember any on *Easter Parade*. She was pretty excited to be working with Fred. The reason I got *Easter Parade* was not because of my great talent. Judy and Minnelli had just finished *The Pirate*, and their psychiatrist said, "I don't think it's advisable for the two of you to do another picture together right away." *Good News* had been a success, and Arthur called me in and said, "I think I'm going to give you *Easter Parade*." I was almost in tears with the thrill of it. The picture had double the budget of *Good News*. I read the script, and it was terrible. It was heavy. Originally Gene's character, the part Fred ultimately played, beat the shit out of Judy's character. I went to Gene and Judy and I said, "We've got to have lunch, and I've got to talk to you very seriously. I have no clout. I'm lucky to get the goddamn picture. But let me tell you something—it stinks. And the audience is going to hate you both. They're particularly going to hate you, Gene, for what you're doing to this poor girl. Don't forget, Judy is always sympathetic in her movies." They said, "What do you want us to do?"

I'd gotten along very well with writer Sidney Sheldon. I said, "I think the script should be taken away from the Hacketts, and let's see if Sid and I can't work on it and lighten it. The picture has got to be fun, it's a musical." So the three of us reached an understanding. Arthur was in New York at the time. They got Freed on the telephone, and Gene and Judy talked to him. I thought my concerns should come from them, so my name was never mentioned. Judy and I had been studying the script and going over it, and she agreed that it was awfully heavy. So that's how we got Sid on the picture. He and I would work on the scenes and then go over them with Judy and Gene. They loved the lightening of the story. By the time Astaire came into the project, the script was fine. It was even better for Fred than it was for Gene.

D: Was Irving Berlin around much?

W: Yes, quite a bit. He loved being around the shooting. I guess he'd seen some of the rehearsals of the tramp number. So when we were recording it, Judy and Fred were naturally standing in front of their mikes. Berlin came over to me and said, "Now Chuck, be careful they don't cover their mouths at any time." He worried that those lyrics might not come out clean and clear.

D: As director, did you continue to keep a hand in the choreography?

W: I did a lot of the things. I did the tramp number in *Easter Parade* and most of the things that concerned Fred and Judy. I did all of Judy's solos. That's how related Bob Alton and I were. Often I did the springboard, and he took it from there. That's how in sync we were in our thinking. I'd learned an awful lot from Bob Alton.

D: Those of you working in the Freed unit must have come almost to a likeness of mind somewhere along the way.

W: Yes. I would say it was the closest with Blane and Martin. They would give me arrangements, and I would say, "Kids, I couldn't be more grateful. This piece is staging itself. It's saying it all right there musically."

D: Was *The Barkleys of Broadway* a difficult film?

W: It wasn't difficult. I wasn't too happy with it because I didn't like the score. I didn't like the score at all. Harry Warren was a sweetheart, but the only song I liked was "You Can't Take That Away from Me," which was not written by Harry. It's an old Rogers and Astaire number written by George Gershwin.

D: Had any of the shooting been done while Garland was still in the picture?

W: No. We were still in pre-production rehearsals. As thrilled as I was when they replaced Gene with Fred Astaire in *Easter Parade*, I really got teary when Ginger Rogers walked down the aisle (we were up on the stage rehearsing a solo with Astaire) and embraced Fred. Metro brought her down from Oregon. I thought I'd died and gone to heaven to be working with Astaire and Rogers. I loved working with Ginger.

D: Did Rogers get back into the swing of dancing easily?

W: Oh, very easily. She did an awful lot of rehearsing, too. I liked the premise of the picture. The fact that the characters in the picture had been a dance team and then separated worked for us. It paralleled what had happened with Fred and Ginger. That helped me in my thinking about the picture.

D: I remember that Ginger Rogers did a very dramatic scene in French.

W: Yes, and Arthur was going to get a legitimate director to do that scene, which hurt me very much because this was my first crack at a dramatic scene. I said, "Arthur, I think I can do that. If I can't do it, then get somebody in." He said, "Well, I think it would be better to get someone else." Ginger went to bat for me, and she said, "Arthur, I want to do it with Chuck." For her to have that much confidence in me made me want to work that much harder. I thought the scene worked all right.

D: I know that there were big problems with Judy Garland during the making of *Summer Stock*.

W: Yes. Do we have to talk about that? That was a real mess. When you start a picture and the bets around the lot are two-to-one that the picture will never be finished, it's not very comfortable. But we did finish it, and the picture made money. And I got an ulcer.

D: Despite the ups and downs, there are some good things in the picture.

W: I would go to dailies and think, "How dare this look like a happy picture!" We were going through absolute torture. Gene was right in there helping, he was marvelous. He'd placate Judy and hold her hand. I just couldn't believe that the rushes looked happy, but they did. It looked like we were having a good time.

D: Am I right that the "Get Happy" number was done quite a bit later?

W: Not that much later, maybe a couple of weeks.

D: Did you enjoy directing non-musicals?

W: I loved them. You see, it's almost twice as much work to do a musical. When you've just got the flow of a straight comedy, it's easier to keep your tempo.

D: As a dancer and choreographer, did you find a sense of rhythm important in a comedy or a dramatic film?

W: Oh, very much so. I was terribly careful that I didn't have my people too busy, so I didn't choreograph them. I even went to the other extreme and would say, "The scene is good. Now sit there and do it. Hold still and do it. Just fascinate me with it."

D: When you had crowd scenes, did you essentially choreograph those scenes?

W: Probably subconsciously. It's like Minnelli being an art director. He couldn't resist saying, "Move that palm a little to the left so that it's in the scene." Whatever your instincts are come to the fore.

D: Did the Esther Williams film *Texas Carnival* offer special problems for you?

W: I don't remember any problems. I think I was probably the first director to take Esther seriously and really try to help her as an actress. Nobody helped me when I started as an actor, and I was left floundering. In *Jubilee* one of my favorite notices was, "And someone we have never heard of came out of a disdainful coma to 'Astaire' around a bit." Nobody told me about sustaining a scene. I was just delivering lines. That's why I was sympathetic to Esther. I told her, "Take your time, and believe it. Go to your dressing room and read the lines, read them again and again, have fun with the fun ones, listen and think." She said, "No one has ever bothered with that before." She wanted to better herself. She wasn't content just to take the money and run and be *the* big money-making star on the lot.

D: Did you work with Williams on the water sequences?

W: Some I did. If they were intimate ones, I did. But the big production sequences usually went to Busby Berkeley.

D: How much contact did you have with L. B. Mayer during those years?

W: Very little. The first time I met Mayer was when we were doing *Summer Stock*. There was a little saloon café just off the lot, and Judy would say, "Let's go over to the Retake Room." We'd go over there, and she'd say, "Now look, Buster, I'm going to have a beer. I'm having a beer if you want me to work this afternoon." I said, "Sure, you can have a beer, as long as you eat and we get back to work." I'd have a martini and she'd have a beer. One day at lunch I got a call to come to Mr. Mayer's office. I opened the door when I was told he'd see me, and the entire upper echelon of Metro was lined along one wall. At the far end of the room at a gigantic desk was Mr. Mayer. He got up from the desk and he said, "I don't know you personally, Mr. Walters, but I feel it is important that I speak to you. It has come to my attention that you are encouraging Judy Garland's drinking." I got myself together and said, "Mr. Mayer, if you want Judy to work in the afternoon she's going to have a beer, come hell or high water. Now which do you want?" That's when I met Louis B. Mayer. I'd been at Metro eight years by then, and this was my introduction to him.

D: I understand that *Belle of New York* is not your favorite picture.

W: Oh, boy! No. I just didn't like Vera-Ellen. I didn't believe her. She was a talented dancer, but who cares? I'd put her in that category. That picture was a duty, I had to do it. Arthur was stuck with the property, and they'd paid a lot of money for it. If it had been my first picture, I swear I think it would have been my last.

D: Do you have special memories of *Lili*?

W: Yes. The studio didn't believe in the film, they hated it. That made making the picture very difficult. We finished shooting, had a rough cut, and I was to go right into something else. I had about a week or maybe ten days between projects, and I always rushed off to New York to see shows and try to get stimulated. I didn't feel any stimulation in California. There was very little theater out here, and looking at other people's pictures wasn't a stimulus. I got back from New York and ran into Keenan Wynn. He said, "Hey, Chuck, I saw the projectionist this morning. They ran your picture last night, and he liked it." I started smelling around, and I found out that the studio didn't know what the hell to do with *Lili* because it was neither fish nor fowl. It wasn't a love story, and it was told through puppets. Leslie Caron is ugly and she had to stay ugly. I couldn't all of a sudden make her pretty. And the story is resolved in ballet form. I wanted the color in the picture to have a soft and muted tone, so the color department bled some of the color, which gave it an unusual look.

Finally Metro decided to preview the picture out in the San Fernando Valley somewhere. I had to go there in a studio car because I would never have found it otherwise. I was scared to death because I'd heard of previews where the audience would walk out or boo the picture off the screen, and they'd have to stop running it. I had a jug of martinis that you wouldn't believe, so I was really smashed. But the cards the audience filled out were fantastic. It was amazing to watch the producer and everybody else climb on the bandwagon. Before that Eddie Knopf, who produced *Lili*, asked Arthur Freed to take a look at the picture, since he didn't know what to do with it. After running the film Arthur told Knopf, "There's nothing you can do with it. Chuck has ruined Leslie."

D: How did you feel about *Dangerous When Wet*, another Esther Williams film?

W: The first thing about *Dangerous When Wet*, I'm happy to say, is that for the expenditure invested it was the biggest money-maker of any of the Esther Williams films. For a company man, that's a nice satisfaction. We had a marvelous time filming the picture. Esther was very comfortable with me and trusted me implicitly. I had given her enough encouragement that she wanted to be the best she could possibly be.

D: In *Torch Song* you danced with Joan Crawford.

W: That was kind of fun, except that I was tired. I had just finished the picture with Esther. The phone rang one night, and it was Joan Crawford. She said, "I have a script, and you're the only one that can direct it. Could I bring a bottle of champagne and the script and a bite to eat and read it to you?" Well, I couldn't say no to Joan Crawford.

Torch Song was Crawford's first film in color, and it was the first time she had danced in twenty-five years on the screen. I said, "We're not going to tease, we're going to open with a number right off. I think we can establish the character that way, too." So that's why we started with a number. We rehearsed and rehearsed and rehearsed, and she said, "Now we've got to bring in somebody, and you've got to teach the number to him so that I can dance with him." Then she said, "I'm so comfortable with you. Would you do it with me in the film?" I said, "All right, if you'll feel better." My hair was getting a little thin at the time, so that's the reason I used the top hat, to cover my head. Joan was always on time, ready to shoot at 9:30. At 9:15 she called me to her dressing room and said, "Chuck, I am scared peeless, I cannot move. I've got to have a drink." I said, "Well, you're no good to us if you're that tense. Go ahead, have a vodka on the rocks." She said, "Thank you. You've got to have one with me or I won't like it." At 10 o'clock we staggered out of her dressing room and said, "We're ready, fellas." I'm exaggerating, but we'd had a few belts before 10 o'clock in the morning to loosen her up enough to start the number.

Michael Wilding, Joan's costar in the picture, was having trouble. He was a little intimidated by Crawford, and I think he was having home trouble with Elizabeth Taylor. So he came in smashed every day. He was playing a blind pianist, and we had to tape his words across the keyboard. He didn't know his lines, he didn't know anything!

D: You referred to yourself as a company man. Is that how you viewed yourself?

W: I wasn't conscious of it until I was told that I was not an *auteur* director. John Darrow, my manager, said this many years ago, that I was not an *auteur*, I was a company director. And I thought, "Gee, I guess I am." I worked so hard and so long to get to MGM, because that's what I wanted. But I finally earned the right there to say, "No, I don't think I can give this picture anything. It's not me, I can't contribute to it." Sometimes I wasn't crazy about a script overall, but I could see how I could help it. So I suppose in those cases I was working for the company. But I would only do that if I felt I could give the script something that was not already there. Another reason I suppose that I was valuable to the studio and stayed there so long is that I was not extravagant with the company's money. I wasn't extravagant with my own money, so I was that much more careful with somebody else's. Wherever we could cut corners, without cutting quality, I would say, "Yes, I don't think we need that. If we find out we do, we can always come back and get it." I didn't trust cutters, so I got so I would only shoot what I needed and what I wanted. I liked my own flow and sense of rhythm and choreography, with the fade-in and fade-out. I would insist that once the writer and the producer and I were in accord on a script, we'd time it and cut it down to the actual release time. If anything, go under a little bit, because you never know when you're going to get to a scene where you want to milk it a little. Some scenes will go fast but some will go slower, too. I wanted the script cut to size before we got in front of the camera. That worked for me, and it was efficient for the studio.

D: What prompted you to do *Don't Go Near the Water*?

W: I did *Don't Go Near the Water* mainly so that I wouldn't be type-cast as a woman's director and a musicals director. I wanted to be more varied in the pictures I did.

D: Did you notice changes at MGM when Mayer left and Dore Schary came in?

W: The big change for me was that Schary and I couldn't stand each other. He was the one that started all the business about "What are we going to do with *Lili*? I don't think we can even release it." Then at the party after the second preview, he and Helen Deutsch were dancing around singing, "Hi Lili," and I thought, "You shits! Where were you when I needed you?"

D: Did you enjoy making *The Tender Trap*?

W: Except for Sinatra. He was a son-of-a-bitch to work with. He had agreed to do the picture on an old commitment, so he was sour. Apparently the money the studio paid him was under the old agreement, too. He'd come in when he felt like it. But I had an old bromide that I operated by: "Give me a son-of-a bitch with talent." When Sinatra learned his lines and did his scenes, he was excellent. He was a hell of a performer. The picture was a challenge because the script was very wordy. It was difficult to stage without being stagey. Those are tough challenges but they're kind of fun challenges, too. You've got to be careful in choreographing that kind of piece, careful not to make it static.

D: How did you feel about *The Tender Trap* when you saw the play on Broadway?

W: I hated it. I wouldn't touch it. I went on suspension. I had just turned down *I'll Cry Tomorrow*.

D: Why did you turn down *I'll Cry Tomorrow*?

W: Susan Hayward came in with the script under her arm. She had played a drunk earlier in *Smash-Up* and had gotten an Academy Award nomination. She'd played a singer before in *With a Song in My Heart*, and now she was to play a drunken singer. I said, "I've seen this already." Do you know whom I wanted in the part? June

Allyson. I wanted to start with this innocent facade and have the fears gradually eat at her. I personally know how tough June can be, and she could have kicked hell out of the part. With that gravel voice and getting drunk—I think she would have gotten an Academy Award. Anyway that's why I walked off the picture. The best scene Susan Hayward ever played was when she came in and met me. She knew I didn't want her, and the scene she played with me was one hell of a scene. They should have gotten that on film. I never really believed her too much on the screen.

D: Was *High Society* a good experience?

W: One of the greatest experiences. And it was rather a coup for me, because Sol Siegel had been a big producer at Fox, and he was the first producer to come to MGM on an independent basis. Sinatra told him, "Well, the only guy to me that should direct this is Chuck Walters." Sol and I got along very well. We got down to him saying, "Who do you want to choreograph the picture?" I said, "It's my bag, it is exactly up my alley." It was the kind of thing I feel I do best and love to do, because the numbers were integrated into the story. Siegel apparently was thinking, "Oh, well, that saves my cash register, two jobs for the price of one." So I did the choreography, and that was very satisfying. That's when I really appreciated my dancing background. I loved the way numbers all of a sudden came from the dialogue. We pre-scored just enough so that when they started to sing, the audience was not even conscious of it. At the bar, when Sinatra sang "You're Sensational" to Grace Kelly, I told them to play it like a scene. I thought she was marvelous, and Frank was, too. Bing Crosby is the nicest man I ever worked with.

D: And you had a Cole Porter score to work with on the picture.

W: When Cole Porter finished a new number, Saul Chaplin, who was head of music on the picture, and I would go to Brentwood to Cole's house for lunch, and he would play his new song. Luncheon consisted of menus at each place, very, very formal. There'd be a glass of wine before, a glass of wine with, all very proper. Then Cole would go to the piano. We would have a demitasse, and he would play his new song.

High Society was the first picture that Crosby and Sinatra did together. So we were all wondering, "What are they going to sing together?" Cole tried to come up with a song for the two of them, and he just couldn't hack it. It was getting late and actually we were into shooting the picture. We were all thinking, "What are we going to do?" Saul Chaplin came up with a song, went to Cole with it, and Cole said, "I think it's perfect." Sol Siegel, Solly Chaplin, and I had a meeting, and Chaplin said, "Chuck, this is what we're going to use for Sinatra and Crosby. It might sound familiar." He showed me the lead sheet, and it was "What a Swell Party This Is," which Betty Grable and I had introduced in *Du Barry Was a Lady*.

D: Did you enjoy making *Please Don't Eat the Daisies*?

W: Yes, I enjoyed it. I didn't want to do it because I was not a Doris Day fan. Then I read the script and I said, "My God, this *is* Doris Day." I loved Isobel Lennart's writing, so I said, "I think the picture might be fun." To know her is to love her, and I loved working with both Doris and Isobel. I wanted to have Betty Grable in the part of the musical comedy star that Janis Paige played. Joe Pasternak and I had lunch with Betty one day, and she loved the idea and liked the notion of our working together again. I knew a side of Betty that, as far as I was concerned, had never been on the screen. It would have been so perfect to do a bad number with Betty Grable, because you can take any of her numbers and say, "She can't sing, she can't dance, but she looks great!" In the number we had planned, Betty would have been satirizing herself. She loved everything about the idea. She said, "It's great, but when does the picture start?" We told her and she said, "That's when Santa Anita is opening." With Betty horse racing came first.

D: Was *The Unsinkable Molly Brown* an interesting project for you?

W: Yes, although I hated the show. It was too stylized. I told Roger Edens when we were in New York scouting locations for *Jumbo*, "I understand the studio has bought the movie rights to *Molly Brown*. You know that we're going to be up for it, so we'd better see the show and be prepared." Roger and I both hated it on the stage. The score was fine, so I said, "Well, the ingredients are there, Roger. It's rags to riches and that always works. If we can just unload some of the crap and concentrate on the good stuff, we'll be okay." So we were ready when the studio asked us to do the picture. I wanted Shirley

MacLaine for Molly. She had the stature. When they told me that Debbie Reynolds would cut her salary to a minimum to get the part, I cried, because I didn't think Debbie was right for the part. And, of course, they let her know that I felt that way, which was no big help to me. All through the shooting of the picture, she'd say, "I know you don't want me." But we got along fine. Sometimes I'm asked, "What do you think is your greatest contribution to the business?" If I could be honest, I'd say, "Getting an Academy Award nomination for Debbie Reynolds."

D: Did MGM change during the time you were there?

W: I was under five regimes, so of course it changed. It changed with each regime. I got along fine with the Jews. When we got down to the Irish Catholics, forget it. It became all dollars and cents, nothing artistic. Whatever they could get the cheapest they used. They were starting to send me real junk, and I had two years to go on my contract. John, my manager, said, "Look, we'll ask for a release. With *Molly Brown* the big hit it is, they're not going to let you go. They'll just stop sending you crap. I'm going to write them a letter." We got a letter back in a week, which said, "We'd be happy to let Charles Walters go." So that's how I got out.

D: When you made *Walk, Don't Run* at Columbia, did you find things considerably different at the smaller studio?

W: Every day, five times a day, I said, "I want to go home. *This* is a studio?" I was spoiled. Columbia was a junkyard compared to MGM. Hollywood's studio heads, if you could call them that, were talking such bullshit that I couldn't believe it. The football player, Mike Frankovich, was the head of Columbia at that time. There was a big production meeting with his assistants. They were all dressed in black, a la mafia, and it was mid-summer. I sat there not saying a word, but I'm smelling what I'm stuck with.

D: How was Cary Grant to work with?

W: He was a darling—except nobody bothered to tell me that he was on LSD. Naturally if I was going to question something, I wouldn't be inclined to question Cary Grant. I'd question myself. So I got an ulcer from *Walk, Don't Run*, too. It was the first time I ever missed a day of work. The ulcer was so bad that I was in bed from Friday night until Tuesday morning.

D: Did you go to Japan on that picture?

W: Oh, sure. We had bad weather, and we'd have to wait in the hotel room until the weather broke. Then boom, out we'd go—Sundays, whenever.

D: You said that you didn't consider yourself an *auteur*, but do you feel there is a Walters's touch in your films?

W: I would look for the heart and the honesty that I could glom onto. I think that was my basic principle. I'd throw jokes over my shoulder if they got in the way of honesty. I think drama has to be amusing and comedies have to have some drama. That's the way life is.

Charles Walters's Feature Films

1947 *Good News*
1948 *Easter Parade*
1949 *The Barkleys of Broadway*
1950 *Summer Stock*
1951 *Three Guys Named Mike*
         Texas Carnival
1952 *The Belle of New York*
1953 *Lili*
         Dangerous When Wet
         Torch Song
         Easy to Love
1955 *The Glass Slipper*
         The Tender Trap
1956 *High Society*
1957 *Don't Go Near the Water*
1959 *Ask Any Girl*
1960 *Please Don't Eat the Daisies*
1961 *Two Loves*
1962 *Jumbo*
1964 *The Unsinkable Molly Brown*
1966 *Walk, Don't Run*

GEORGE SIDNEY

Son of an Entertainment Executive

Screen director George Sidney, the son of Loew's executive L. K. Sidney, was born in Long Island City, New York, in 1916. He worked at Metro-Goldwyn-Mayer from 1933 until 1956, directing his first picture at the studio in 1941. Later Sidney made films at Columbia for eleven years. He specialized in lavish musicals (*Anchors Aweigh, Show Boat, Annie Get Your Gun*) and period adventure movies (*The Three Musketeers, Scaramouche*), most of which were box-office hits, but he occasionally directed straight drama. Sidney retired from filmmaking in 1968 and died in Los Angeles in 2002.

The following interview was taped in the director's office in Beverly Hills, California, on August 22, 1980.

D: I know that both of your parents had been actors, but I'm wondering at what point you decided on a career in show business.
S: Yes, my parents had been actors, although that wasn't really their profession. I think show business was for me because when my mother was pregnant with me, she sat in a theater box for ten months waiting to give birth. So I suppose you could say that was my early exposure. Then I was carried on stage at eighteen months, and at three years of age I rode my tricycle into someone's vaudeville act. At six I costarred with Tom Mix in a movie billed as "the littlest cowboy." I also played the lead in one of the silent versions of *Little Lord Fauntleroy*. After this auspicious occasion and a few other parts, I realized that acting wasn't for me.

I wanted to get on the other side of the camera. At six or seven years of age I was taking pictures like mad. The best toy I've ever had in my life was a miniature silent movie camera that my father had

61

made for me. I used to go down the streets of Denver, Colorado, with my cap turned around backwards and make believe that I was taking pictures. In the early 1920s no one knew anything about motion pictures; they were just something you heard about. So people thought I was a midget cameraman.

D: Didn't you appear in a film called *The Cohens and the Kellys*?

S: That was my uncle George Sidney, who was an actor, writer, producer, and composer. He had been a Broadway actor, and he came out to California and did many, many films. He did a series called *The Cohens and the Kellys*. It was possibly the first attempt on the screen to deal with the issue of tolerance. Kelly was a big, tall Irishman, a stereotype, played by a man named Charles Murray. The other man in the story was Jewish, short and fat, and he was played by George Sidney. The two fellows were great friends, but they were constantly beating each other's brains out; then they'd get back together. I was named for my uncle.

D: Didn't you work as a musician for a while?

S: I played four instruments, and I still play. I've written some music. I'm a member of ASCAP. I've arranged, composed, conducted, and play instruments. I have a piano here in my office. If I get inspired, I'll run over and play a medley of my hits.

D: What was your first job at MGM?

S: I came to MGM as a messenger boy. I walked and walked and walked until I worked my way up to office boy. I continued doing all kinds of assorted jobs. My ultimate aim was to become a director. I went through that whole halcyon period at MGM, and I guess I did about every job on the lot. You could do that in those days. You could move from one department to another. There was so much work to be done that I would take two jobs, and the studio wouldn't even know it. I'd be working on one company in the daytime and another company at night, and no one would catch on. I'd just take my card out of one rack and put it in the other. That way I built up muscle.

I learned every job in a motion picture studio. Later on I did second unit work on musical numbers. In those days you could devise numbers for someone else's pictures, and I did choreography and staged numbers. At the same time I was also the test director, and I made all the screen tests at MGM. I made thousands of screen tests, which I found most exhilarating. It was exciting to take a person, mold them, try to find what they looked like, and decide how they should look. Also I made short subjects and kept going until finally somebody said, "Well, I guess we'd better let him direct."

D: Your father was an executive at MGM.

S: No, he was with Loew's Incorporated in New York. Loew's was the parent company of MGM. My father was busy helping to run that company in the East. He had the Capitol Theater in New York, he produced the shows there. He had a radio station called WHN, and he produced the shows that went all over the country. My father came to California about twelve or fourteen years after I went to MGM.

D: Was *Free and Easy* the first feature film you directed?

S: Yes, the first one that was completely mine. Up to that time all the things I had done had been in other people's pictures.

D: By then did you have a pretty good grasp of camera work and all the film technology?

S: I thought so. I had become a motion picture cameraman as well as a still photographer. I modestly thought I was quite good with the camera.

D: Did you work closely with cinematographer George Folsey after you became a director?

S: Yes, sure. I don't know how many pictures we made together, but we made several. I had a great time with Harry Stradling, a wonderful cameraman, and Charles Rosher and Karl Freund. But when we did the more complicated musical numbers, I would operate the camera myself. When you're doing big musical numbers, where the camera has to stop in twenty-one or twenty-five different places and then move on, it's awfully hard to give that responsibility to the operator, who hasn't conceived the movement. If I ran the camera, I would know exactly what I got. And it gave me something to do during takes other than bite my nails.

D: Did you work well with Robert Cummings on *Free and Easy*?

S: Oh, yes. I had known Bob Cummings when he was still Brice Hutchins. He came to Los Angeles in 1935 or 1936 in a Shubert musical, and I think I made a screen test of him. When we were making *Free and Easy*, Bob would come on the set with his health foods and his can of tomato juice. I haven't seen him in years and years, but I understand he's still a health food fanatic.

D: Was *Pacific Rendezvous* an interesting film for you?

S: It was interesting for one mechanical factor. I was not supposed to make the film. It was ready to go into production, and they didn't have a female star for the picture. They asked me to make a test of one of the contract girls at the studio, and Lee Bowman, who was in the film, was also going to be in the test. We were going to do a scene from that film. The sets were already dressed and ready to go. I made the test, and the higher-ups liked it so much that they decided to give the girl, Jean Rogers, the lead in the film. And they said, "By the way, why don't we let Georgie make the picture, too. He did the test so well."

Louis B. Mayer got hold of me, and he took me for one of his walks. When he really wanted something, he walked it out of you. He walked me up and down that lot, back and forth. I said, "Look, this picture is ready to go. Two days' preparation is not enough time for me to get ready." And with my bad feet, Mayer walked me into doing it. Also my ego got the better of me. The man who was going to direct the picture, George Seitz, was a speed-king. He had started with the *Perils of Pauline* serials and made films very fast. Seitz was going to make *Pacific Rendezvous* in twenty-four days. So young fellow that I was—I was maybe twenty-five years old at the time—I said, "I'm going to make it in twenty-two days." And I did.

Actually, since I'd made the test, I had one scene already shot. When I started the picture, I was already eight minutes of film ahead. I simply inserted the test. That's the only time I ever shot a picture where on opening day I was already ahead of schedule.

D: Did you have a great deal of contact with L. B. Mayer during your years at MGM?

S: Oh, yes, because he had a great belief in young talent being the life blood of the industry. No matter what was going on in the studio his ear was always available. When I said, "I've found someone, Mr. Mayer, that I think we should make a test of," he always had time to listen. He was an unbelievable man; he was a giant, a giant among giants.

Mayer came down on the set one day after I'd made a few pictures. He called me aside and said, "How's it going, boy?" I said, "Oh, fine, except that they're pushing at me because I'm slow." He said, "Are you getting what you want?" I said, "Yes, but they want me to stop making close-ups, and I think this way we're creating a star." He said, "Boy, get what you want. However, if you tell the production department that I told you this, I'll deny it!" What he was doing was putting steel into my spine to stand against the system.

Mayer was totally committed to making stars and developing talent, whether it be writers, directors, cameramen, or whatever. He never saw a film until it was completely finished, because he wanted to go in and see that picture in a theater and get the audience's reaction. He held himself in the background. But if you needed him, he would come in and carry the day. They don't make executives that way any longer.

D: Was *Pilot No. 5* a rewarding film for you?

S: Yes, because we took Gene Kelly, who had been a hoofer, and gave him a straight acting role. We used some brand new people, Van Johnson for one. I needed a fellow with a face, who just looked up after an air raid, and that was Peter Lawford. It was Lawford's first picture. *Pilot No. 5* was an exciting experience. It was a kind of avant garde way of telling a story, and it was an attack on Fascism. That and *The Red Danube* are probably the only two really serious films I made. I veered away from serious material because I was only interested in making films that would entertain. I preferred big entertainment. I did not feel that motion picture audiences should get propaganda for their money.

D: When you say serious films, you mean message pictures.

S: That's right. That's why I specialized in musicals and did some adventure pictures, things I really enjoyed. I didn't want to make propaganda. I didn't believe that was the kind of film to make when audiences were being told, "Come on in, you're going to have a great time." So I always tried to make pictures that entertained, and I think by and large I was fairly successful in doing that.

D: How was Gene Kelly as a dramatic actor?

S: Very good. It's interesting that most people who have a feeling for music—Judy Garland, Frank Sinatra, Bing Crosby—can cross over. I think the really consummate musical talents can do most anything. It's the other way around that you get into trouble.

D: So you enjoyed big musicals like *Thousands Cheer*?

S: Yes, they were all exciting. This was a period in Hollywood when we kind of made those pictures up as we went, and that was fun. I'd get up in the morning and say, "Gee, what are we going to do today? Let's do this and do that." It was exciting because there was a lot of young talent, and we were all running and pushing and shoving and getting results that at the time we never thought about. You go to Europe and to film seminars in this country and they talk about the classic days of the MGM musical. But at the time we were too busy, day and night, making those pictures to think we were making a classic anything. Far from it. We enjoyed the work, it was great fun.

D: Did you find that there was a team spirit at MGM?

S: Oh, yes, there was great camaraderie. And there was a great backing by the studio, more than we realized. We were down there shooting the bullets on the set and didn't realize that the higher-ups were looking over our shoulders in a beneficial way. As director I'd say, "Oh, I need something else," and they'd get it. They were putting all the ammunition in our hands. The more you did and the more successful it was, the more you asked for. There was no self-aggrandizement at that point; we were never conscious of the press or of reviews. We were just making movies. We didn't know about four stars on the marquee and *Time* magazine and the rest. We weren't paying any attention to those things.

D: Was Joe Pasternak an agreeable producer to work with?

S: Joe was wonderful. Joe was a believer in what we all called Pasternak Land. There were rules in Pasternak Land. There were no terrible people, and everything came out well in the end. Mothers and fathers were respected, the country was respected, the flag was respected—things that are considered corny today.

D: Was there a difference in making a Pasternak musical at MGM versus an Arthur Freed musical or a Jack Cummings musical at the studio?

S: Completely. They were three completely different types of people, as well as producers. They each had their own particular foibles and their own approaches. They were all very successful, but technically there were differences. Metro's musical units were powerhouses.

D: Could you give me examples of the differences between those three producers?

S: Pasternak was a little more saccharine. In his pictures the little girl from nowhere found happiness. Possibly the root of his approach was a little more European. The stories he selected were fables, fairy tales. Freed was a tunesmith; he was one of our great songwriters. He was Tin Pan Alley, and he saw everything from Tin Pan Alley. Arthur lived in that kind of world, and his pictures reflected Irving Berlin, Cole Porter, the Gershwins, all of the great songwriters who were his comrades. That was the kind of sophistication that his pictures had. Jack Cummings had an adventuresome quality which caused him to reach out for the unusual and get a whole different panorama.

Cummings, Pasternak, and Freed were three completely different people. They were only similar in that their pictures came out well and entertained. David Belasco said, "The audience should only know one thing—where the counter is to put its money," and that's about right. The audience should never know, as it's sitting there enjoying a show, what goes on technically. Today everyone knows that that darn shark over at Universal isn't real. In our time we would never have told that.

D: One of the key men in the Metro music department was Roger Edens. What kind of person was Edens to work with?

S: Roger was a man of the greatest musical taste. Rog was a musical intellectual. He was well read, he was well versed, and his hand was a very important one in everything Arthur Freed did, certainly in everything Judy Garland ever did. I first met Roger briefly when I was playing in vaudeville and he was playing second piano for Ethel Merman. The first piano player went on to write some notable songs; his name was Harold Arlen. We played on a bill at the Paradise Theater in New York. But Roger had great musical integrity and creativity. Having Roger around a film was a great backstop, it was a step up. Rog supervised fellows like Connie Salinger, the arrangers, and Adolphe Deutsch, key figures in the MGM music department. Roger never came on strong but he was a giant.

D: Did working in Technicolor in the 1940s present problems?

S: I ran into major problems working with it much earlier when we used two-strip Technicolor. Originally MGM made a contract to do six reels in color, and they made a picture called *Hollywood Party*, in which they did a number called "Hot Chocolate Tears." It was awful. They had five reels left, so Mr. Mayer, being a big man, said, "It's a mistake. Pay them off." Dr. Kalmus, the inventor of Technicolor who had formed the company, said, "Oh, no, you've got a contract to release five more reels of Technicolor, and you have to do it." So MGM said, "All right, we'll make some shorts." Those were the days of two-strip Technicolor. We made some terrible shorts in that process.

Then when I started making musicals, we were using three-strip Technicolor. We had to use so much light that the performers would fall apart. You'd feel that the set was a house of wax, your face would just melt. The Technicolor people set up all kinds of photographic rules. Finally on *Anchor's Aweigh* we said, "Oh, we're not interested in those rules." They wanted a complete fill-light so that everything looked like a picture postcard. And we said, "We won't do it." They used to have so-called Technicolor experts who would run in and put a red handkerchief in the set or something, and they were afraid that stark white would blast all over the screen.

All of a sudden we found the right color by going back to the painters. It was just impressionism, and it was no different than any other film. We just shot it like it was black and white, and that's when we started to get good color films. But the heat, until the film became faster, was just terrible. If you had a small set, there wasn't enough room to get all the lights in, so we had to figure out high intensity arcs and pull away so the actors' faces wouldn't be wet. There were also a lot of problems in printing. Then when we got monopack, where you only had one negative and it was a faster film, we didn't have these problems. Of course, I don't think that any color has ever surpassed three-strip Technicolor, because you had three separate negatives. You had thirty-two filters. You had complete control, which you never had with monopack.

In the three-strip days the crew was dealing with a camera that weighed 1,200 pounds before the operator and this and that were on the end of the boom. The logistics of moving it were troublesome. The camera was a big blimp, and people had to push these things.

D: Did you enjoy making *Bathing Beauty*?

S: That was wild. That was truly wild, because this was the first so-called water picture. And again we were working with three-strip cameras that weighed all this weight. I wanted to be able to go down underneath the water and come back up. So we had to invent all kinds of things. We had to invent wet makeup, wet hair. We had to put glass in front of the camera to go under water and not have it drip. For that six months my hair was always wet, because we were always in the water trying to invent, doing choreography for swimming, making the swimmers move like dancers.

Bathing Beauty was a fun picture because, in a sense, that was a silent picture. Red Skelton did the comedy routines, and they were silent. The swimming with Esther Williams was silent, just music. And the Harry James and the Xavier Cugat numbers were just musical. So this picture, oddly enough, was a very big success in all countries of the world because they didn't have to dub it. People loved the spectacle of the thing.

I made Esther's first screen test. She had been in the World's Fair, not in New York, although she had worked in New York. She was in the San Francisco Fair. We made a screen test of her, and the studio signed her and put her in this picture and built the whole picture around her. With *Bathing Beauty* we made the screen wet.

D: Was Esther Williams easy to work with?

S: Oh, sure. Needless to say, she was a complete amateur as an actress. She was a swimmer. But that was part of the fun of it—taking people and molding them. She was certainly glorious to look at in the water. Just unbelievable.

D: Wasn't Buster Keaton a gag man on *Bathing Beauty*?

S: Yes. Buster worked with Red Skelton a lot. Skelton did some of the routines that Buster had done in silent films and updated them.

D: What was Keaton like personally?

S: Very affable, very warm. I met Buster originally in 1920. Of course in his work he was the dead pan comedian. I was amazed that in real life he always had a laugh and a smile. Keaton was a great perfectionist. He would work a gag out—how he should walk, how he'd make a move. I think he was one of our great comic geniuses, but he himself was completely different from that dead pan character he played. That, of course, was a shock. There are some people that you meet—Bob Hope, for instance—who are exactly the same as when they're performing. Others contradict their public character.

D: You mentioned *Anchors Aweigh*. Was that one of your favorite films?

S: Oh, that was a lot of fun because we were kind of making it up as we went. A lot of new things went into that picture, and we put everything we could into it. It proved very, very successful.

D: Did Gene Kelly contribute a great deal to the creative aspect of the production?

S: Yes, he always created part of his dancing. He was very strong in that area.

D: He was the choreographer on the film, wasn't he?

S: We didn't even have that kind of title in those days, everyone did everything. I don't know whether anyone else was working on the choreography or not; it was too long ago.

D: I remember so well the animation, where Gene Kelly danced with Jerry, the mouse.

S: That was something, because we never knew whether it would work or not. We shot this thing and put it together the best we could. Originally Walt Disney was going to do the animation, and then he couldn't do it because he was too busy with other pictures. So we got Hanna-Barbera to do it over in the cartoon department at MGM. We shot it and it was all fine, except there was one little thing we'd forgotten. Gene had a shadow on the floor, because he was reality, but the mouse dancing beside him had no shadow. So the boys had to go back and draw 20,000 mouse shadows to put in. No one had thought about that.

D: Did you work well with Frank Sinatra?

S: Frank was just great. We've been friends throughout the years. If Frank is your friend, you don't need anyone else. I was just recently at his fortieth anniversary in Las Vegas. And I did *Pal Joey* with Frank over at Columbia. He was an unbelievable professional. He's an amazing, great talent, with great sensitivity. I would say that he has greater knowledge of an orchestration than anybody. He knows more about a song than anyone. When we'd run through an orchestration, we'd watch him. If those shoulders went up in the air a little bit, something was wrong. He's practically infallible with a song. His phrasing is magnificent. In that period when I was making musicals, it was the time of the musical giants—Judy Garland, Gene Kelly, Frank Sinatra, Fred Astaire. That's what made those pictures great, along with the songwriters—Rodgers and Hart, Oscar Hammerstein, Irving Berlin, George and Ira Gershwin, Jerome Kern, Cole Porter. They made a difference. We made musicals because we had music.

D: Did you like doing *The Harvey Girls*?

S: That was great fun. I had made Judy Garland's first screen test. There was a theater here in Los Angeles called the Wilshire Ebell. It was connected with a temple, and they used to put on vaudeville acts on certain nights of the week. This little girl came out with her two sisters and her mother playing the piano. She did a little number with a baseball bat. We took her out to the studio and made a test on a soundstage right opposite the commissary. I don't think she was Judy Garland yet, she was still Baby Frances Gumm. She did this little number with the baseball bat in the test, and the studio signed her.

Judy was an unbelievable heavyweight. The number "On the Atchison, Topeka and the Santa Fe" in *Harvey Girls* was shot in one take. We'd lined the thing up for two weeks. Judy came down after lunch, and we walked through the number once, the dance and everything else. Judy was amazing, because you could stand there and say this and that, and you'd swear that she wasn't listening. But in the take she crossed every "t"; she never forgot anything. Giving her a song was like putting money in Fort Knox.

D: Was Robert Alton good to work with?

S: Bob was fine, a good contributor and a fine choreographer. He was easy to work with. Bob was a real New Yorker out here, and he had a lot to contribute to the Freed unit.

D: MGM also had a wealth of contract players to draw from.

S: You'd just reach in and choose whomever you wanted. They were there; it was incredible. On *The Harvey Girls* I had Marjorie Main, Virginia O'Brien, and Cyd Charisse as supporting talent. Everything was right there on the lot.

D: At MGM productions were done on such a lavish scale. Were there ever budget problems on the pictures you made there?

S: Not really. Sometimes we might want to build three mountains and we could only have two. Everything in the picture business was making so much money in the 1940s. As time went on, then budgets became a bigger problem.

I remember when I was going to make *The Three Musketeers*, I wanted very much to go to France and shoot the picture there. The studio said, "No, it's out of the question." In those days we didn't go on location. So I decided that instead of wasting a lot of money on the background I'd put it all in the foreground. I put all the money on stuntmen. In the *Three Musketeers* that I made everything happened in the front, and no one ever saw the background.

D: What was Benny Thau's role at MGM?

S: Benny Thau poured oil on the troubled waters. He was a very quiet man, a gentle man. Technically you could say he was a talent executive, but that's almost a demeaning designation for what Benny did. He was much more important than that. He would sit and kind of quiet things down when they got out of hand. He was a people-to-people person. If Spencer Tracy was upset about something, they'd say, "Benny, go talk to Tracy." Benny spoke very quietly. You could almost never quite hear what he said. But he would talk to this one and that one and had the ability to calm things down.

D: Was *Holiday in Mexico* an interesting picture for you?

S: Yes, as I recall. Harry Stradling photographed that film, and we did some interesting things art-wise, building sets and things. It was one of little Janie Powell's first pictures. She came into the studio as Suzanne Burce, I think her name was. Her father had a little hot dog stand up on Sunset Boulevard. She was cute and wonderful to work with. The picture was fun.

D: Did you enjoy making dramatic films such as *Cass Timberlane*?

S: Yes, I enjoyed that. *Cass Timberlane* wasn't really that dramatic a film, it was a personal film. It was a Sinclair Lewis study of an older man who married a younger woman. It was a challenge to have Tracy and Lana Turner playing husband and wife. How can you do that? But I always wanted that casting, I felt it could work. Lana was a big glamour girl, but she had great talent if she really wanted to dig into it. I think the two of them came off reasonably well in the film. But that was another form of challenge.

D: How did Tracy work as an actor?

S: With great economy. Tracy would never use two words if he could get by with a nod. He had a great open face, and he could use it effectively. We had known each other before, but it was a little shocking to him that the kid was going to direct him in a picture. He said, "You know, I'm like a wounded tiger on the set." I said, "That's not what I heard. I've heard that you are an absolute bastard. But you must remember, Spence, that I'm half Irish and half Hungarian." We never had one confrontation.

Acting was about Tracy's whole life, unlike Clark Gable, who wasn't that crazy about acting. But Spence enjoyed it. When the cameras weren't on, he loved to ham it up and do wild things. He'd tear his clothes and pull off his hat. But working with him was a most happy experience.

D: You mentioned *The Three Musketeers*, and that was one of my favorite pictures as an early teenager.

S: It was fun. People said to me, "Why make *The Three Musketeers*?" I said, "I'm making a Western musical." They said, "Who's writing the music?" I said, "I've got a great guy, he's Russian. He's called Tchaikovsky but he's great." They said, "But *The Three Musketeers*, that's a costume picture." I said, "Yes, it's a Western with costumes." And that's exactly what I made. I didn't approach it as a classic. The dueling was pure choreography, and the fights are pure Western stuff. It was one of the most successful films I ever made. I just set out to make a rip-roaring kind of film. We had the back-up of all that MGM stock company. I think the picture cost $900,000. The big dueling scene was shot over in Busch Gardens in Pasadena. We shot on the back lot, in a public park, on golf courses. We had to wait one morning until a fellow got through shooting a hole on the golf course in back of the studio. I had the King of France and all the horses ready to go, and here came this fellow in his undershirt playing golf. We had to sit there and wait until he got through. I got some phony peach trees and pear trees and had them carried around in a truck to dress different sets, and I'd take paper flowers and put them everywhere. So I created France in places right around the studio. It didn't quite look like France, but the action in the picture was good enough that people forgot.

There were holes in those sets we used, but no one saw them. Bob Planck was the cameraman, and I said, "Let's project color on walls." We put colors here and there and had a little fog machine going. That was exciting to create as we went. Sometimes it's much more fun when you haven't got everything, and you're covering up something. It was all in a day's work, but that's what made it fun.

D: If I'm remembering correctly, Lana Turner did not want to play Lady de Winter.

S: I don't think she wanted to do it at all. She got into it and she enjoyed it. She was just wonderful in the part. People thought making *The Three Musketeers* again was ridiculous, but it worked.

D: How about *Key to the City*, did you like making it?

S: Well, I loved Clark Gable, I loved Frank Morgan and Gretchen [Loretta Young]. It was just a little tiny picture but it was a lot of fun. I've enjoyed all of the films I've made, I really have. People say, "What is your favorite film?" That's like saying, "Who are your favorite children?" I have no favorite film. Each film I made had its own life, its own start, its own finish, its own group of people who worked together. Sometimes you like the people more, or sometimes you fall madly in love with the people, but then the picture is over and that feeling is never quite recaptured again. You start on another project.

D: Weren't there big problems on *Annie Get Your Gun* before Judy Garland had to back out?

S: I wasn't directing the picture when Judy Garland was doing it. They only shot a few days. They stopped the film, and it just laid there. I saw Ethel Merman do the part opposite Ray Middleton on the stage. I loved it, it was fine, but there wasn't any picture there. Then I saw Mary Martin play it with the touring company, and Mary played the story so you knew there was a character. The studio called me and asked if I'd be interested in making *Annie Get Your Gun*, and they sent me the recordings of Judy. I thought about it and said yes. They said, "Who do you want to play Annie?" I said Betty Hutton, and the people at MGM said, "Oh, she's crazy." I sent for Hutton, and I said, "Look, no one except me wants you. I understand that you're crazy, but don't try to be crazy with me. I'll hit you right over the head." So we got that straight and had a marvelous time. She was acclaimed in the part and got great reviews.

Annie Get Your Gun was a funny picture. I saw it six or eight years ago at some university and had to laugh, because I did such outrageous things in the film. There was a train and the Indians were setting the train on fire, and they were shooting bows and arrow and hitting people's posteriors with these arrows. I thought, "Oh, what an outrageous kid you were in those days." But I sat there laughing; it was a real hunk of entertainment.

D: Was Irving Berlin around much during the making of the picture?

S: I'd known Irving Berlin for years. There's a place called the Strand Barber Shop in New York; it's around the corner from the Strand Theater. All the people from show business used to go there. I was taken to that barber shop from the time I was seven or eight years old by my father. And Irving Berlin always came in. When I did *Annie Get Your Gun*, Irving came out to California. They ran the picture for him in the projection room. He came to me and said, "George, I just saw your *Annie Get Your Gun*, and it's great." The show is always billed as Irving Berlin's *Annie Get Your Gun*. But that was the size of the man. Such giants no longer exist.

D: That was Howard Keel's first film, wasn't it?

S: He'd been in England and made his motion picture debut over there. But *Annie Get Your Gun* was his first picture in this country. He had a great voice. We always kidded him about his dancing and called him Slewfoot. We all joined in the skeet shooting. I was hot in those days, shooting skeet and all that. We formed gun clubs. I did some of the trick shooting in *Annie Get Your Gun*. It was all a wonderful world, a great life. But when that kind of world is over, it's over, and you go on to other things.

D: *Show Boat* has always been one of my favorite musicals.

S: That was a classic musical, and we shot the picture in twenty-eight days. We spent five or six days down in Natchez, Mississippi, shooting some atmosphere. We built the boat on Lot Three at MGM and floated it there. We had our bad experiences, such as the boat catching on fire. Originally we had two Sherman tank engines in the boat to run it.Everyone said, "You can't use Ava Gardner as Julie in *Show Boat*. The only girl you can use is Dinah Shore." I made a test of Dinah Shore, and she wasn't right. I made a test of Ava singing to a Lena Horne sound track, and everybody said, "Pretty good, pretty good." Ava played the part and was wonderful; she got applause.

D: Did she do her own singing in the picture?

S: We dubbed her, we recorded someone else singing. Then when the picture was finished, Ava went back and sang to her own image. That is her voice in the picture. I have the sound tracks here to prove it.

D: Was *Scaramouche* interesting for you?

S: Oh, sure, it was a continuation of the dueling. I always felt that *Scaramouche* should have been a musical. It would have needed the most crafty score, but it could have been terribly exciting.

D: Was Eleanor Parker a solid actress?

S: Yes, excellent. I decided that she had to be a redhead for this part in *Scaramouche*, and she didn't want to dye her hair. So I had wigs made. We went through the wigs, and there were problems, problems, problems. A few days after we finished the picture I walked into the old Romanoff's and there she was. I walked by and I thought, "My God, she's still wearing her wig." I stopped at her table and said, "What did you do?" She said, "Well, I think you were right, so I dyed my hair red." I said, "After all the problems I went through, now you dye your hair red!" But Eleanor was a fine actress.

D: How about *Young Bess*, did you like it?

S: *Young Bess* was interesting. I would have liked to have been able to open it up and shown the exterior of the period, instead of just showing the interior of Bess's world. I could almost have made a corollary film. Being a kind of Anglophile, the subject was terribly interesting to me, and I had some wonderful English actors in the picture. After making it my English accent was quite broad for a long while.

D: Wasn't *Kiss Me, Kate* shot in 3-D?

S: Yes. We did it in 3-D and flat as well. I made two versions at the same time. The original 3-D version, when shown in a laboratory condition with expensive Polaroid glasses, was just wonderful. We really worked on that. But they hustled 3-D for a dollar and just ruined it. We had some wonderful people in *Kiss Me, Kate*. Bobby Fosse was one of the dancing boys. Bobby Van was another. Carol Haney was one of the dancers; she danced with Bob Fosse. And Ann Miller was in the picture; she's still going strong.

D: What about Kathryn Grayson, was she an effective performer?

S: Yes, she was what was needed. She was a singing soprano ingenue, and that's how the parts she played were written. She was kind of a product of the studio. I made her first test, and we made five or six pictures together.

D: Were there problems in transferring a successful Broadway musical like *Kiss Me, Kate* to the screen?

S: There always are because basically in most musical shows the whole thing takes place in the first act, and the second act is just musical numbers. So you have to rearrange. You have to take the finale of the first act and make that the finale of the show. You always have to drop out numbers and add others. In *Kiss Me, Kate* we took the number "From This Moment On" from one of Cole Porter's other shows. Somehow things don't always work, and you have to change them around. But you must change them in a way that audiences will think that they're seeing the show exactly as it was done on the stage. Sometimes filmmakers tamper too much.

D: Why did you leave MGM?

S: I left MGM because I wanted to do *The Eddy Duchin Story*. I went to Columbia to do that. Originally *The Eddy Duchin Story* was to be made at MGM, and I was going to make it there. Averell Harriman was kind of a godfather to Eddy Duchin. He saw the Jolson pictures and liked the way Columbia handled the Jolson story. So he gave *The Eddy Duchin Story* to Columbia. Harry Cohn had been trying to get me to come to Columbia for years. So I called up Harry and said, "Harry, I'm coming to Columbia. I'm going to make *The Eddy Duchin Story*." He was thrilled. I went over to Columbia, and the Duchin picture was the first one I made there. I was on a loan-out to make it. After that film I went back to MGM, and it wasn't the same MGM. Mr. Mayer wasn't there, it was a whole different studio. I enjoyed working at Columbia, so I went back and stayed with Harry Cohn for about eleven years.

D: So things really changed at MGM when Mayer left and Dore Schary came in.

S: Completely. The types of films that were being made were totally different. They were films that I was not particularly interested in making. There was nothing wrong with them, but I didn't care to make them. *Bad Day at Black Rock* was a fine picture, but I didn't want to make it. So I went over with Harry, and we just had a great time for eleven years.

D: Apparently you got along with Harry Cohn, despite his tough reputation.

S: Just wonderfully. Cohn was a man who was really out for quality. His studio was on the rise whereas other Hollywood studios were on the descent.

D: Did having your then wife, Lillian Burns, as Cohn's assistant complicate matters for you at Columbia?

S: Not particularly, not particularly.

D: Were you happy with *The Eddy Duchin Story*?

S: Yes, I enjoyed it, because I had taken piano lessons from Eddy Duchin. I'd been to New York to see the Harrimans and was getting on a plane, and who sat next to me on the plane but Tyrone Power. Tyrone said, "What are you doing in New York?" I said, "Oh, I'm getting ready to do a picture called *The Eddy Duchin Story*." Ty said, "I knew Eddy Duchin. I knew him from up in the snow country. Who's going to play Duchin?" I said, "You are." He said, "That's impossible. I've got pictures lined up for the next four or five years." I said, "I don't care, you're going to do it." And he ended up playing the part. Harry Stradling photographed the picture, and we went to New York. I must say, I enjoyed that because I was having an exhilarating affair with New York City, where I had been raised.

D: I remember one shot in the picture where Power and Kim Novak are walking in the rain.

S: Oh, that was great fun, working in the park. Harry Stradling and I just took the camera and made those things up. They weren't in the script. I got Carmen Cavallaro to play the piano for Ty. Ty wasn't a musician but he practiced and practiced at the keyboard. We had people to teach him the fingering. We got Moss Hart to write the script. Then Moss was taken sick and went off the film. Samuel Taylor, who had just finished *Sabrina*, came on, and ultimately Clifford Odets finished the screenplay. That's some trio of writers! The final script was a blending of the three.

D: How about *Pal Joey*, did you enjoy that?

S: Well, that was just a riot, that was a real ball. I always loved working with Frank Sinatra, and the material in *Pal Joey* is just a gasser. We went to San Francisco and shot up there, then came back to Los Angeles. Frank decided that it would be better to work in the afternoon rather than in the morning, so we started working at one o'clock. We worked from one till eight every day. We whizzed through that picture and finished a number of days under schedule. Frank would come in and he'd be wound up ready to go, and we'd knock off two or three days work at a time. It was great fun.

D: You altered the show's score considerably.

S: Oh, completely. We added "Lady Is a Tramp" from *Babes in Arms* and put in "My Funny Valentine" and "Small Hotel," all Rodgers and Hart songs. Naturally we had to drop some of the songs from the original score.

D: Was Rita Hayworth good to work with?

S: A real doll. She's terribly shy, but Rita was terrific.

D: Did *Pepe*, which had a big cast, pose problems?

S: There were problems dealing with the logistics of making a picture in two countries with a writers' strike going on at the same time. It was difficult trying to schedule around this person and that person and getting all of the people together. Shooting in Mexico with two sets of crews down there posed problems. I was moving back and forth, and any time I was in one place I needed to be in the other place. Because of the writers' strike, Jimmy Durante and Cantinflas had to ad-lib a six or eight minute scene. We were lucky, it turned out to be pretty funny. The studio thought we had hired writers on the black market.

D: Was *Bye Bye Birdie* a satisfying film?

S: That was a great deal of fun. Originally I was going to produce the picture and have Gower Champion direct it. He had directed the show on Broadway. But Gower said, "I just can't see this as a picture. I'm out, there's nothing more I can add to it." So I took over. It was a young people's picture, with a lot of bright, gay, noisy cast members yelling and screaming.

D: Had MGM changed a great deal when you went back to the studio in 1963 to make *A Ticklish Affair*?

S: Yes, it was a whole different studio again. Studios reflect the personalities of those who control them. At Columbia people could walk in and sense whether Harry Cohn was in the studio or not. After Harry died, people would walk in and sense a void. A spark or a flame had gone out of it. It was no longer the old Columbia.

D: What about *Viva Las Vegas*, an Elvis Presley picture, did you look forward to making that one?

S: That was one of those cases where we had no script, and we had a commitment. Originally it was something about an Arabian or something, I don't know what it was about. But we turned it around, and we wrote the script in about eleven days. I produced the picture with Jack Cummings. We changed the whole thing and decided to do it in Las Vegas.

D: Was *The Swinger* a satisfactory film for you?

S: Again we did the script in ten days. The studio had a commitment and needed to fulfill it. I produced and directed that. We devised a script that would give Ann-Margret an opportunity to show her facets. And boom, boom, boom—off we went.

D: How about *Half a Sixpence*, was that a good experience?

S: That was quite an experience because they'd never made a musical film in England. The only one they'd ever made there was a picture Wesley Ruggles made called *London Town* thousands of years ago. And Jessie Matthews's musicals, but that's going back some. They'd never worked with playback in England, and when I went there they didn't have a music cutter. So I had to bring some people in. I had to bring in a music cutter to teach people there how to cut music, and I had to bring in playback equipment. It wasn't fast working in England, not by a long shot. But I must say I enjoyed it, and the picture was a real smash over there. In the United States *Half a Sixpence* did less than nothing because it was an English picture. The film didn't have anyone in it that anyone in this country knew. Unfortunately Tommy Steele had just made two very bad pictures in this country. We followed those and had nothing to build on with him. Also something else happened. By the time we started to make *Half a Sixpence* a thing called Beatlemania had taken over. That brought in a whole new sound. Maybe if we had been two or three years earlier with the picture, it might have been more successful with American audiences.

D: Do you feel that a director should put a personal stamp on a film?

S: Not at the cost of the film. I think sometimes people go out of their way to put some little shtick in. I don't know that I have a personal stamp, whatever that may be.

D: I wondered if you thought there was a "Sidney touch" in your pictures.

S: Not consciously. I love beautiful people.

D: Critics have said that your work is filled with dazzle and vivid coloring. Would you agree with that?

S: I like beauty. Since I'm interested in painting, I'm greatly influenced by painting. I'm influenced by music and influenced by pleasant things to look at. I tried to do things a little different, not for the sake of doing them different, but to keep the project interesting. I think people can wreck themselves by trying to make their work too unusual.

George Sidney's Feature Films

1941	*Free and Easy*
1942	*Pacific Rendezvous*
1943	*Pilot No. 5*
	Thousands Cheer
1944	*Bathing Beauty*
1945	*Anchors Aweigh*
	Ziegfeld Follies (portions)
1946	*The Harvey Girls*
	Holiday in Mexico
1947	*Cass Timberlane*
1948	*The Three Musketeers*
1949	*The Red Danube*
1950	*Key to the City*
	Annie Get Your Gun
1951	*Show Boat*
1952	*Scaramouche*
1953	*Young Bess*
	Kiss Me, Kate
1955	*Jupiter's Darling*
1956	*The Eddy Duchin Story*
1957	*Jeanne Eagels*
	Pal Joey
1960	*Who Was That Lady?*
	Pepe
1963	*Bye Bye Birdie*
	A Ticklish Affair
1964	*Viva Las Vegas*
1966	*The Swinger*
1968	*Half a Sixpence*

VINCENT SHERMAN

Actor Turned Writer Turned Director

Director Vincent Sherman was born in Vienna, Georgia, in 1906, the son of working class parents. After acting on the stage in New York, Sherman turned to screenwriting and directing, working mainly at Warner Bros. He became recognized as a skilled technician with a special flair for melodrama, making such pictures as *Mr. Skeffington* with Bette Davis, *The Unfaithful* with Ann Sheridan, and *The Damned Don't Cry* with Joan Crawford. Sherman lives in Malibu, California, and remains a keen observer of the film industry.

The following interview with the veteran director was taped in his home on August 5, 1981.

D: Mr. Sherman, I understand that you are a Southerner.
S: Yes. My father was Russian, he came to this country at the turn of the century. I was born in a little town in Georgia about fifty-six miles below Macon, Georgia. As a youngster I was very interested in public speaking and debating. When I went to Oglethorpe University in Atlanta, I was on the debating team and became president of the Debating Society. I thought I was going to become a lawyer because Clarence Darrow had been my god. At the time of the Scopes trial in Dayton, Tennessee, I was selling films in the South. I had finished college and was selling motion pictures throughout eastern Tennessee, parts of Georgia and Alabama, and part of South Carolina.
D: What brought you to New York?
S: I had always had an interest in drama, and I think I read almost every play that was in the Atlanta Public Library. At one point I had ambitions of becoming a playwright. Theater appealed to me greatly,

although I had seldom participated in it because there wasn't much theater in the South in those days. In my last year at college there was a professional stock company in Atlanta, and they needed someone to play an old man in *Seventh Heaven*. I was all of eighteen years old, and I had to play this man in his sixties. My English teacher at Oglethorpe, who had seen me in a little one-act play the preceding semester, suggested that I try out for the part. The company paid me $40 for the week!

Also in my last year in college I got an idea for a play. A former schoolmate of mine named James Larwood and I sat down and wrote a play about a fraternity house and, after I finished law school, we took the play to New York. I never practiced law. Larwood and I hoped to become writers in the theater. We had several nibbles on the play but didn't sell it. In the meantime, to make a living while we were trying to write plays, I got a job as an extra with the Theater Guild for $16 a week. That allowed me to stay in New York. I remained an actor in New York for over ten years.

Around 1930 I met Moss Hart, the playwright. My wife was working in a play broker's office and I met him there. The broker for whom my wife was working had just sold Hart's play *Once in a Lifetime*. Moss was charming, and he said to me, "What do you do during the summer?" I said, "Well, I get a job in summer stock or something like that." He said, "Do you think you could direct plays?" I said, "I don't know, I'd like to try." He said, "Well, I have been directing plays in summer camps." He couldn't go to the camps that summer because he had to stay in New York and work with George Kaufman on *Once in a Lifetime*. So Hart sent me over to apply for the job, and I got it.

My first summer directing was tough but it was exciting. We had to put on shows every Friday and Saturday night. I did a lot of plays that were new to me and a lot of plays that were tried and proven. It was wonderful training, because in one week's time or less I had to put on a show for the guests and visitors at the camp, many of whom sat on their hands. If they didn't like the show, they told us about it. But the challenge of having to do a show weekly sort of conditioned me for doing the B pictures I did later on. Even though the scripts were bad, I said, "Well, we'll fix them when we get on the set."

In New York I met Elmer Rice. I had been in two of his plays, and he knew that I wanted to write and direct. So Rice invited me into the Federal Theater, which he headed in New York for a year and a half. The first play I directed for the Federal Theater was a play about the abolitionist John Brown called *Battle Hymn*. Then Sinclair Lewis gave the Federal Theater his play *It Can't Happen Here*, and I was called upon to direct that. When I got the script, I didn't like the Lewis play at all and wanted to get out of doing it. But Hallie Flanagan, who headed the Federal Theater Project, told me how necessary it was to do something important for the Federal Theater, because there were many Congressmen sniping at the project and determined to kill it. So I felt obligated to do the best I could with Lewis's play.

D: Tell me about your association with the Group Theater.

S: The Group Theater was formed in the 1930s as a rebellion against the old florid ways of acting. I acted with them in one or two productions in New York. Clifford Odets, who became the favorite playwright of the Group Theater, had been an extra with me at the Theater Guild when we were both in *Marco Millions* and *Volpone*.

D: How did your first film work come about?

S: I came to Los Angeles in a West Coast production of *Dead End*, the Sidney Kingsley play. I played the part that Humphrey Bogart played in the movie. I met a producer at Warner Bros., Bryan Foy, one of the Foy family, and he offered me a job at Warners as a writer. He offered me $100 a week, and I said, "No, I make more than that as an actor." My wife didn't want me to stay in California anyway. She wanted me to go back to New York and work on a play. Finally Foy said, "Go to lunch and I'll talk to you after lunch. Let me speak to Mr. Warner."

Apparently Foy went to lunch and ran into Jack Warner, and I met with him again afterward. On the back of a piece of Spearmint chewing gum paper Warner had written that if I signed a seven-year contract and agreed to either act, write, or direct, he felt safe in offering me a contract. Evidently during the lunch period the studio's casting director, a man named Max Arnow, had said, "Well, Sherman's a good actor. If he doesn't work out as a writer, we can always use him as an actor."

D: Hadn't you made some films as an actor before that?

S: Yes. I had played the part of a young radical in the Chicago company of *Counsellor-at-Law*. When William Wyler was ready to make the movie with John Barrymore, Elmer Rice recommended that they look at me for the picture. I flew out to Hollywood, met Mr. Wyler,

and acted in that picture. I stayed out here and did about eight or nine
B pictures. I played gangsters. Finally a call came from Mr. Rice asking
me if I wanted to play in *Judgment Day* in New York, and I went back
to New York. I started working for Warner Bros. in July 1937.

D: During the making of *Counsellor-at-Law* did you get to know
John Barrymore?

S: Yes. He treated me marvelously. The poor man was having trouble retaining his lines, and on the scene I did with him we had to do
twenty-seven takes. He was very apologetic, but he would get to a
certain point and it was like a black-out. He even had a blackboard
that he would read off of. The day that he did a scene with my friend
John Qualen, they did fifty-five takes and finally had to quit.
Barrymore could not remember his lines. I was waiting for Qualen
back at the hotel to have dinner, and he came in about nine-thirty or
ten. That night apparently was the night that Barrymore went home
and called his next-door neighbor and said, "I think I'm losing my
mind." He had a great fear of that.

Barrymore was a very intelligent man, cultured and very well read.
He had been a cartoonist in his young days, and as we were sitting at
the desk working, he had a pencil and was sketching faces. I looked
over in between takes, and the expression on the faces was the
expression that he was supposed to have in the scene.

D: How would you describe the general atmosphere around the
Warner Bros. lot when you came to the studio in 1937?

D: It was like a factory. It was a factory with talented people, but it
was a very business-like place. They made a certain number of A pictures a year, which were under the wing of Hal Wallis, and a certain
number of B pictures, which were under the supervision of Bryan
Foy. I started there as a B writer, and after two years they made me a
B director. Then after one or two pictures I became an A director.

Jack Warner didn't have too much to do with the details of each
story. He had very little to do with the B pictures, they were just sort
of a side issue. Very often he wouldn't even look at the rushes of the
B pictures. Those were pictures that cost around $150,000. In those days
Warners had around 1,600 theaters, so the studio supplied them with
one A picture and one B picture on a double bill. Foy usually would
remake old A pictures, what he called switches. The writers and directors would take an old picture and switch the setting. I later switched
some A pictures myself. I had to do a picture with Ann Sheridan, and

we didn't have a script for her. So producer Jerry Wald had the idea of taking Somerset Maugham's "The Letter" and making a modern piece out of it. We switched the story, which had been made into a picture with Bette Davis earlier, and filmed it as *The Unfaithful*.

When it came time to renew the option of an actor or a writer or a director, Warner would look at a list of their pictures and ask, "Did they make money?" If the person had been associated with a picture that did well, the option was automatically picked up. If the person had been involved with some flops, the option probably would be dropped.

I'd finish a picture on a Friday, and many times I'd come in Monday morning and they would hand me another script. Three days off were a vacation. But later, when I became an A director, things eased up a little bit. There was nothing chi-chi about Warner Bros., but it was a vital place and they paid comparable to other studios. I would say that Warners was closer to the earth than MGM and most of the other studios. Many of the writers at Warner Bros., like myself, were from New York. We were kids who had experienced the Depression, and our fathers had dirt under their fingernails. In the 1930s Warners dealt with pretty meaty subjects. Their pictures were more down-to-earth than those made at Metro or Paramount.

D: Was Warners a friendly lot?

S: Yes, very friendly. Everybody was always beefing with the front office. We always complained that we didn't have enough time to make our pictures, that the studio was tight with money, and so forth. But among the people who were working on the lot there was great camaraderie. The actors and writers and directors were very friendly. It was really a big happy family.

As a director, I'd come to the studio around eight o'clock in the morning, stop off at the makeup department to say hello to the leading lady or leading man, see how everything was, maybe have coffee and a doughnut in the makeup department, go down to the set, and we'd start shooting at nine o'clock. It was a very friendly atmosphere, and we all respected each other's work. I don't think any of us regarded ourselves as artists. Filmmaking was a business. There was definite artistic consideration in the preparation of scripts, but we didn't go out and parade that. We knew that we had to make successful pictures. We knew that if the pictures did no business, there would be no studio. It was an industry. Warners knew that if they made a picture, it would at least play in their theaters, and they had to have pictures for their theaters.

D: Part of the challenge must have been to make pictures of quality yet also something that would be successful at the box office.

S: That's exactly right. You always had two eyes. One was on the artistic merit, on the credibility of the material, seeing that the characters behaved reasonably and that we had serious themes in our pictures. We dealt as much as possible with real life problems, and as much as possible with real life solutions. But still, we had to make pictures that entertained and did well at the box office.

Jack Warner never stood over a director and dictated how pictures should be shot. We knew that we had to cover the subject sufficiently so that the studio's editors weren't tied down to any one shot. We knew that audiences at that time wanted to know where the scene took place and who was involved. That didn't mean that we had to start every scene with a long master shot. We could start it with a close-up and then reveal the location later. That was up to the individual.

Directors had a certain amount of freedom. I never felt any pressure to do things a certain way, and I don't think any director did. We just knew that we had to have enough coverage for the editors to have some leeway in doing their work. In general directors told the story the way they thought was most effective.

D: Was *Crime School* the first script you wrote at Warner Bros.?

S: Yes, that was the first one. Since I had been in *Dead End* and since the Dead End Kids were under contract to the studio, Foy chose me to help put together a script for them. We very quickly came up with *Crime School*, which was half of *The Mayor of Hell*, which James Cagney had done for the studio, and half of *San Quentin* that Pat O'Brien and Ann Sheridan had done. We put the two together. Bogart was in *Crime School*; that was the first time I met him. And the Dead End Kids were in it. I was also dialogue director on that picture. It turned out to be a big box office success and cost, I think, $186,000 to make.

We were about four or five days late on the picture, and in those days it was a criminal offense to be on a B picture four or five days over schedule. The production man was raising hell, and he blamed me for the delay because I was rewriting scenes for the director, who was an old-timer named Lew Seiler. But when the picture came out and got four stars in New York, I got all the credit, which was equally unjust. I had something to do with the success, but so did the director and the actors. That's the way the picture business goes. From being a villain during the making of the picture, I found myself overnight the fair-haired boy. That's how crazy the picture business is.

D: Was *My Bill* an interesting project for you?

S: No, no. Believe it or not, after *Crime School* I got a call from Foy one Thursday afternoon, and he said, "I've got to have a script ready for Kay Francis by Monday." They were going to start shooting toward the end of the week, and John Farrow was to direct. Kay Francis had been a big star at the studio, but her last few pictures hadn't made money and Warner wanted to break her contract. He thought that if he said to her, "You're going to make a picture with Brynie Foy," she would be indignant and walk out on her contract. She was getting, I think, $5,000 a week, very big money in those days. Kay, however, said, "As long as they pay me, I'll sweep the stages for them."

Foy gave me an old play that Warners owned called *Courage*. It was an old-fashioned piece about a woman whose husband dies and she's left with a couple of kids. I had to have a script finished by Monday morning. I got my secretary and started to work on Friday morning, and we worked until about eleven that night. We worked all day Saturday and Sunday, and on Monday morning I gave Foy a script. By the end of that week Farrow was shooting it. That was *My Bill*.

D: Was *Return of Doctor X* your first assignment as director?

S: That's right. It was a mystery-horror picture. Foy called me into his office and said, "Warner wants to make some new directors, and I recommended you. I've got two scripts. One is a comedy remake of *Kid Galahad*, and the other is a kind of mystery-horror picture." He told me a little bit about the mystery-horror picture, and I said, "I think I'll do that." He said, "Okay." I said, "I don't know too much about the camera." Foy said, "That's all right. I'll put you with Sid Hickox, a good cameraman, he'll help you out with the cutting and so forth." And he did. Sid was an old-timer on the lot and had been Kay Francis's cameraman. I admitted to him that I didn't know one lens from another and had no idea where the camera should be. Sid said, "Go ahead and line the scene up the way you think you want it, and then we'll talk." Little by little I picked up what I needed to know.

I didn't really feel in control of everything on the set until after I'd done five or six pictures. It took me that long to learn how to stage a scene for the camera, because you stage for the camera differently than you do for the theater. I also had to learn how to cut most effectively and how to motivate movement. I finally realized that the best pictures are those in which an audience is not conscious of the mechanics of what's going on in the making of a film. As time went on I tried to do less and less camera movement. I tried to make the camera as unobtrusive as possible, let the actors come to the camera if possible. It took time to realize the power of a camera, that I could select what I wanted an audience to see. The camera was frightening to me at first. We used to call it the One-Eyed Monster. Once I got familiar with it, then my senses became attuned to when the camera should move. A director's concentration becomes so fierce that every nerve in the body is responding to what's happening on that set. I became so sensitized that I could see a mike shadow sometimes when nobody else had noticed it.

D: Was Humphrey Bogart a rewarding actor to direct?

S: Yes, he was a real professional. He came from the theater, and he was a very hard working guy. Bogie was always grousing, always annoyed. First of all, he was making very little money in those days. When I worked with him on *Return of Doctor X*, he was considered merely a villain. In the late 1930s nobody in their wildest imagination ever dreamed that Bogart would be a leading man. But almost every director on the lot thought of him whenever they needed a heavy. I don't think he was very happy about that. I never thought that Bogart was a great actor, but he was very skillful and a real personality.

D: How did you feel about *Saturday's Children*?

S: I loved it. It had my friend Claude Rains, whom I'd known in the theater in New York, in it and also John Garfield, whom I'd worked with in *Counsellor-at-Law* in Chicago. The script of *Saturday's Children* had been written by the Epstein brothers, and the picture was supposed to have been directed by Anatole Litvak. Originally it was to star Jimmy Stewart and Olivia de Havilland. But Stewart turned the part down for some reason, and when he turned it down, Litvak didn't want to do the picture. The Epstein twins then went to the front office and said, "There's a young kid here from New York who's just started directing. Why don't you give him a chance to direct this picture?" So *Saturday's Children* was my second directorial assignment. It was what we called a small A picture. It got wonderful reviews in New York. I enjoyed making it, and the picture had a wonderful script. The Epsteins were good writers.

D: What kind of a fellow was Hal Wallis to work with?

S: Wallis was a very efficient studio manager, a very competent, skillful man. I was not personally too fond of him. I suppose working for Warner he had to be a strict disciplinarian. Producing thirty or forty A pictures a year, he had to be on his toes all the time. I never got close to him. On one or two occasions we exchanged a few harsh words. When Wallis was making *Air Force* with Howard Hawks directing, I got a call from Warner one day. He said, "Listen, Howard Hawks is sick, and we want you to go in for a day or two to shoot some scenes on this picture he's making. Go in and talk to Wallis." Wallis gave me the script and told me to go look at the film that Hawks had shot so far on *Air Force* and acquaint myself with it. He said, "You start shooting in the morning." Then I began to hear rumors that Hawks wasn't sick, that he and Wallis had had a fight.

Since I was under contract to the studio, I had to go in and shoot. So I came to the set the next day and started working on one of the scenes. Wallis came on the set and said, "See if you can't get some life out of these people, they're all so dead-ass." I said, "Well, Hal, based on the film I saw, that was the whole approach that Hawks took, that's the style of the picture." The characters in the film were in a plane. They couldn't run and shout, they had to keep their heads cool and fly. The drama had to play itself.

Anyway I shot on *Air Force* for damn near ten days. After ten days I was suddenly told that Hawks was coming back. Hawks finished the picture and re-shot some of the stuff that I'd shot. I bumped into him one day and said, "Hi, Howard. I just want you to know that I did the best I could filling in for you on *Air Force*." He said, "You don't have to tell me. I knew everything that was going on." I found out later that he had an assistant on the set who would call him every night and tell him what had taken place that day. That's just a sidelight of what can go on in this business. After that episode my friendship with Wallis went out the window.

D: Did you find Bette Davis easy to work with?

S: Davis was a most talented actress and a great screen personality. During the making of *Old Acquaintance* we got along very well. She had some problems with Miriam Hopkins on the picture, but looking back on the whole thing, their trouble was more amusing than dramatic or serious. On *Mr. Skeffington*, the second picture I made with Bette, we had some difficulties. She was going through a reaction to her husband's sudden death. It was a difficult time for her, and I attributed most of our problems to that. Also in the latter stages of that picture, when her character is an old woman, she had this difficult makeup to put on. It took hours to apply, and by two or three o'clock in the afternoon her face was itching so that all she wanted to do was claw it off with her nails. But she had to work until five or six o'clock with it still on. So *Mr. Skeffington* was a hard picture for Bette. I'm sorry that we had words while we were making it.

Davis almost became a caricature of herself. She had such a strong personality and had such success playing the neurotic kind of woman. There was a quality in what she created as Mildred in *Of Human Bondage*, her first big success, that she carried over into other things. Even great actors sometimes develop characteristics in a certain role, and they feel a comfort and a safety in that. Those characteristics sort of hang on and they're very difficult to get rid of.

D: As director, did you work closely with the Warners music department?

S: I'll tell you what the situation was. If Franz Waxman was going to score the film, I'd have a long talk with him before I ever started the picture. When the picture was finished, we'd first run a rough cut for Warner, then make a few adjustments if necessary. Sometimes there would be a retake, but not too often. Then the music people would look at the film. Leo Forbstein was head of the music department, and he'd bring Franz Waxman or Max Steiner or whoever was going to compose the music. We'd all run the film together—the producer, the director, and the music people. We'd each make suggestions about where the music should be, but most of that was left up to the composer. After the score was added, Warner would listen to it, and sometimes he would say, "I don't think we need music in that place, let's take the music out." But this was all a harmonious relationship.

I've found that most of the time real artists are tough, hard boiled, hard working, practical people with their feet on the ground. Their artistic opinions come out of an honest and real relationship to life and to people. There's none of the preciousness of people who live in a rarefied atmosphere. We were not just making quantity, we were trying to do quality work as well.

D: Warner Bros. had such marvelous character actors, among whom was Sydney Greenstreet.

S: I knew Greenstreet from the theater. He was in the Theater Guild. We worked together in *The Good Earth* in New York. I played a small part in *The Good Earth*, and Sydney was in that and so was Claude Rains. Sydney was in *Volpone*, too. The first picture I made with Sydney, I think, was a comedy with Ida Lupino called *Pillow to Post*. It was just a little comedy that the studio had picked up for peanuts, and they needed a property for Ida.

Let me explain something. There were a certain number of stages at Warners, I think twenty or twenty-two. There were people on the studio's payroll. When pictures weren't in production, Warner was bothered, because he had to turn out so many pictures. In other words, when the stages were unoccupied and people were sitting idle and not doing anything, he was losing money. Whether the pictures were good, bad, or indifferent, Warner wanted pictures being made. In fact, I remember one time when he called me about a picture that I didn't want to make, and he said, "Listen, I've got eight actors sitting on their ass doing nothing, getting paid. I want to put them to work. Take this script and do the best you can with it and give me twelve reels of film." He knew that whatever we gave him, whether it was a good or poor picture, was better than nothing. He had 1,600 theaters, he could always put the picture in those theaters. That's the way Jack Warner operated. So under pressure, we did the best we could with the material.

D: Did you enjoy making *Janie Gets Married*, which I presume was a little film?

S: No, I hated it. I liked the people in it. I liked working with the young girl, Joan Leslie. I had directed her in *The Hard Way*. She was a very nice, sweet girl and a hard working youngster. She was talented but unappreciated in many ways. She was under contract to the studio, and she did everything they gave her to do. The girl who starred in the original *Janie* [Joyce Reynolds], which was a lightweight comedy, didn't want to make the sequel. The studio had the script, and Warner wasn't about to throw away a script that he'd spent money on. Mike Curtiz, who had directed the original *Janie*, didn't want to make the sequel either, so they gave the picture to me. I wasn't busy at the time. I didn't like the script, and I wasn't that fond of the producer. It was not a good picture in my opinion.

D: You mentioned Ann Sheridan, and I'm wondering what kind of a person she was?

S: I loved her. She was a wonderful gal, very regular, very down-to-earth, no put-on, no affectation, very honest, and great to work with. She'd had the misfortune of starting out as an Oomph Girl, and she did a lot of B pictures. That always colored you to some extent in the eyes of the studios. Annie's was a slow development, but I think she became a very proficient actress. She was one of the most skillful comediennes in this town. Annie knew how to toss away a line with a kind of cynical quality and had a wry quality. I think she did a marvelous job for me in *The Unfaithful*. She also did an excellent job for me in *Nora Prentiss*.

It was funny about *Nora Prentiss*. I got a call one day from Warner, and he said, "Listen, you know Sheridan. I need a picture for her, we've got to put her to work. Can you think of anything we can do for her?" I had a story that I had bought myself for like $2,500 that I planned to make some day on my own. I told Warner, "Gee, I've got a story, Jack, that I bought about a year ago. It's really a man's story, but maybe I could do something and make a story for Annie Sheridan out of it." I told him the story, and he said, "We'll buy it from you. See if you can get Sheridan to do the picture."

I flew to New York to see Annie and told her honestly what the situation was. I've always been honest with actors and actresses. I may not be honest always with producers, but I've got to work with actors and actresses day in and day out, and there has to be a mutual trust if the project is going to succeed. I told Annie the story Warner wanted her to do, and she agreed to make the picture. The story I bought had a melodramatic finish, with a guy changing his face. But when I started to work on the first part of the script, it became a very human drama and not melodramatic. So when we got to the end of it, I almost was ready to change the plot, because we'd already done a very real, human story. We were stuck, and I didn't have any solution. So we just went ahead with the original story and stuck with the melodramatic finish, which was really just a gimmick.

D: Was making *The Adventures of Don Juan* with Errol Flynn a good experience for you?

S: Yes and no. Errol Flynn was a marvelous guy personally, but difficult to get on the set. He'd come to the studio sometimes a minute before nine o'clock in the morning, then wouldn't appear on the set until ten-thirty or eleven. Around five o'clock he'd start to slow up and start drinking. That part was difficult. When he worked, he was delightful to work with. He was a charming man with a great sense of fun. I think he was making more money than anyone else on the lot. His pictures had been very successful, but by the time I worked with him, he was beginning to slip a little.

I wasn't supposed to make *Don Juan*, originally Jean Negulesco was supposed to direct the picture. For some reason Flynn apparently called on me to do it. I later heard that Ann Sheridan had told him, "Get Vince. He'll play straight with you." By that time Flynn had fallen out with Mike Curtiz and Raoul Walsh, with whom he had made highly successful pictures. Initially the script of *Don Juan* was a very delicate, charming little script. In fact the first writer said to me, "This is like a piece of Venetian glass." I went to Warner, and Warner said, "To hell with that, this is Flynn. He's either going to be fighting or screwing. Get some guts into the thing." That's when I got Harry Kurnitz in to do some rewriting, and we boosted the script up as much as we could.

Flynn was a great prankster. He'd pull capers like a high school kid. He never really matured, and he loved to thumb his nose at the establishment. I think he realized that the distance between being a big star making $5,000 a week and being flat broke, and not having money to buy a meal with, wasn't that much. He just felt the falseness of the whole thing. I think stardom had sort of caught him off-guard. It was difficult for him to handle. I think Flynn thought, "Well, if becoming a star is this easy, how phony is all this?"

D: Do you have fond recollections of making *The Hasty Heart*?

S: It was one of the most pleasant experiences I ever had. I worked under difficult conditions in London; it was one of the hardest winters they'd ever had. The fog was so thick that one day I had to open the stage door and get a fan to blow the fog out of the stage so we could shoot. But I had a wonderful cast, and it was a property that I liked very much. Warners owned forty per cent of the Associated British Pictures Corporation in London, so Jack sent me over to England to make the picture with Ronald Reagan and Patricia Neal. I was to cast the Scotsman over there. Warner told me that he wanted to spend no more than $1.2 million on the picture, and I made it for $800,000.

Reagan did a fine job in *The Hasty Heart*. I think it was one of the best jobs that Ronnie ever did. He had originally wanted to play the

Scotsman and was disappointed that he didn't get the part. But he agreed to play Yank, and we got along fine. Richard Todd, who was actually Irish, played the Scotsman. I got somebody to teach him the Scottish brogue. *The Hasty Heart* is a beautiful story, and Todd gave a wonderful performance.

D: How about *Backfire*, did you like that?

S: That's the picture I said I didn't want to do. That's the time when Warner said, "I've got eight actors that I need to put to work." They were Viveca Lindfors, Dane Clark, Gordon MacRae, Virginia Mayo, Eddie O'Brien, and three more who were under contract to the studio. That picture had an involved story, with flashback within flashback, and I hated it. The interesting thing is that not long ago I saw the film, and it looked better than when I made it.

D: Was Virginia Mayo a competent actress?

S: Yes. She was a beautiful girl, very sweet. As you say, she was competent. She was very easy to work with and had a nice screen quality. I don't think she was any intellectual giant or a gal with any great depth, but very worthwhile to have in the studio under contract. She photographed beautifully.

D: I know that you made something like three Joan Crawford films almost in a row. Was Crawford good to work with?

S: There was a consummate professional. No question about that. She knew every trick of the trade, knew lighting, where the camera was, knew cutting. She'd been working in pictures for so many years and was very, very smart about what she could do and what she couldn't do. She knew what would work for her and what wouldn't work. She was knowledgeable about story, too. I had no problems with Crawford whatsoever, it was a real pleasure to work with her. Sometimes she'd get a little annoyed with other people. She didn't like kidding around.

D: One of the Crawford films that you directed, *Harriet Craig*, was made on a loan-out to Columbia. How did you find working conditions at Columbia after having been at Warner Bros.?

S: I guess I'm one of the small group of people who liked [studio head] Harry Cohn. I found Cohn a very knowledgeable man, tough, and he could be crude at times. But he had impeccable taste when it came to pictures. He was shrewd, with a keen nose for what the public would buy. Those old-timers had that in common. They couldn't intellectualize about a subject, the theme of a picture, or the fine points of characterization, but they had a feel for the overall piece. They knew whether it was something good, whether it was real, whether it was honest, whether the public would like it.

I didn't want to direct *Harriet Craig* because it was a remake of *Craig's Wife*, an old Rosalind Russell picture. I tried to get out of it but I couldn't. The deal was made before I knew about it. Crawford wanted me to do the picture with her. I called Warner Bros. and said, "What happens if I say no to this loan-out?" And the studio said, "You'll break your contract." I had a five year straight deal with them at pretty good money, and I didn't want to break that contract. So I went over to Columbia and we rewrote the script for Crawford, and I did the best I could with it.

D: I remember that you made *Affair in Trinidad* at Columbia.

S: After I left Warner Bros. I directed a Western with Clark Gable at MGM. When I finished it, I went over to talk to Harry Cohn, and he said, "How would you like to make Rita Hayworth's first picture now that she's back from her marriage to Aly Khan?" I said, "Why me? Who wouldn't want to make it? She was so hot when she left." Cohn said, "I like you. Listen, I'll give you the first twenty pages of the script. Go sit in that office and read it." I read the unfinished script he had for Hayworth, and Cohn asked what I thought of the story. I said, "Well, it's a springboard, Harry. What about the rest of it?" He said, "It's great. Will you direct it?" I said, "Well, if you say you've got a good story, okay." We shook hands, and I went downstairs, talked to the writer and producer, and found out that there was no story. They had five stories, which means that they didn't have any. Cohn said, "Give me an exotic background, a few dance numbers, a love-hate relationship, and get me twelve or fifteen reels of film." So I put a picture together. It was really a synthetic job of stealing a little from this and a little from that and slapping something together, because Rita had come back unexpectedly and they had to put her to work. I knew that the film was a piece of junk but, to my surprise, Cohn gave me a piece of the profits and offered me a contract after that. *Affair in Trinidad* did business and was fair entertainment.

D: How was Rita Hayworth to work with?

S: She was a lovely girl, very insecure, but a much better actress than people gave her credit for being. Rita didn't have the capacity or background to handle being a world-wide celebrity.

D: You referred to *Lone Star*, the picture you made at MGM with Clark Gable. Was filmmaking at Metro different from other studios?
S: Not terribly different. I didn't like the script and didn't want to do the picture, although I had great respect for Clark Gable. I'd never met him but I'd heard wonderful things about him. I went over to Metro and met the producer and Gable and told them that I thought the script needed work. Then I went home, and I got a call from my agent saying not to worry about *Lone Star* because Howard Hawks was going to direct the picture. I said, "Well good, maybe Hawks knows what to do with it." Three days went by and I got another call from my agent. He said, "Vince, the Hawks deal didn't work out, and Gable said he liked the fact that you were honest with him about the script. He'd like to have you direct the picture. They're going to have it rewritten."

I went to work looking for locations. The producer and I talked about things to do with the script, but I never saw a writer. They hired a writer and didn't let me talk to her. Apparently she worked on the script for two or three weeks. Finally the producer told me, "Vince, her stuff was so bad that we didn't want you to see it. We fired her." So they brought the original writer back in, a writer I didn't like in the first place, a guy named Borden Chase. I didn't like him personally or his politics. He was a right-wing reactionary, and I was a left-wing liberal. So the joy of that picture was working with Gable and Ava Gardner and Broderick Crawford.

Gable was king of the MGM lot, but he was as humble as you can imagine. If he respected you, he listened to you, and if he thought what you were saying made sense, he'd go all the way with you. He was one of the easiest and nicest people I ever worked with in this business. I'd come on the set in the morning, and he'd say lines that I didn't like myself as they were written. I'd say, "Clark, does that line bother you?" And he'd say, "Yeah." I'd say, "What do you feel like saying there?" And we'd work it out together. Gable was a delight, a real gentleman.
D: Why did you leave Warner Bros.?
S: I had two more years to go on my contract. Warner was getting rid of all the high-priced people at the studio, and I was getting a very big salary. I suppose if I'd wanted to I could have stayed, but Warner and I had had a fight about *Goodbye My Fancy*. Jack cast a guy named Frank Lovejoy in the leading role. Lovejoy was an old friend of mine from New York, whom I liked very much, and he was a good, solid actor.

But I did not think he was right to play Joan Crawford's lover. I thought he was miscast. Warner and I had an argument about that, and I got very annoyed. Jack said something to the effect that he was running the studio, that he was paying Lovejoy, and Lovejoy was going to do the picture.

Then one day during the making of the film, Warner called me and said, "I don't want any more close-ups of Crawford. She's getting too old, stay away from close-ups." I said, "Well, Jack, I've got to have some close-ups in the picture." He said, "Well, all right, make close-ups of the other people but not of her." I said, "I can't do that. She's the star of the picture." Warner got sore at me and we exchanged some harsh words. I said to Jack's assistant, Steve Trilling, "I'm sorry but I'm not going to ignore Crawford in close-ups. If that's what you want, put somebody else on the picture."

I think underneath there was something else involved, which I only found out years later. I have no proof of this, but I suspect that my name was on a gray list of radical actors. I was never a member of the Communist Party. I was solicited by the Party and always turned them down. But I was a left-wing liberal, and my name was on many different committees and many organizations that were liberal and left-wing in intent. Maybe there were some Communists involved with those groups, but I had nothing to do with the Communist Party. I suspect that Warner was told that I was on this list and he wanted to get rid of me. He was very frightened because there were many writers at Warners who were left-wing and even some who were Communist Party members, as the House Committee on Un-American Activities found out later. I think Warner was nervous about my political affiliations and used our argument as an excuse. He was cowardly that way. Also the money I was making had something to do with it. Harry Cohn put me back to work. Cohn had more guts than Warner had.

D: I understand that you took over *The Garment Jungle* at Columbia when Robert Aldrich bowed out?

S: That's right. Aldrich and the producer were not getting along. Neither one of them were getting along with Harry Cohn, and Cohn was unhappy. Harry asked me to re-do two or three scenes, and I couldn't turn him down. Then he decided that I should finish the picture. I didn't know what the hell was going on. I re-shot, I would say, about seventy per cent of the picture in about ten days time.

D: Did you find Paul Newman a talented young actor when you worked with him on *The Young Philadelphians*?

S: Oh, yes. He didn't really want to make *The Young Philadelphians*. He hated the script and did the part reluctantly. I thought Newman did a very good job, and it was one of his better pictures. He was very pleasant to work with and a highly talented man. There again I feel that Paul is a person who's capable of doing much better work than he has normally been given the opportunity to do. I thought he did a marvelous job in *Somebody Up There Likes Me*, and he did a good job in *Sweet Bird of Youth*, but beyond that he hasn't had many really good parts. Good roles are few and far between.

D: As you think back over your years at Warner Bros., do you feel that the studio gave you a chance to develop your talent?

S: Yes, to some extent. I would have loved to have done *Casablanca*, I would have loved to have done *Treasure of Sierra Madre*, but I didn't get those. I don't think that there was any concerted effort not to give me top pictures. That's just the way the schedule worked out. It's true that if you did a successful picture, you could demand a little bit more in the next one. I was always what I thought was a fairly good company man. I felt a certain loyalty to the studio. They were paying me good money. If I didn't do a picture and was off too long, I felt a little self-conscious about it. I was a guy who had had a rough time in the beginning and started at the studio at $200 a week. When I finally got up to $3,500 and $4,000 a week, I felt an obligation to deliver. Many times I'd have to do things that I didn't like. Warner would beg me to do the picture, and I'd do the damn thing. Some of the pictures I wish I hadn't made. An old director told me when I started in the business, "If you get one out of six that's really good, that's a good average," and he was right.

Vincent Sherman's Feature Films

1939   *The Return of Dr. X*
1940   *Saturday's Children*
          The Man Who Talked Too Much
1941   *Flight from Destiny*
          Underground

1942	*All Through the Night*
	The Hard Way
1943	*Old Acquaintance*
1944	*In Our Time*
	Mr. Skeffington
1945	*Pillow to Post*
1946	*Janie Gets Married*
1947	*Nora Prentiss*
	The Unfaithful
1949	*The Adventures of Don Juan*
1950	*Backfire*
	The Hasty Heart
	The Dammed Don't Cry
	Harriet Craig
1951	*Goodbye My Fancy*
1952	*Lone Star*
	Affair in Trinidad
1956	*Difendo il mio Amore* (in Italy)
1957	*The Garment Jungle*
1958	*The Naked Earth*
1959	*The Young Philadelphians*
1960	*Ice Palace*
1961	*The Fever in the Blood*
	The Second Time Around
1968	*Cervantes* (in Spain)

MICHAEL GORDON

Leftist Intellectual

Stage and screen director Michael Gordon was born in Baltimore, Maryland, on September 6, 1909. He entered the movie business in 1940 as a dialogue coach and made his debut as a film director two years later. He worked at Columbia, Universal, and Twentieth Century-Fox and made films ranging from low-budget crime pictures to such serious dramas as *Another Part of the Forest* and *Cyrano de Bergerac*. Blacklisted from the industry following the House Un-American Activities Committee's hearings in Hollywood, Gordon returned to filmmaking in the late 1950s and directed *Pillow Talk* and *Move Over Darling*, both successful comedies. He died in Los Angeles in April 1993.

The following interview was taped in the director's office at the University of California at Los Angeles in three sessions, August 7 and 12, 1981 and July 26, 1982.

D: How did you, a boy from Baltimore, first become interested in the theater?
G: There was a fellow who moved into my neighborhood, who oddly enough came from Richmond, Virginia, who was into what was called declamation in those days. I was about twelve years old. He got me interested in such things, and I began working on pieces like "The Traitor's Deathbed," dramatic monologues where you gesticulated and made all the appropriate gestures and motions. Much to my astonishment, I got involved in a few competitions and did very well. I won a declamation contest in high school. Then I went to a boys' camp in Massachusetts, where in addition to the athletic program they had a very intensive dramatic program. I had quite a

successful experience there over a period of years, because I was a camper for four years and subsequently became a counselor at the camp. I had almost the identical experience when I went to college. So far as I can recall there were no formal classes in theater at Johns Hopkins, but there was an extracurricular undergraduate dramatic club. In my sophomore year I tried out for it and became something of a wheel in the drama club, the Barnstormers. I had been accelerated in the lower grades in school, and I graduated from Johns Hopkins at nineteen. I had two uncles in New York and my mother was from there, so we made frequent trips to New York. My favorite uncle was something of a gypsy musician, and he suggested that I go to Yale Drama School. He sent me a catalogue from Yale, and it was astonishing. Here were all the things I wanted to do for sheer fun, and this was a field of study. I was enormously turned on. In the community I grew up in, a middle-class Jewish community in Baltimore, if I had said that I wanted to enter a Benedictine monastery, it wouldn't have been any more exotic than going to Yale Drama School.

D: Was George Pierce Baker still at Yale?

G: Baker was still there. Actually he taught for one year after my class. I got my MFA in 1932. Baker taught playwriting and one survey course in dramatic literature. In playwriting terms he was very conventional. My attitude toward him at the time was that he was an old fuddy-duddy. He was using Sir Arthur Wing Pinero and Henry Arthur Jones almost as exemplars of contemporary playwrights. Baker was a strong advocate of the well-made play form. I actually majored in playwriting.

D: After Yale did you go immediately to New York?

G: Yes. I think I had the feeling that if I didn't give Broadway a try, I'd always regret it. I had no contacts in New York at all, but I got very lucky. I perhaps had seen two or three professional plays before I went to Yale. My fellow students in New Haven would talk about Guthrie and Kit and Alfred and Lynn, and I didn't know who they were talking about. I was really an illiterate in the theater.

D: What was your first job in New York?

G: I was a chorus boy in a musical. I could do a respectable time step, but I think I was really engaged because I could speak lines.

The show was a revue, and they needed people to fill in the skits. The revue was called *Walk a Little Faster*, and Beatrice Lillie was the star. I kind of maneuvered myself into being the second assistant stage manager. It was a reasonably successful show that might be remembered today for a song in it called "April in Paris." Vernon Duke was the composer. He and I roomed together for a while. Oddly enough that's when I first met Dimitri Tiomkin, who later won all kinds of Academy Awards for scoring, but who was then merely the consort of Albertina Rasch, the choreographer on *Walk a Little Faster*. The show closed about a week after Roosevelt's inauguration when they closed the banks.

D: Was your goal to become a director?

G: That was something that took shape while I was at Yale. I had enough sense to realize that my prospects as an actor were limited, but the fledgling director has the hardest time of anyone to find a job. There are no small parts for directors; it's the whole bit or nothing. I had doors shut in my face a lot of times. But nobody ever worked on preplanning on a script any harder than I did.

D: How did your first directing assignment come about?

G: Luck was a very important factor. Albert Maltz and George Sklar, whom I'd known at Yale, got involved with Theater Union, a labor theater. This was in the early 1930s. I became the stage manager of their first production, a play called *Peace on Earth*. The next production they did was called *Stevedore*, in which they gave me billing as assistant director as well as stage manager. That play closed in the summertime but reopened with about a twenty-five percent cast replacement the following fall. The director was in Europe at the time, and I was called upon to put the show back together again. They let me direct their third production. I had been trying to get into the Group Theater from the time I arrived in New York. So I left Theater Union, where I had my introduction to directing, and went to the Group in the very subordinate capacity as stage manager. Then I began to design the lighting for the Group's shows.

D: How long were you with the Group?

G: I left the Group in September 1940. That was about the tenth year of their existence. I joined them in about their fifth year. I wrote some people I knew in Hollywood, and within a few days I got a call from one of the guys saying, "I can get you a job at Columbia. It's a terrible job but it's a job." So I left the Group and went to California. Leaving the Group Theater was like leaving the Church, but I was thirty years old and needed to make some money. Joe Bromberg, a member of the inner circle of the Group, had already gone to Hollywood. So had Franchot Tone. These defections were something that agitated the people in the Group a great deal.

D: What was your reaction to Columbia when you arrived in Hollywood?

G: For me it was an interesting experience. I saw working there as a job of transition. I knew damn well by then that I was going to be a director. I had the snobbish attitude toward Hollywood that most people from Broadway had. But I did recognize that the screen could be an effective medium and had many more resources in terms of story telling than the stage offered. I had fooled around a little bit with film in New York with a group that had originally been still photographers. So I'd had a taste of filmmaking. But Columbia offered me a security I'd never known.

D: You went to Columbia in what capacity?

G: First I was a dialogue director and subsequently a director. What I said to myself was, "This is going to be a learning experience." The things I needed to learn really broke down into three categories—the camera, the sound track, and the cutting room. I got books and cultivated people who were specialists in those fields and picked their brains. Also I observed. Being a dialogue director was the lowest position on the totem pole. My fundamental duty was to make sure the actors knew their lines when they got on the set. Anything more depended on the dialogue director, the kind of relationship he or she established with the director, and the kind of rapport the dialogue coach established with the actors. In some cases I did a certain amount of directing. In other instances it was clear that I was to keep hands off. I watched what was being done by experienced directors I was working with. After perhaps three or four months, when I began to get some sense of what the nature of the operation was, I began taking the next day's call sheet and working on it as though I had to shoot those scenes tomorrow. Then I compared what my planning was with what the director in charge did. So being a dialogue director wasn't a drudge for me at all. I enjoyed it. I didn't feel that the time was squandered. Much of it was amusing.

In New York, where everybody in the theater operated on a shoestring, you had to be very much on your guard in financial matters. In Hollywood you could rely on someone's word in meeting contractual obligations. I hadn't learned about what would later be described as "creative bookkeeping." In old Hollywood if somebody said, "That's a deal," it was a deal. You didn't have to have the agreement on paper, you didn't have to have payment in advance. That impressed me tremendously. The studios weren't operating on a shoestring financially, and the honesty and reliability of producers and executives was something I hadn't anticipated. The other thing that surprised me was how good movie actors in the top category really were. I discovered to my astonishment the craftsmanship of Loretta Young, Roz Russell, Joan Crawford, Mel Douglas, and people of that caliber. I was really bowled over by their dedication.

D: Who were some of the directors you worked with at Columbia?

G: Edward Dmytryk was one, Charlie Vidor and Al Green were two more. Alexander Hall was the first director I worked with at the studio. I read the script he was doing and had some critical comments to make about it. I didn't know what the hell my duties or responsibilities were really, so I wanted to talk to Hall. I finally reached him on the phone, set up an appointment, and he said, "Look, I've never had a dialogue director before and I don't need one now, but Harry Cohn's got this cockamamy idea that you could be of some help. Just stay on the set and keep out of my way and we'll get along fine." I'm proud to say that he asked for me on his next picture and his next and his next. But I had to learn about such things as the impact of montage and the juxtaposition of images, which directors like Eddie Dmytryk, who had been a film cutter, already knew.

D: How did your first directing assignment at the studio come about?

G: It came as kind of a fluke. I was working as assistant director on a picture with Charlie Barton in the B unit at Columbia. There was a mix-up in scheduling or something. Barton had to start another picture before he finished the one he was working on with me. He said, "Let Mike finish the one I'm working on. He knows the story, he knows the script, he knows the people, he knows what it's all about." We had four more days to go on a twelve-day picture. So that's how I began. Apparently Cohn was satisfied with my work, because within a month I had my own picture to direct.

D: How did you get along with Harry Cohn?

G: My relationship with him was distant and guarded, like a dog with bared fangs. But he and Darryl Zanuck, of the studio executives I've encountered, were the true movie-makers. Cohn was a vulgarian but he knew how to make movies.

D: What kind of money were you making as a director at Columbia?

G: I directed four pictures at Columbia below scale. When I started there, I was making $125 a week. Even my assistant director was making more than I did. I was working in the B unit, on ten-day or twelve-day pictures. In my third year at the studio I was placed on lay-off. I'd directed these four cheap pictures, the last of which was *Crime Doctor*, and thought I was ready for something better. I was told that the studio only had good pictures coming up. I said, "Well, I'm ready for a good picture." The answer I got from Irving Briskin, the head of the B unit, was, "How can we give you a good picture? Look at the money you make." In other words somebody who was making $125 a week couldn't direct a good picture. That's when I walked out on my contract and was threatened with never being able to work in Hollywood again. I went back to New York and soon got *Home of the Brave* to direct on Broadway. That play was the turnaround for me. Three years later I was back in Hollywood at ten times the salary I had been making.

When I started directing *Boston Blackie Goes Hollywood*, my first picture at Columbia, I thought, "Man, this is my big chance." I wanted to make the picture a marvelous critical triumph. I fell half a day behind schedule, and I was called into Briskin's office. He explained to me very carefully what the financial setup was. If we made a good B picture, it probably wouldn't gross much more than a bad B picture. "I don't want it good," he told me, "I want it Thursday!" That was the way Briskin operated.

D: You returned to Hollywood in 1946.

G: Yes, exactly. I went to work for International Pictures and then my contract was taken over by Universal. I was to start work for International in September, but the summer before International merged with Universal and my contract was transferred. When I arrived in Los Angeles in 1946, I was under contract to Universal-International.

D: Was *The Web* your first film for U-I?

G: Yes. When I got the script of *The Web*, I read it and I had a number of ideas about what ought to be done. I was given assurance in advance that the script was going to be given a revision. Much to my astonishment I was called by the producer one day, and he said, "Are you all ready?" I said, "Ready for what?" He said, "Well, we start shooting a week from Monday." I said, "On what script?" He said, "On *The Web*." I said, "I won't do it." That created a tremendous uproar, and I was hauled up in front of Leo Spitz, who was sort of a legal officer at the studio. I was lectured on what my responsibilities were under my contract. I said, "Look, it takes just as much effort and just as much money to make a bad picture as it does to make a good one. Why don't we make a good one?" So they put another producer on the project. His name was Jerry Bresler. We made three pictures in succession together, and it was a very helpful association. Bresler had a great deal of savvy about filmmaking, particularly in terms of work efficiency. *The Web* turned out to be something of a sleeper. Then immediately after that we did *Another Part of the Forest* and then another film with Freddie March and Florence Eldredge called *An Act of Murder*.

D: Was *Another Part of the Forest* a satisfying film for you?

G: The most of any I've ever done. I feel that my work in *Another Part of the Forest* was probably more gratifying to me than any other picture, even though in terms of financial success, it was by no means the best. We had ample time for preparation. Although by virtue of Guild regulations I didn't get screen credit, I did in effect collaborate on writing the screenplay. I was strongly influenced by William Wyler, whose depth of photography, which he used in *The Little Foxes*, had become kind of a model. It seemed to me that by virtue of the consanguinity of those two plays there was justification for using an approximation of the same stylistic approach. I remember with great satisfaction and pleasure how good Fredric March was in the film. Working with Florence Eldredge, his wife, was difficult at first because she had only acted in one film and had to make a readjustment. I think on an unconscious level she was influenced by what she'd seen Mildred Dunnock do in the stage version of the Hellman play. Florence and I had lunch together and she said, "You must be more patient with me, Michael. I know what you're looking for and I think I'm moving toward it." I had to say to her, "Florence, do you remember that shot we printed at a quarter of ten last Monday? That was opening night for that much of the picture. I can't be patient." In her thinking she hadn't made the transference from the way things were done on the stage. In film your first rehearsal is your dress rehearsal for all practical purposes, and it is opening night when you say, "Print it."

D: Was Ann Blyth a skillful actress?

G: No, not really. She was charming and she was not without some talent. But hers was a relatively minor talent, I think. Frankly that was the role in the picture that satisfied me least, compared to the young Patricia Neal, who had played Regina on Broadway. Neal almost had the quality, whether she was consciously striving for it or not, of the young Tallulah Bankhead, who had played the same character twenty years older on the stage earlier. Pat Neal was really majestic on the stage. She was tall and strong-faced, and Ann Blyth was like a little Dresden doll. I strove to give her a little more iron, but it was not native to her. While she certainly did a creditable job, it fell considerably short of the image I had in mind.

D: How was Dan Duryea to work with?

G: Dan was marvelous. He played the father of the role he had played in *The Little Foxes*. He was a very interesting actor to work with. I thought he gave not only a very good performance but actually provided a leaven of comedy that occasionally got broad but never unreal. It didn't for a moment become hokey. I had known Dan slightly in New York. He had good solid theater training.

D: What was the philosophy behind production at Universal-International?

G: There was a strange dichotomy. Bill Goetz, according to his
lights, really wanted to do quality things. Universal, of course, had
been one of the oldest studios and made Abbott and Costello comedies and jungle pictures and that kind of stuff. A great deal of the pol-
icy there was determined by Nate Blumberg, who had been head of
Universal but was then based in New York. The man who was head
of sales, whose name I forget, had an astonishing degree of influence,
particularly in the area of marketing films, but spilling over into
what was saleable. That began to verge on artistic decisions, especially in determining titles of pictures, some of which were ridiculous. The original title of *An Act of Murder* was *Live Today for
Tomorrow*, which made no sense at all. Bill Goetz had had a successful picture with the word "tomorrow" in the title, and he thought
that was a good luck charm or something. We got an enormous
spread in *Life* magazine, with still photographs and all, under the
title *Live Today for Tomorrow*, and then the studio released the picture under a totally different title. All of that publicity value went
down the drain.

D: *An Act of Murder* deals with mercy killing, and I understand
that you had problems with the censorship office on that film. How
did the Hollywood censors work?

G: The normal operating procedure was that the studio would send
the censorship office the script, and they would send back some comments and make a list of things they found objectionable in the script.
Then there would be consultation. Two men from the censorship
office usually came out together, and we would sit down with them
and confer. I remember the opening line in the conference we had
on the script of *An Act of Murder*. One of the censorship guys said,
"This is a very interesting script, boys. It's too bad you can't make
the film." Mercy killing was an absolutely verboten subject. We
argued back and forth and did some give and take and ultimately
came up with a sorry compromise. That was that the judge, the character played by Freddie March, set out to perform a mercy killing
on his wife but it was later discovered that she had died of natural
causes. It was an awful cop-out, but that was the way we got the
censorship office's seal of approval.

D: But as you were saying earlier, Universal did some quality films.
G: Yes, they did quite a few. The Universal-International merger
occurred during the halcyon days of the post-war boom. By 1947
there had been some profound changes, not the least of which was
the emergence of television. I remember going to New York on the
train and seeing this forest of television antennas as we came through
the Bronx. Little by little the commercial orientation in filmmaking
became dominant. I remember being compelled to sit at a meeting
in the office of the production manager in which he read a list of
twenty-five pictures that had been made in the past year and all but
two were in the red. So the pinch toward economy became increasingly forceful, and that affected programming. The artistic aspira-
tions of Bill Goetz gave way to more popular fare.
D: Did you enjoy making *The Lady Gambles*?
G: Yes, except I didn't like the title. The title suggests a kind of
philandering heiress with a chauffeur. We really researched that
material, that is to say the subject of a compulsive gambler, with
the most thorough responsibility. We really attempted to study the
subject and develop a film that would deal with it in a realistic way.
Interestingly enough, I got more insight into compulsive gambling
from Dostoevski than I did from any of the psychiatric material
that I read. Barbara Stanwyck, who played the lead in the picture,
was one of the most rewarding actresses I've ever had the pleasure
of working with. She was going through a period of travail in her
personal life at the time. There were rumblings of the dissolution
of her marriage to Robert Taylor. During the time we were shooting
he was in England making a film, and there were rumors of dalliances
of one kind or another over there. Stanwyck was in a pretty disturbed
frame of mind, but she was marvelous to work with—conscientious,
always talented, always truthful, with a great personal sense of humor.
She gave herself to the job. I think *The Lady Gambles* is a better movie
than the title would ever lead one to believe.
D: How did you feel about *Woman in Hiding*?
G: I enjoyed that film less than many I've made. There are some
films or plays that are about concept, an idea, or a theme of some

sort. There are others that are simply anecdotal. *Woman in Hiding* was in the latter category. It was simply a melodrama and that was all. We tried to make it as effective as we could. But it was kind of a pot-boiler really.

D: Did you work well with Ida Lupino?

G: Very well indeed. As a matter of fact, toward the end of the picture she was preparing to direct her first film. I read her script, I discussed it with her, and I showed her how I would break down the shooting preparations. I even sat with her on the location where they were shooting. We talked about editing and so on. So we had a very good relationship, I liked her very much.

I discovered that while I was shooting a scene, no matter what it was, that became the most important part of the picture. Sometimes I might waste twenty minutes or half an hour on something that wasn't really very important at all. Even when I was working on commercials, which I mercifully did anonymously, I worked on them just as hard as I did on important pictures. If you have a sense of craft and pride in your work, you do that. When I was doing a picture, I became fully absorbed in it. I've had occasion to say to students, "To be a professional means that activity is the way you earn your living." It becomes important for the professional to recognize the fact that he or she takes the best job available at the time, especially if you're not wealthy and have family obligations. Not everything one does necessarily is the purest. *Woman in Hiding* in my personal calendar was not what I'd call an important experience.

D: *Cyrano de Bergerac* clearly was.

G: Yes, that was very exciting and great fun to do. That was the only picture I made on which I can honestly say we had meaningful rehearsals. I knew José Ferrer casually in New York. He was interested in film but hadn't been in one. He came out to Hollywood perhaps a month in advance of shooting the picture. I knew that we were going to be making the picture on an incredibly tight time schedule. I asked Ferrer to bring with him the production book of the Broadway production he'd starred in. I read it and we went over it page by page. Every day for about three weeks we met for a couple of hours. By the end of that time I knew what they had done in New York in as great detail as he did. Even though we shot the picture under the most enormous time pressure, it was a relatively calm and placid voyage. The picture was made in about twenty-one days. Ferrer knew his character well; all we had to do was effect some modifications. His performance on the stage had been excessively operatic.

One of the problems we faced was what to do about Cyrano's nose. We worked on that very assiduously. I studied photographs of practically every Cyrano that had ever been done. We knew that we were going to have to withstand the scrutiny of the close-up. The noses that might have been reasonably effective on the stage would not be able to withstand the glare of a close-up. So we worked on the nose with the greatest care. One of the things that I perceived in studying the photographs of earlier Cyranos was that everyone had merely appended something to the tip of the nose. In no case was there any attempt to enlarge the nostrils in proportion. I wanted an aristocratic quality, a little bit of an up-tilt for panache. First an artist drew a portrait, and then we made a plaster of Paris mask. I think the nose in the film worked quite well. Joe Ferrer looked better with the nose on than without it.

D: Mala Powers played Roxanne.

G: Mala was certainly not our first choice, because she was relatively unknown. We wanted Arlene Dahl for the part. That deal fell apart simply because MGM, who had Dahl under contract, made exorbitant demands that producer Stanley Kramer felt he couldn't meet. Mala was about nineteen years old at the time, and I think she did a very creditable job. Somehow she never had the charismatic quality that makes a star.

D: Did you work closely with writer Carl Foreman on the script?

G: Oh, yes. We sat cheek to jowl on the whole development of it—in developing the scenario, developing the outline, and in the actual writing of the text. I was involved with the project for a number of months before we actually went to work. We departed quite a lot from the primary text of Rostand in two respects. One I call negative, that is to say the elimination of a lot of material that we felt would be incomprehensible to a contemporary American audience. The more positive thing we did was to ask ourselves what might the dramatist have been inclined to dramatize in his play were it not for the limitations of the stage. The duel with the hundred men and the actual assault that ultimately proved fatal for Cyrano are obviously treated narratively in the play. We opened up the play to make it cinematic. We had Cyrano run down by a couple of horses and a heavy cart in a narrow alleyway, which made pretty good film footage.

D: Shortly after you finished *Cyrano* you went under contract to Twentieth Century-Fox.

G: Yes. Fox, I thought, was the epitome of film studios at that particular time.

D: More than MGM?

G: Oh, much more. Fox was doing a lot of very good things. Zanuck really was a filmmaker. When I did *I Can Get It for You Wholesale*, the first film I made at Fox, I got detailed notes from Zanuck for the first week of shooting almost every day after he'd seen the dailies. I got them twice a week after that, then once a week. He really viewed all the material with scrupulous care. I didn't necessarily always agree with his judgment, but his remarks were generally very rational and sensible. I came to have considerable respect for that aspect of the man. He was an indefatigable worker, enormously conscientious, and very knowledgeable. So I enjoyed working at Fox.

D: Was Susan Hayward good to work with on *I Can Get It for You Wholesale*?

G: I had a similar experience with Hayward that I'd had with Ida Lupino on *Woman in Hiding*. There was one point where we needed a certain emotional kind of letting go, and she was having difficulty getting it. With Ida I merely went up to her using the most male register that I could summon vocally and, with gentle pressure on her arm, said the deathless words, "Take it easy, baby." Just the man-woman thing kind of softened her up, and Ida played the scene exactly as I wanted it. I thought it was perhaps the most brilliant and successful direction I'd ever given an actress. I tried the same approach with Susie and she said, "Don't handle the merchandise, that won't get you anywhere." It just didn't work with her. A director has to deal with every situation in its own idiosyncratic terms.

D: Did you find Hayward generally a solid actress?

G: Oh, yes. She was a very guarded person, she was a very difficult person to get to know. I felt that while we worked together. She really built a solid wall around herself. But we had a good working relationship.

My relationship with Dan Dailey during the making of the picture was an interesting one. He was on the verge of a crackup that sent him to the Menninger Clinic right after we finished shooting the picture. I found out later that he didn't even remember doing some of the scenes. He was that near the edge of the precipice. Yet he worked hard on the picture and gave a fine dramatic performance. I found working with him enormously gratifying.

D: How was George Sanders as an actor?

G: He was very strange and the antithesis of what one would anticipate. This man, with the dazzling urbanity one saw on the screen, was one of the tensest actors I've ever worked with. The tension manifested itself, for example, in profuse sweating, so that he would have to change four shirts during the course of a take. I found Sanders difficult to work with. He did have certain qualities, and I simply went with those qualities. He was not very malleable. He was married to Zsa Zsa Gabor at the time, and I had the feeling that that was not a marriage made in heaven. She was around a bit, and I had the feeling every time she was around that he became increasingly tense.

D: Did you enjoy making *The Secret of Convict Lake*?

G: Yes, very much. I had a beautiful cameraman on it, Leo Tover. He was a really fine artist. He had such velvety values. The quality that he got in black and white, through the gradation of grays, was truly spectacular.

D: Did you work well with Gene Tierney on the picture?

G: Yes, on the whole. I got to know Gene much better than I ever got to know Susan Hayward. Gene was a more open kind of person. She was also a very troubled person. She extraverted her problems, brought them out into the open. She wasn't a concealer. I had problems with Glenn Ford on *Secret of Convict Lake*. He and I didn't get along too well, but you can't win them all.

D: How about Ethel Barrymore?

G: What shall I say? She was a national monument. She was pretty elderly at the time. You didn't direct Ethel Barrymore, you just hoped the performance came out right and said, "Beautiful, darling." But her role in *Secret of Convict Lake* was a fairly confined one, and she was a majestic presence.

D: Let's talk about the blacklisting.

G: Have you got a weekend to spend listening? It's hard to know where to begin in talking about the blacklisting. The first onslaught against the motion picture industry occurred in 1947. Hollywood was really running very scared. The studios were in the throes of a severe financial pinch and executives felt they were at the mercy of any kind of adverse publicity. So the motion picture industry was particularly vulnerable and susceptible to the kind of onslaught that occurred. Long before I was involved, the Hollywood Ten had been subpoenaed and testified. In Hollywood there was a very substantial counter-reaction on a variety of levels. Then came the astonishing turnabout, namely a meeting of all the heads of major studios at the Waldorf-Astoria Hotel, in which there was total capitulation. That's when the blacklist started at the instigation of the House Committee on Un-American Activities. That was two and a half years before I became in any way embroiled in the situation. There was a genuine atmosphere of terror in this town. People were losing their jobs and, in many instances, even losing their personal liberty. There was an atmosphere of suspicion and mistrust and anxiety that was as pervasive as today's smog.

D: When your name appeared on the blacklist, did Twentieth Century-Fox drop your contract?

G: Yes, in mid-term. I must concede that Zanuck, in personal terms, urged me to cooperate with the Committee. But when the axe fell, I was terminated. I must say in fairness, however, that the studio paid me the money coming to me under the terms of my contract. Others weren't so fortunate. I was just invited to get my personal belongings and vacate the premises, which I did.

D: So you went to New York and back to Broadway.

G: That's right. I had to hang around Los Angeles for quite a while, and that was really weird. My name was named early in the year. I had in fact been a member of the Communist Party. I hired a man named Abe Wirin, who was head of the American Civil Liberties Union here in Los Angeles, as my attorney. I needed guidance on how

one should comport oneself both in front of the Committee and outside. There was great anxiety anticipating what would actually happen when we were finally in front of the Committee. We faced
incriminating others and possibly contempt of Congress, which could
mean jail. It was a very narrow path and involved very great perils.
There was a period of about eight months between when I was terminated by Fox and the time the Committee reconvened its hearings
out here. Meanwhile I was in the process of disposing of our house
in Los Angeles. At the last moment there was a two-week delay
before the hearings started again. I had to vacate the house that I
had sold, and a friend took my family and me in for a couple of
nights. We were all packed and ready to drive back East as soon as
I had testified. I remember at dinner the night before the hearings
resumed, I suddenly said, "What if they ask me where I'm living?
What will I say?" So I went and slept in a motel that night so that I
could give the motel as my address and would not compromise my
host who had been gracious enough to take my family in for a couple
of days. We lived under that kind of terror. The day the hearing was
over, we got in the car and drove to New York. We didn't know the
degree to which the ripples of the blacklist would affect the Broadway theater. As it happened, the anarchy in the Broadway theater
was a blessing. I was able to hack out a career there during the blacklist period

D: By the late 1950s you were back in Hollywood and working at
Universal again. Had Universal changed a great deal?

G: No, not yet. MCA hadn't taken over yet, so the studio was pretty
much the same. Ross Hunter, who was a producer at Universal, had
seen *The Tender Trap*, which I directed on Broadway, and he liked it
and felt that the play exhibited the general temper and spirit that he
wanted for a film he was preparing, which was *Pillow Talk*.

D: Did you enjoy making *Pillow Talk*?

G: Oh, yes, it was a lot of fun. Up until that time I had been viewed
as that intellectual, intense Jew out of the Group Theater, and I wasn't
associated with comedies. But I've always like comedy and relished
working in comedy. I told Rock Hudson, who had never done a comedy
before *Pillow Talk*, "There's no magic in doing comedy. You play it

very real, and the comedy comes not because you do things in a funny way. We find funny things for you to do, and you play them with the utmost seriousness." The juxtapositions and the incongruities that come from those juxtapositions are what make the comedy. Rock responded to that advice and played his role with total earnestness.

I was very happy to be gainfully employed in Hollywood again, although I must honestly say that deep in my heart I had some misgivings about the rampant chauvinism of *Pillow Talk*. But it was fun to do, and I enjoyed working with Doris Day very much. I had problems with Marty Melcher, her husband, who was also her manager, because he could not understand why I said that Doris was not going to have a number to sing. She sang in the picture, but informally. I said, "She's an interior decorator in this film, not a singer." Doris herself was willing to go along with that.

D: Was *Portrait in Black* an interesting film for you?

G: Being the melodrama that it was and based on a very well-contrived, well-made play, I thought it was dramatic literature, but not what I would call a monument in dramatic literature. It was interesting but not something that made my heart leap with joy and ecstasy. I didn't enjoy doing the picture at all.

D: Was Lana Turner good in that kind of part?

G: Lana was, in my judgment, a very talented actress whose chief liability was what I regarded as impoverished taste. She did a serviceable job in the picture. A number of actresses have a certain image that they expect to maintain. Lana was not a dummy, and she would give me wonderful rationalizations why she should wear pendant earrings. They had nothing to do with the role, but they had to do with her particular self-image. I felt we might have done better to concentrate on areas of her ability. If we had, hers might have been a more gripping kind of performance.

D: What kind of a fellow was Anthony Quinn?

G: A man of bottomless talent. My mother used to have a saying: Little children, little problems; big children, big problems. One can transfer that to talent: Little talent, little problems; big talent, big problems. So the sailing with Quinn wasn't always the smoothest, and there were differences of opinion. But Tony was exciting to work with, even with the problems that he had. He gave himself to the work with a real commitment and dedication. I respect him very much.

D: Did you strive for striking visual images in your film work, Mike? Did you like to play with the camera?

G: There's a character in a play, I think it's by Odets, who says, "The function of the parent is to make himself unnecessary." I sometimes extrapolate that to say that one of the functions of the director is to make himself invisible to those watching the film or play. To be a show-off may be an enormous accelerating factor in one's career, but I have serious doubts that it contributes to an artistic achievement. Certainly I had visual interests. As I read a script I'd see it with a certain style, a certain feel, a certain atmosphere. That inevitably involved considerations of visual composition and organization. But I didn't suddenly shoot down at the street from the top of an eight-story building. Ceiling shots might be spectacular, but I didn't find them useful.

I feel the same way about cutting. My ideal would be to edit a sequence so that the audience is unaware of how the film's cut, unless the cutter is deliberately striving for a shock effect.

D: Was *Boys' Night Out* an interesting film for you?

G: That's a picture that really started from a five-page dirty joke that the writers sold to the producer. We didn't have censorship ratings at that point; a picture either got the seal of approval or it didn't. I was forced to clarify my ideas about that picture in a way that I think proved constructive. It forced me to recognize that the principal business of comedy is to expose certain aspects of human or social folly to ridicule.

D: Was James Garner good to work with?

G: He was so good in both of the films I did with him that it made me feel I was stealing the money I was paid. All I had to say was, "Roll 'em" and "Cut." He is very, very gifted.

D: How about Kim Novak?

G: Kim is really a very nice gal. She wasn't the most skilled, but she was very honest in her work. While she wasn't the easiest person to get an effective performance out of, I didn't mind working with her. She really tried very hard. She just wasn't the most adept comedienne.

D: Was making *Texas Across the River* a good experience?

G: Yes, from most points of view. I didn't enjoy working with Dean Martin because he didn't have the attitude toward work that I do. He liked to play around and just wing a performance. We were on totally different wave lengths. But I liked the idea of the picture, and some of the things in it I thought were very funny. Ben Starr worked on that screenplay, and he and I had a very close collaboration.

D: Why did you leave filmmaking?

G: Every career has a profile, and it reaches a kind of apogee and then descends. I had a feeling that on the basis of the offers I was getting, both in terms of quality and quantity, that my career was spinning out. I sensed that film producers were reluctant to hire people my age. It was a hard thing to face. The moment I reached that conclusion I sat down and wrote a letter to UCLA. About seven or eight months later I got a call asking whether or not I would be interested in teaching in the summer session. I had the opportunity to direct a play and teach a class. After that the department asked me to join the faculty on a lectureship basis.

D: Do you feel that your approach to direction changed through the course of your career?

G: I don't quite know how to answer that. Fairly early in my career I was enormously influenced by the Group Theater and the so-called Method approach to acting. I've had occasion in the past to describe myself as a small m "methodist," as opposed to a completely orthodox Methodist. I don't think that has appreciably changed, because I don't think that the art of acting is the art of lying. Acting is the simulation of experience. One must employ the total persona of the individual to make that happen. I'm not a total Methodist because I readily acknowledge that the relationship of the inner life to external behavior is a reciprocating phenomenon. In a certain sense that belief was something that evolved. I've always believed that the best plays have something to say. Huxley says in *The Doors of Perception* that the function of art is to provide a sense of order to the chaos of existence. I think that's what our job is.

D: Do you feel that your professional life has contributed to your personal development?

G: That's a hard thing for me to assess. I can't separate the two really. In my early professional life I think I tended always to place work very high on my priorities. I think my capacity to love either my wife or my children has been in some respects modified. I was fully absorbed in work in my early years. To a certain degree I still am. I get a kick out of doing a damn good job. Fortunately I have relationships outside of work that are gratifying to me. Possessions don't interest me enormously, but I'm enjoying my dotage profession, which is teaching. What else would I do with myself? My daughter, who has a different value system from mine, asked me recently, "What gave you your drive for work?" I thought for a moment and I said, "Fear." Coming out of school in the midst of the Depression, I had to work. I was propelled to be an achiever as a child and skipped grades in elementary school. I don't think zealous achievement is an active element in my life now, but I think the dedication to work has continued. In this business you betroth yourself to insecurity the day you say, "Theater and filmmaking are going to be my profession."

Michael Gordon's Feature Films

1942   *Boston Blackie Goes Hollywood*
            Underground Agent
1943   *One Dangerous Night*
            Crime Doctor
1947   *The Web*
1948   *Another Part of the Forest*
            An Act of Murder
1949   *The Lady Gambles*
1950   *Woman in Hiding*
            Cyrano de Bergerac
1951   *I Can Get It for You Wholesale*
            The Secret of Convict Lake
1953   *Wherever She Goes* (In Australia)
1959   *Pillow Talk*
1960   *Portrait in Black*

1962   *Boys' Night Out*
1963   *For Love or Money*
            Move Over Darling
1965   *A Very Special Favor*
1966   *Texas Across the River*
1968   *The Impossible Years*
1970   *How Do I Love Thee?*

FREDERICK DE CORDOVA

Fast Enough for Television Production

Frederick De Cordova was born in New York City in 1910 and entered the motion picture business from the stage in 1944. He directed many medium-budget films at Warner Bros. and Universal, among them *Her Kind of Man*, *Wallflower*, and *Bedtime for Bonzo*, which starred Ronald Reagan. Turning to television in the early 1950s, De Cordova produced or directed weekly shows that featured George Burns and Gracie Allen, George Gobel, Jack Benny, and the Smothers brothers, and in 1971 he became the producer of the *Tonight Show*, then hosted by Johnny Carson. De Cordova died in Woodland Hills, California, in 2001.

The following interview with the film and television director-producer was taped in De Cordova's office at the NBC studio in Burbank, California, on July 16, 1982.

D: Since you grew up in New York City, I suppose that it was almost inevitable that you would become interested in theater.
De C: I guess I was interested in the theater prenatally. Both of my parents had been involved in it. I grew up in an atmosphere which certainly was theatrical. My father worked with George M. Cohan and Sam Harris. My mother was a truly beautiful Irish girl and worked in shows either as a showgirl or as an actress. So I grew up knowing an awful lot of people in the business. That led to my attempting to be an actor in stock companies during the summer season, and that in turn led to my selecting a university with a strong theater program. That was Northwestern. Later I went to Harvard Law School, where I formally got involved in show business because a classmate of mine was Johnny Shubert, the only son of J. J. Shubert

and the only nephew of Lee Shubert. When we finished law school Johnny said, "Why don't you come to work in the Shubert office?" I went to work for the Shuberts and was Johnny's "go for," although we didn't call it that in those days. Then I went into stage managing, and that led to directing in New York.

D: What shows were you involved with in New York?

De C: On my first show in New York I was assistant stage manager, working with a well-known star, Joe Cook, at the Winter Garden Theater. Cook's head stooge was Dave Chasen, in whose restaurant, Chasen's, I ate dinner last night. I was associated with several rather prestigious shows in New York—*At Home Abroad* with Bea Lillie, *Life Begins at 8:40* with Ray Bolger, *Ziegfeld Follies* with Bob Hope, Fanny Brice, and Josephine Baker—although my efforts were not particularly prestigious.

My first real directing job was at the Winter Garden in a musical revue, *Ziegfeld Follies* with Milton Berle, Ilona Massey, and Arthur Treacher. Then I directed a very good show (and not too many of my shows have been good), a Dietz and Schwartz musical called *Between the Devil*, which starred Jack Buchanan and Charles Walters. I also directed summer operas in Louisville, St. Louis, and Nashville for the Shuberts. Eventually some fool said, "Why don't you come to California and direct?" I went to Warner Bros., and I was there for five years and at Universal for five more.

D: Didn't you start at Warner Bros. as a dialogue director?

De C: I was a dialogue director for a year, and it was a rather good proving ground. Presumably I knew what I was doing so far as performance and script were concerned. But what I didn't know was where to place the camera and how to use a camera effectively. Warners was one of the studios that used to bring out potentially good directors from the stage and assign them to one or two very good directors working on the lot. The novice would be of some use to the director, and the director would be of enormous use to the newcomer. I was assigned to one of the wonderful filmmakers, Michael Curtiz, and was his dialogue director for such shows as *Mildred Pierce*. Then I was assigned to David Butler on *San Antonio*, a picture that starred Errol Flynn. One day Curtiz in his broken English said to me, "Jack Warner wants to see you. Go upstairs and talk to him." That sounded ominous. I went upstairs, and what Warner said was that Curtiz had told him that I was now capable of directing my own pictures.

D: What kind of man did you find Curtiz?

De C: I was an enormous fan of his, only perhaps because he seemed to like me. He was harsh and gruff and had a sense of humor that was often misunderstood. He was satirical. He was sarcastic. He was educated, but he'd been a strong man in the circus. Curtiz had a magnificent knowledge of what to do with the camera, as anyone can see in *Casablanca* and *Yankee Doodle Dandy* and many of his other pictures. I was flattered that he thought I was being of some value to him. He would say to me, "All those people over there should be saying something. Tell them what to say." And I would get a chance to create something on the spur of the moment that he would use in a scene.

I also found the Warner brothers wonderful. I had an extremely good relationship with Jack Warner, who put up with what I didn't know and was helpful, although sometimes critical. Eventually he fired me in a legitimate fashion after I had done several pictures for him. He said that I was being ungrateful, and in a sense I was. But I thought the time had come for me to be doing better pictures than I was getting. Later Warner saw me at a party and said, "There are five people in this room that I've fired. As I look back on it, I was correct in every single case."

D: How would you describe the general climate around the Warner Bros. lot?

De C: Fear. Then when most of us got away from the lot, we were rather proud to have been there. It was an era when people had the security of being under contract to a studio, working forty or fifty-two weeks a year depending on their contract. Those who were rebellious were the same ones who started the new system, which allowed stars, directors, and producers to choose their own pictures. Although some wonderful things have come out of that, there is not now the alma mater feeling that we used to have back in the days of the big studios.

D: You used the word "fear." I've heard tales of soundstages and dressing rooms at Warners being bugged. Was that true?

De C: If it was I didn't know it. The fear I meant is that by a purely social slight or a show of independence you might be fired. There was a fear of losing a guarantee of income.

D: Did you find Warner Bros. a status conscious studio?

De C: I think that all of the studios were status conscious. I did not find, as I've read, that the stars spoke only to stars, the featured people only to featured people, and bit players only to bit players. They were all as nice to other people as people are today and just as rude. I didn't see at any time that people weren't invited to somebody's home because they weren't a big shot. God knows, I wasn't a big shot, and I was treated as nicely by stars and producers and their wives as anyone could be.

D: It seems to me that one of the strengths of the big studio system was the team that each studio created.

De C: The character people as well as the stars were carefully chosen. During my time at Warners we had Jack Carson, Bobby Hutton, Joan Leslie, contract people that we knew we could drawn on and have a solid cast if we got a script that was good. These people weren't big stars, but we knew that they would perform at least fairly well and sometimes extremely well.

D: Was *Too Young to Know* your first film as a director?

De C: Yes. And it was very exciting for me. It was not a large budget, nor a long shooting schedule. That was with Robert Hutton, a young star of the war years who was very good. I also had Joan Leslie, Dolores Moran, Dorothy Malone, and Craig Stevens, all of whom were contemporary with me. I enjoyed that picture very much, and some of the notices were better than I had expected. Some of the New York notices were fairly good, and the picture became a stepping stone for others.

D: Was Dorothy Malone a skillful actress?

De C: I believe she might have been had it not been for my directing. All of those players were young and new. Warner had seen something in them that he thought would be good picture-wise. Dorothy Malone became a far more important actress later than she was when I worked with her. That's true of many of the people I worked with, until it got to the point where I was making everybody's last picture. I made Deanna Durbin's last picture, Sonja Henie's last picture, not Ronnie Reagan's last picture but certainly one of his last.

D: At the outset of your career as a film director, what did you find to be the major problems?

De C: The problem was, and rightly so, that there was a success caste with scripts. The fine directors—Mike Curtiz, Irving Rapper, people like that—would be much more likely to be assigned the scripts that I wish I'd gotten. I would get the ones those directors didn't want to do. I didn't have access to the top scripts.

D: Did that mean that you were also not given the best designers and a top crew?

De C: In many of the early pictures that I did I had what was called a short schedule. I would be expected to shoot a picture in thirty-five days, which meant seven weeks. While that was a long time compared to the quickie productions, it was a short time compared to what the major directors and big stars had. I never found that I was given short shrift in my crew. I may not have had Bette Davis's set designer, but I had someone who had done good work. Craftspeople didn't stay at the studio if they weren't competent.

D: Was *Her Kind of Man* an interesting film for you?

De C: Yes, it was a gangster picture. I had a cast comparable to the early Warner Bros. films. I had Dane Clark, the Julie Garfield replacement. I had Faye Emerson, a possible Bette Davis replacement. I had Zachary Scott and Janis Paige, both solid performers. It was great fun to work with those people, and I had a rather good script. I also had a man on the picture named Harry Lewis, who has gained bigger fame as owner of the Hamburger Hamlets that are now all over Los Angeles. He's made a real fortune in the restaurant business.

D: Was Zachary Scott a talented actor?

De C: Yes, I thought he was extremely good. I think he was one of a small group who actually was better than the parts he was getting at the time. Later he moved up to better roles. Scott made a highly convincing villain, as he proved in *Mildred Pierce* and other pictures where he played the sophisticated heavy.

D: What about *That Way with Women*? Was making that picture a rewarding experience?

De C: Yes, for two reasons. It was the first time that I got to direct a marvelous actor named Sydney Greenstreet. And again I had Dane Clark in the cast, along with a pretty girl called Martha Vickers, who had made quite a success in *The Big Sleep*, a Raymond Chandler picture that starred Bogart and Bacall. Clark and Vickers and Greenstreet were the solid kind of actors that Warner would give us for the smaller number of days that we had to shoot B pictures. If the director knew what he was doing when he walked on the soundstage, they sure knew what they were doing.

D: What kind of man was Sydney Greenstreet personally?

De C: Absolutely darling. He was intelligent, backgrounded, had a good sense of humor, was a fine cook, and in no way was hostile to younger actors. He was helpful and couldn't have been nicer.

D: You worked with Martha Vickers again in *Love and Learn.*

De C: That was not a particularly great picture for anybody, except that it was fun to make. Bobby Hutton was in it, Jack Carson was in it, and a whole list of those small bit players of those days who were extremely efficient and knew their craft. But the picture was not a success and I think deservedly so.

D: Did you work closely with Steve Trilling at Warner Bros.?

De C: Trilling was a close friend. He was the man between me and Jack Warner. Warner did not have time for all the details of film projects unless he chose to. Parenthetically he did indeed have time to watch every day's rushes with all the directors who were shooting. He would set up a schedule so that he would sit with each director in a screening room at the finish of a day's work. Negulesco and his people would leave, and somebody else—Rapper or whoever—would come in. Then I would come in with my people, and Warner would be there to see our rushes.

But Trilling was a wonderful buffer. I think he probably took quite a beating from Warner, but he didn't turn the beating back on us. If something went wrong, Warner would blame Trilling. Steve was a good man to have between the creative element and the studio boss.

D: Did Warner have a keen sense about film editing?

De C: Warner and Darryl Zanuck both had the reputation of being astute editors. Whether they cut by the seat of their pants or whether they cut from instinctive knowledge, I don't know. But Warner had a feel for what was wrong with a scene and when a closeup could help.

D: Do you have strong recollections of making *Always Together?*

De C: I do because every once in a while I get wonderful notices for something I do, and on that picture I got excellent notices in both New York and Los Angeles. It was another picture that I enjoyed doing, but about that time I began to feel that I was entitled to be making something better than light spoofs with young leading men and women. Probably Warner thought I hadn't done enough for him.

D: Did you work closely with the publicity department at Warner Bros.?

De C: I had no particular relationship with the top publicity people, although I knew some of them. I would know the publicists assigned to my pictures. I was not particularly publicity conscious, nor do I feel that whatever I did with those people would have had any effect on their campaigns. Later perhaps my input would have been greater.

D: Was *Wallflower* your last film at Warners?

De C: I have a feeling that *Always Together* was, but *Wallflower* was from a Broadway success by Henry and Phoebe Ephron. It was a definite success in movies, but again, outside of a first-class group of character actors, I was back working with a young group of actors and actresses, many of whom were to become more important as time went by. That picture I happen to like very much, but again I felt that I was getting into a syndrome of "here is a young director, here are two young stars, let's give them that script and bolster them with Eddie Arnold and character people of that caliber." The picture was delightful, but there were down periods when I felt that I should be getting ahead faster. I began to say, "I'd like to move on." So when I got an offer from Universal, I took it.

D: Did you feel that Universal and the general atmosphere there were appreciably different from what you'd known at Warner Bros.?

De C: Yes. In the first place things were appreciably different for me because I moved way up in class, not personally but so far as my pictures were concerned. I had a nice father-son relationship with Bill Goetz, who was one of the people running Universal. I had a longtime relationship with the man who succeeded Goetz—Bill Dozier, who also was a major official at the studio. I became a close friend of a well known producer on the lot named Robert Arthur, who had a fine list of credits. And I started off at the studio with a picture that showcased Deanna Durbin, which immediately moved me up into a higher echelon since I was directing a major star's picture.

D: In your opinion was Universal a well-administered studio?

De C: It was starting to be. In the days way before me it had been kind of a schlocky studio. When I went there, it had just become Universal-International. There had been a new influx of personnel on upper levels, and they were attempting to make better pictures than the old Universal had. I found that they had begun to invest in pictures and to look for outside stars and outside directors. I thought the studio was very well administered.

D: *For the Love of Mary* was the Deanna Durbin picture that you directed. Did you find Durbin easy to work with?

De C: Wonderful is the answer to that. I was lucky. As a bachelor I knew a lot of people—boys and girls, men and women—whom I would be involved with socially, either at dinners or parties or nightclubs. Durbin was one of those, so we were not strangers. She had directorial approval on her pictures, so when I was offered *For the Love of Mary*, I knew that I had her sanction and felt that I was now in the big time.

D: Was Durbin a comfortable actress?

De C: She was comfortable, although she was getting to the point where she was uncomfortable making pictures at all. She knew that she was an established star. She was very pleasant to work with. She worked hard. She did have several clauses in her contract, like a two-hour lunch, that could have posed problems, but I knew about those before we started the picture. Otherwise she was fine. I couldn't have been more pleased working with her.

D: What kind of film was *Illegal Entry* for you?

De C: Interesting and good and brought me back to the *Her Kind of Man* type of picture. It starred Marta Toren, who was one of the many attempts at finding another Garbo. She was a good actress and couldn't have been nicer. I again was surrounded by very fine actors—Howard Duff, George Brent, whom I adored, and a number of small-part actors who played regularly in gangster pictures. There were a lot of locations on that picture, and it was the second one I made with Duff. Later I worked with him and Ida Lupino in television.

D: I know that you did at least two films at Universal with Yvonne DeCarlo. Was she good to work with?

De C: She was a doll. Maybe I sound like a Pollyanna, but there have been very few people that I've worked with who were a pain in the behind. DeCarlo, I believe, was underrated as an actress. She was most professional, worked hard, was very good at her craft, possibly was not a first-class star, but she came in on schedule. She knew her lines, she sang and danced rather well, and she wanted very much to be a bigger star than she ever became.

D: What kind of shooting schedule did you have on DeCarlo's films?

De C: Forty days, eight weeks, something like that.

D: I remember her well in *The Gal Who Took the West.*

De C: That picture was originally intended for Durbin. And when Durbin said, "I'm finished," we thought of a lot of people for the part and came up with Yvonne.

D: Did Technicolor in those days pose problems?

De C: Nothing technical ever presented a problem for me, not because I was particularly good at anything, but because I was always surrounded by people who would say, "This is what you do." Technicolor was a problem in that it cost a lot more money to make a picture in color than in black and white. Most Technicolor films were shot outdoors. They took a little longer to light and to shoot, but I was always pleased when I saw the rushes in color.

D: You made several pictures with Rock Hudson at Universal. Was he agreeable to work with?

De C: He was nice and very professional. He wasn't always delighted with the pictures he was in. It was a long time before Universal recognized that he was a major star. Rock made a whole different type of picture before he got big. We used him as a gladiator in *The Desert Hawk*, but it was pretty obvious that he and Tony Curtis would move into better things.

D: Of course, I have to ask you about *Bedtime for Bonzo*, since so much public derision was placed on that picture after Ronald Reagan became president. How did you feel about the film?

De C: I was pleased about it then, and I'm pleased about it now. The fact that Reagan worked with a chimpanzee and the title had Bonzo in it has given the picture a kind of derogatory connotation. I see it often, since people seem to think they're doing me a favor by showing it, and it's a very good picture. Ronnie was always a most capable actor, Diana Lynn was good, and the script was very funny. The pictures that followed with Bonzo were spin-offs like the spin-offs from *Francis* [the talking mule]. Universal made a lot of money with one picture, so the studio did another one. I made *Bonzo Goes to College*, but I drew the line at *Bonzo, Private Eye.*

D: Did you enjoy making *Little Egypt*?

De C: Oh, maybe a modicum. At least the picture got me back into the musical area where I had worked in New York. Mark Stevens was an attractive, competent actor, and Rhonda Fleming was a very pretty girl. We tested a lot of women for that part. Whoever played it had to be voluptuous and able to move sexily. The picture was kind of a pot-boiler, but we got paid for it. The results weren't terrible, although I don't think I heightened Fleming's career or that the picture heightened mine.

D: Why did you decide to leave filmmaking?

De C: I think that picturemaking kind of left me about that time [1953]. I began making some Westerns like *Column South* with Audie Murphy and a couple more desert pictures, what the industry called "tits and sand" movies. I didn't feel there was an enormous future in the way I was going. I still had a year to go on my contract with Universal. We settled the deal because I knew that CBS was beckoning for me to come over there. Television was a new world. I was kind of a big shot going into television, whereas I was kind of a shrinking shot in motion pictures. God knows, it has worked out wonderfully for me in television.

D: Was directing *The Burns and Allen Show* your first job in television?

De C: No, I did a couple of things for CBS before that: *That's My Boy* and another series before that. *The Burns and Allen Show* was the first big, major television show I did with a big star. I was finally in the big time when I directed that.

D: Did George Burns himself have a lot of impact on the show's scripts?

De C: Yes, George was a major writer. There was always a head writer on the show, but George was in on every line and in on the direction as well, which sometimes was a help and sometimes was a pain in the behind. He was a protector of Gracie, who was a sensational lady, and the protector of the show and how it was being done.

D: Did you find directing for television vastly different from movie directing?

De C: No. Really not at all. If I had been one of the hundred-day directors in motion pictures, where I did things a million times and looked for whether the sun was exactly in the right place, I might have had trouble adjusting. But in television I was actually functioning pretty much the way I had in motion pictures. I worked quickly, I was organized, and I was able to get along with my stars and featured players. I was somewhat talented rather than outstandingly talented and found the "hurry up" system of television not a great deal different from my "hurry up" system in motion pictures. Television welcomed my way of working, and I certainly welcomed that my method of working was easily applicable to television production. In television everything is done quickly, but I didn't have much problem adapting to the short schedules.

D: What would an average work week have been like on *The Burns and Allen Show*?

De C: Since we did a show a week, we actually shot two days, rehearsed one day, worked with the writers one day, and spent a day casting. I worked ever day, not twenty-four hours every day, but I was involved in every aspect of production, as I was in such shows as *December Bride*. Those were among the first multiple camera shows. *December Bride* was shot in front of an audience, whereas *The Burns and Allen Show* was not. The multiple camera show, which Desilu had pioneered, was a great technical advance for a director who knew what he was doing.

D: Of course Spring Byington, the star of *December Bride*, was a veteran motion picture actress.

De C: *December Bride* was one of those great ensemble shows. Verna Felton and Harry Morgan, who later gained great popularity in *M*A*S*H*, were both excellent, as was Spring Byington. Frances Rafferty had been a well known young leading lady at Metro, much like the girls I used to work with at Warners. Working on that show was a fabulous experience.

D: Later you worked on *The Donna Reed Show*.

De C: Yes, that was a strange situation. Bill Dozier, whom I'd worked with at Universal, was in charge of production for Screen Gems, and he brought me in to be vice-president in charge of programming. About a week after he brought me in, Dozier got fired, and that meant that my days as an executive at Screen Gems were numbered. Instead of quitting, which I had no intention of doing, although they'd have liked for me to do that, I worked out my contract by directing and producing. I was involved in the directing of the pilot of *Bewitched*, many episodes of *Donna Reed*, and many episodes of *The Farmer's Daughter* with Inger Stevens. Whatever was available I was doing as a director there. Then I moved to Eddie Small [a producer] and directed some more movies, one with Bob Hope and one with Elvis Presley. From there I went to Four Star to do the Smothers brothers' first show and some pilots. That led to *My Three Sons*, and *My Three Sons* led to the Johnny Carson show. My deal on the latter was to produce the *Tonight Show*; there was never any thought of my directing it. The director of the *Tonight Show* had been with Johnny Carson for many, many years.

D: I know that you've compared Carson with Jack Benny, with whom you'd worked earlier.

De C: They are both giants in the industry. I think that one of the people Johnny drew on for his comedic methods was Jack, but then so did a hundred other people in this business. Johnny and Jack are totally different in style. Johnny's fast, whereas Jack was slow. Johnny is a totally different kind of comedian. Johnny is not a character comedian at all. If he plays parts in sketches on the show, he is Johnny in a far-out performance.

D: Do you miss directing?

De C: No, I "miss-directed" enough. I suppose if a wonderful script came along at this time and somebody said, "Would you like to take a crack at it," I would be flattered and would do it. But it would have to be a very good script. It would have to be peopled with interesting performers, and the conditions under which I worked would have to be pleasant. If all of those things were going to happen, they could probably find someone else to do the job better.

D: Did you develop an overall philosophy of directing?

De C: I'd like to be that articulate about my craft. No, I knew then and I know now that I have an ability, except in rare instances, to involve myself in the thinking of the performer. The technical end of directing seemed very simple to me once I learned it. I think a person has to have some of that instinctively, and some of it you learn over the years. A director has to know what is funny and how to present it to an audience so that it *is* funny. I was not an *auteur* director. I was efficient, competent, a technical director whose ability to get along well with people was my major asset.

D: Was your emphasis always on entertainment?

De C: Oh, yes. I had very little desire then or now to contribute to the welfare of the world. I was never that kind of person.

D: Do you feel that your professional life has contributed to your personal development?

De C: Certainly. It's made me a lot of money, and that has contributed to my wife's personal development. I come under the heading of extremely lucky people. Not since I came out of college have I ever had a day off salary. Some of the salaries were $35 a week. They're slightly higher now. I am a surviving member of many areas of show business, and that gives me great pleasure.

D: I've read the criticism that you're too conservative in your approach to television.

De C: Maybe. Conservative does not mean that one does the same thing all the time, but it does mean that the person walks slowly and doesn't run and fall over the toilet. I've been with enough shows that had superior credentials and didn't need somebody to come in and change the format. I don't believe that I'm a stick in the mud, but God knows I am not rushing to change the format of something that is doing well. If a show begins to sag, it's time to look for new things. Otherwise leave it alone.

Frederick De Cordova's Feature Films

1945 *Too Young to Know*
1946 *Her Kind of Man*
1947 *That Way with Women*
Love and Learn
Always Together
1948 *Wallflower*
For the Love of Mary
The Countess of Monte Cristo
1949 *Illegal Entry*
The Gal Who Took the West
1950 *Buccaneer's Girl*
Peggy
The Desert Hawk
1951 *Bedtime for Bonzo*
Katie Did It
Little Egypt
Finders Keepers
1952 *Here Come the Nelsons*
Bonzo Goes to College
Yankee Buccaneer
1953 *Column South*
1965 *I'll Take Sweden*
1966 *Frankie and Johnny*

Henry Hathaway (center) with John Wayne and Dean Martin

HENRY HATHAWAY

Stern Taskmaster

Screen director Henry Hathaway had the reputation of being a delightful man socially but an ogre on the set, particularly tough on actresses. Born in Sacramento, California, in 1898, Hathaway worked primarily at Paramount and Twentieth Century-Fox. He directed a wide variety of pictures but is remembered best for such Westerns as *The Sons of Katie Elder* and *True Grit* and his realistic crime dramas, among them *Kiss of Death* and *Call Northside 777*. A skilled craftsman, Hathaway pioneered in the use of actual locations in his work, most notably in the filming of *The House on 92nd Street*, a near-documentary. He continued making motion pictures into the 1970s and died in Los Angeles in 1985.

The following interview was taped in the director's home in Bel-Air, California, on January 6, 1983.

D: Mr. Hathaway, how did you first become involved with the motion picture business?
H: I quit school in 1914 to help support my family and went to work at Universal Studio the day it opened in the San Fernando Valley.
D: I know that you came from a show business family.
H: My mother was an actress. In the early days they used to have road companies, and there weren't any unions. If the company went broke on the road, the actors had to get home on their own. We lived in San Francisco when I was a boy, and all the vaudeville acts for the Orpheum and Pantages circuits were booked out of there and traveled down the coast. A road company my mother was in went broke

in Goldfield, Nevada. She took a job as a waitress in a hotel to earn enough money to get back to San Francisco. Another company went broke in San Diego, and my mother saw an advertisement for actors to perform with the American Film Company. She applied and got the job. Allan Dwan directed her. My mother played character parts and heavies, and the movie company liked her enough that she got the whole family to move down to southern California. Later she worked for Thomas Ince and for Universal, when the studio was at Sunset Boulevard and Gower. She worked mostly in serials. Then Universal closed that studio and moved to the Valley. That's when I quit school and went to work.

D: Hadn't you been a child actor yourself?

H: Yes, whenever they needed a kid they used my sister or myself. We'd be kids stolen by the Indians and that sort of thing.

D: You mentioned Allan Dwan. What kind of a man was he?

H: He was strong. Strong physically and strong mentally. He was a good director. I worked for him later as a prop man at Paramount when he was shooting some pictures with Gloria Swanson.

D: You told me earlier that when you were at Paramount the two people who influenced you most were directors Josef von Sternberg and Victor Fleming. How did they influence you?

H: Fleming was a realist and von Sternberg was a master at fantasy. Von Sternberg would say, "Here's a situation. How can you fantasize it? How can you make this *seem* like what it is?" Vic, on the other hand, would say, "If it's a shoe, then get me a shoe. If I need a palm tree, then get me a palm tree." Fleming was the realist. He wanted to shoot on location, whereas von Sternberg didn't. Paramount had a contract with writer Zane Grey, and every time Fleming directed a Zane Grey story, it had to be filmed on the exact location that Grey mentioned in his story. We slept in bedrolls up on the Carter Rim, where they made *Heritage of the Desert* the first time. We worked on a reservation one time and went down to Texas another time.

D: What was Fleming like personally?

H: Strong, decisive, but with good humor. When you see Clark Gable as Rhett Butler in *Gone With the Wind*, that's Victor Fleming on the screen. Gable dressed like Fleming, he talked like him, he walked like him, he stood like him, and his attitude toward women was the same.

D: Had you been interested in the frontier West before you started making Western movies?

H: I wasn't a Western nut, no. The arrangement that Paramount had with Zane Grey was that the studio could remake a picture as many times as they wanted, but they had to pay the author $12,500 every time they did. So when I started making Westerns, I'd get an old script that Fleming had filmed, find a writer, and work the script over. The first picture I made was *Heritage of the Desert*. This was the same story that Fleming had filmed before. I would have worked on any kind of picture. I didn't care what the hell it was, just so I got to direct.

D: In the big studio era did you essentially do whatever the studio wanted done?

H: I did the kind of picture the studio wanted. They'd give me a script and say, "We want to do this picture." I'd make it. It wasn't that I'd make any old thing. But if the studio believed in it enough to buy the property and put a star in it, it wasn't up to me to say, "I don't like it" and refuse to do it. I made over fifty pictures. *Nob Hill* is the only one a studio ever handed me that I said I didn't want to make, and I finally made it anyway.

D: Was *The Lives of a Bengal Lancer* an interesting film for you?

H: Oh, just marvelous. Most of the Westerns I worked on were shot up near Lone Pine, which is desert country and it's got big mountains behind it. I'd been to India and knew that country, and I thought the area around Lone Pine could stand in for Tibet. But I said, "Do me one favor. I need an elephant in the first scene I shoot. That'll make it look like India." The day before we left to go on location, the assistant director said, "I don't think they're going to send the elephant." So I went to the front office and I said, "Look, I'm arriving in Lone Pine tomorrow and if there's no elephant, I don't work." I was making the film on a financial shoestring. A couple of directors had been assigned to it, and the budget had been so expensive that they cancelled the picture. Then they rejuvenated it with me—a fast director and cheap. Right after dinner the assistant director told me, "They're not going to send the elephant." So I called the studio and said, "Send the elephant or another director if you want work done tomorrow." The next morning I got word that they had stopped in Maharvey to get gas, and the elephant had put his trunk around a neon sign and wouldn't let go. They had a hell of a time. They finally got him loose and called to say that they were on their way. They finally got to Lone Pine and were coming down a little dirt road. Coming up a hill the driver shifted gears and stopped under a tree, and the elephant put his trunk around a branch of the tree and wouldn't let go. I said, "Send a guy down with a saw and saw the branch off. So they arrived at the camp around noontime with the elephant still holding on to the branch they'd sawed off.

D: Once you got a script and had agreed to direct the picture, how did you begin your preparation?

H: It depended on the script. I started from scratch. From the script you determined where you would like to make the picture. If the place you wanted was impossible, then you tried to get the next best place. You wanted to find the best art director for that kind of picture. I did a lot of my work on location and went to whatever environment that script needed. For *Spawn of the North* I went to Alaska. For *The House on 92nd Street* I went to New York City. It's awfully hard to create reality on soundstages, and I mostly made realistic pictures.

D: I've been through one of your scripts at the American Film Institute, and I was amazed at all of the notations you made.

H: Every notation in those scripts was made before we started the picture. Often I suggested where dialogue might be cut. Placement of characters in scenes was important. There's always one principal character, and the director has to place that actor so that it doesn't seem like he's favoring that particular character.

D: How much of a hand did you have in the writing?

H: A good deal. I wrote the script for *Home in Indiana*. I didn't like it, so we got other writers and I told them some things I wanted. But when the writers turned in the script, I was halfway through the picture. I just forgot the script and improvised. The writers wanted a conference, and they wanted to argue about this and that. So I just left and went down to Lexington, Kentucky, and went to work. When I came back to do the interiors at the studio, the writers still hadn't finished the script.

D: Was part of your job to simplify a script?

H: You simplify everything, not only the script. You simplify the acting. You don't want to get too spread out on the location; you try to hack the geography so that there isn't too much outside interest. I never liked sets that were too elaborate, because I didn't want audiences looking over the shoulders of actors. I made people the focus of my scenes. I didn't want too many distractions.

D: I believe that *Trail of the Lonesome Pine* was the first time you worked in color. Did color pose problems for you?

H: Only for the cameraman. I had worked on a couple of color pictures in the early days. One was with Richard Dix and Lois Wilson. The first ones only used two colors. *Becky Sharp* was the first picture made with the three-color process, and that was made completely in the studio. But *Trail of the Lonesome Pine* was the first outdoor picture in color. I made a lot of tests. The studio wanted real colors, not just tones. Natalie Kalmus was the color consultant. I selected the clothes I wanted for the actors and got to the set and found that she'd picked other wardrobe. So I quit work until I got the clothes I wanted back. We had an awful fight. Finally I said, "You either take her off the picture or take me off." I got a letter from the head of Technicolor after the picture was released complimenting me on the color. I just approached color naturally. The Technicolor people soon threw out their rules. The first Technicolor camera was so big that it took three men to carry it. There were three strips of film—red, blue, and yellow—that ran through the camera and three magazines.

D: What kind of an experience was working with Mae West on *Go West, Young Man*?

H: Well, she was the director, the star, the photographer, the designer, the art director, everything on her pictures. If she hadn't had those big breasts, I'd have thought she was a man. She was strong. West knew what she wanted and she got it. I thought I'd do a few extra things to try to have a little fun with her, rather than her having fun with everybody else. For the first scene in the picture we rented Constance Bennett's Rolls Royce. I had Mae West in the car, a footman came around and opened the door, and out came a bulldog on a diamond chain. Then Mae West got out. As she and the bulldog walked away their butts were moving the same way. It was really funny. When West saw that in the rushes, she went crazy. "No god-damned dog is going to steal laughs from me!" she said. "I'm the one who gets the laughs." So she had that cut out. Xavier Cugat was the bandleader in the picture. When she saw him, she said, "Get that guy a toupee. I'm not going to work on a picture with a baldheaded guy." So we had to wait until Cugat got a hairdresser to fit him with a toupee. West was a big star, and she ran her movie.

D: Why did you leave Paramount?

H: I don't remember. There wasn't a fight or anything. I think my contract came to an end and Twentieth Century-Fox offered me more money.

D: I know that you and Tyrone Power became close friends during your years at Fox.

H: Yes. I made five pictures with Ty and sold him a house. But I think my best friend among the actors was Gary Cooper. I'd worked on Coop's pictures as a prop man, an assistant director, a production manager, a second unit director, and I directed him in five pictures. I knew him through all of his love affairs. Ty Power was charming, but everybody thought he was a little swishy. He was so handsome and always so beautifully groomed. Not a hair was out of place. You'd see Cooper working in his vegetable garden, and he looked like a farmer. Coop was a very rare person. He was sensitive, a very gentle man, and it showed on the screen. He was no actor, but he was so natural. He could make action films believable and play in any kind of picture. Cooper *was* the Virginian. I was an assistant to Vic Fleming when Coop made that picture. That's the kind of guy Coop was.

D: Did you enjoy making *Brigham Young*?

H: We had so much trouble with that script. So many people wrote on it. I didn't like the characters too much. Brigham Young I liked, but I didn't like the love story. We had such a hell of a time with the grasshopper siege. Then I read in the paper where they were having one of those big influxes of grasshoppers in a city in Nevada. I left the next morning and took only one actor with me, Mary Astor. When we got to this town in Nevada, there were grasshoppers all over the ground and up the walls of houses. Guys were digging big trenches and were going to try to burn them. If it hadn't been for that, I'd never have gotten that sequence in my picture. But the grasshopper

siege looked pretty convincing in *Brigham Young*. We filmed the
seagulls up at Mona Lake. They had a breeding ground up there. The
shots of the Mormons going through the mountains were done at Big
Bear. If you could make a picture all on the back lot, it was a little
picture. What made *Brigham Young* a big picture was the background. I made the same picture that was in the script, but the locations made it big. The crossing of the frozen river, however, was
filmed on the back lot. I needed a space of ice twenty-five yards wide
by one hundred feet long. The studio had every ice company in town
bring ice to the set. They laid blocks of ice down for the wagons to
cross on.

D: Was studio head Darryl Zanuck intimately involved with every
production at Fox?

H: From stem to stern. From the beginning of writing to the final
cut. Zanuck was a whiz with scripts. He was not a literary man, but
his instincts were so good. He knew what would work and what
wouldn't work. He could sense what was too long and what was too
short, what was silly and ridiculous and what was sound. He had
great instincts about a script. I think that was his forte. Zanuck
would get up in the morning and sit in his robe and read a script
while he had breakfast. About eleven o'clock he'd have a shave, then
get in the car and come to the studio in time for lunch. He'd go to
lunch and spend the afternoon in script conferences. Then he'd have
a massage and go to dinner. After dinner he'd watch rushes and first
cuts. He loved movies so much. Many times we'd finish work at
twelve or one o'clock, and he'd say, "I've got a French movie I hear is
good. Do you want to watch it with me?" If I didn't, he'd sit in a projection room and look at it alone. He absolutely loved movies. I never
saw anybody work like he did. He worked from the time he got up in
the morning until one or two o'clock the next morning.

D: How closely were you involved with the music in your pictures?

H: Al Newman, who wrote many of the scores for Fox pictures,
was marvelous. That was one thing about Zanuck: he never hired
bums. He had great respect for talent and always got top people.
Newman was one of the best in the business. When you heard that
Alfred Newman was going to write the music for your picture, you
had confidence in him.

D: What was your method of dealing with actors?

H: I found I must always be truthful. I never believed in treating them like children.

D: You've been called an extremely harsh taskmaster.

H: Well, only to the extent of wanting people to be on time and know their lines. I had the best crew, and I expected them to do their best. They were getting a lot of money. If anybody sloughed their job, they caught hell or got fired. I had no patience with them.

D: Did Zanuck pretty much give you a free hand to do your job the way you thought best?

H: He had a half dozen directors that he trusted. Joe Mankiewicz had a completely free hand, I had a free hand, Henry King had a free hand. Zanuck never bothered people that he had faith in. If he saw something he didn't like, he'd call you in and say, "Why did you do this?" If your explanation made sense, he'd say, "Okay." But he was a bastard with people who didn't do their job. He was worse with people he thought didn't try. He never condemned anybody because they made mistakes. It was just when they didn't try. He was paying them a lot of money and expected results.

D: What kind of money were you making?

H: In the late 1930s and early 1940s I was getting $3,500 a week. In those days that was a lot of money. When I had my cancer operation and was gone for four months, I got that check every single week.

D: Did you like making *The Shepherd of the Hills*?

H: That was the first time I worked with John Wayne. He was having a love affair with Marlene Dietrich at the time. We were working at Big Bear. Dietrich stayed in a hotel over by the lake. One morning Duke was rushing to the set, he was late, and coming in he hit a corner and turned over in his station wagon.

D: Was Wayne already a pretty good actor?

H: He never was an actor. And because he wasn't an actor, he had to do everything real. There wasn't anything in Duke that would allow him to pretend he was something. He couldn't be French or have an accent. He couldn't be an Olivier. Whatever the actor was called upon to do in the script, he *did* it. With Duke it wasn't a question of acting, it was a question of reality.

D: I've heard you say that Gene Tierney was one of the actresses you got to know best.

H: Yes, I got to really care for Gene. She had a lot of troubles, but she was a charming, lovely girl and a good actress. Gene had a mysterious quality about her. A lot of times she had a deep look in her eyes, like she was thinking more than she was telling. She had such wonderful eyes. If you looked into her eyes, you could tell instantly whether she was happy or sad. She didn't have to talk.

D: Was *The House on 92nd Street* a favorite project of yours?

H: That was one of the first films done entirely on the streets with nothing shot in the studio. The picture was really a documentary. It was a true story. It was very exciting to invent new ways of doing things. I put a screen around a manhole and had a glass in it to photograph through. I worked in a station wagon shooting through a one-way mirror. I used real houses and worked inside the houses. I never shot one thing in the studio. Later I made *13 Rue Madeleine* in Boston and Quebec. I was supposed to make that picture overseas, but we only had James Cagney, our star, for fourteen weeks and he wouldn't fly. If we'd gone to Europe, half of the time would have been taken up with travel. So I told Zanuck, "Look, I've traveled quite a bit, and the old city of Quebec looks just like France and parts of Boston look like England." We went down the St. Lawrence River to where the farms are and used that area for the countryside. We always found something that looked like the actual places in the story.

D: Were you enthusiastic about making *Kiss of Death*?

H: That was another of the pictures I made in New York, and it was a true story. An assistant district attorney wrote it. I loved the picture because I liked working outside. It was exciting to maneuver things and get work done without people on the streets knowing that you were filming. The only pain in the ass on that picture was the leading man, Victor Mature. He was carousing all the time and up all night and sleeping all day on the set. He was dirty. I bought him a couple of new suits, and I found him in the men's toilet, lying on the floor asleep in one of the new suits I'd just bought him. But he was a good actor.

D: How did you feel about *The Black Rose*?

H: I don't know. I was with a doctor all the time during the making of that picture. That's the first picture I made after my cancer operation. In the first place, it was cast badly. Jack Hawkins, the English actor, was too old for the part. It should have been played by someone like Van Johnson. And Cecile Aubry, the little French actress, didn't have a lick of sense. I tried to get Leslie Caron, but Caron said she loved ballet and didn't want to be in pictures. Cecile Aubry was way wrong for the role. So I didn't have a good time making that picture. If you don't have a good time, the picture doesn't turn out well.

D: How did you and Orson Welles get along?

H: Terrible. I worked all one day on a scene with him and finally said, "We'll come back tomorrow." He said, "No. I've done it every way I know how to do it. What do you want?" I said, "Orson, you've done it every single way except the way I asked you to do it. And if we're here for two weeks, you're going to do that scene the way I want it done." He looked me in the eye and went in and did it correctly. It pleased him to outwit people. That was the trouble with him throughout his whole career.

D: Was *Rawhide* more your kind of film?

H: No, I don't know how *Rawhide* happened. I guess it was just a story that Fox had, and Zanuck put Ty Power in it. I don't remember much about the picture.

D: Was Susan Hayward, Power's costar in *Rawhide*, good to work with?

H: She was temperamental. She was a strange girl. She made a bad marriage and never really got out of life what she was entitled to and was bitter about it.

D: Do you remember *14 Hours* as a good experience?

H: We had two endings for that. The night we previewed the picture with the original ending, where the man jumps, [studio executive] Spyros Skouras was in the theater. He had found out that day that his daughter jumped out of the tenth floor of a hospital where she was being treated for being a little wacky. She jumped out of a tenth-floor window and committed suicide. Skouras said, "No picture is ever going to be released from this company with anybody jumping out of a goddamned window." So we had to make another ending where the guy was rescued.

D: What kind of a man was Skouras?

H: He was a blustery Greek, but a good businessman.

D: Did you find *The Desert Fox* an interesting picture?
H: That was marvelous. I went to Germany and photographed there. We actually used Rommel's house in the picture. His wife and I sort of hit it off. She gave me his leather coat, his sunglasses, and the little whip that he carried all the time for James Mason to use in the picture. I had read everything I could find about Rommel before we started filming.
D: Were there signs in the 1950s that the big studios were beginning to get nervous and scared?
H: It wasn't the big studios, it was the big men who ran the studios. The whole business was disturbed by television. In that period there was a slump, no question about it. Here came a strange new medium created by outside people, and the studio heads were trying to figure out what to do about it.
D: How did you feel about *Niagara*?
H: That was the first big picture with Marilyn Monroe starring. She was a bright girl. She knew every goddamned thing she was doing, but she liked playing dumb. I had no difficulties with her, absolutely none. Her dumbness was all acting.
D: What was your opinion of *Legend of the Lost*?
H: That was my original story. I paid Ben Hecht to write the script. That was a fiasco. Everybody tried to change the story from what it was. I only wanted to see three people through the whole thing, and they tried to make it more.
D: Was Sophia Loren, John Wayne's costar in the picture, good to work with?
H: Yeah, but she's a one-dimensional actress. She has no depth, just beauty.
D: Did filming *How the West Was Won* in Cinerama pose problems?
H: They were having trouble with the script. Sol Siegel was a friend of mine, and he was the head of MGM at that time. He was having so much trouble with *Mutiny on the Bounty* and Marlon Brando that he couldn't devote much time to this picture. Everybody worked for half-salary on *How the West Was Won*, because the Catholic Church was to receive a cut of the profits. Siegel was having trouble with the story, and he called me over to Metro and said, "See what you can do with it." I ended up directing the first segment of the picture and

wrote the script for the second segment. Then I made the second one. The third segment was the war, and John Ford directed that. George Marshall directed the part about the military that Richard Widmark was in, and I did the last segment. We had more goddamned trouble. They had an idiot for a producer, and Sol Siegel was drunk most of the time. We spent so much money on the picture that they almost decided not to do the last part. We had a meeting and I said, "You can't quit. You've got to show how the West was won. The West was won when the law took over."

D: Was *The Sons of Katie Elder* a favorite of yours?

H: It sure was a good picture. I liked it, but I liked *True Grit* better. There's a funny story about *True Grit*. Hal Wallis called me and said, "I've got this book, and by five o'clock I have to say whether I'll buy the rights or not. It's going to cost me $100,000." He said, "I want you to read the book and tell me what you think." I read it, and I ran right back in and said, "Jesus, buy it! The dialogue is delicious. The way this girl talks is sensational." Charles Portis, the author of the book, objected to our decision to film the picture in Colorado, since the story takes place in Arkansas. I said, "Look, in Arkansas nobody's been ten miles from their home in their whole life, and when they see the picture, they'll be happy to know that some part of Arkansas looks like that." Portis also didn't want John Wayne to play Rooster Cogburn, even though the part won Wayne an Academy Award.

D: Did you work well with producer Hal Wallis?

H: Yes, he left me alone. He only had his eye on the money. Wallis wanted me to make the follow-up, *Rooster Cogburn*. I thought the combination of Hepburn and Wayne would be absolutely sensational. But when I read the script, I thought it was ridiculous.

D: Do you feel that your professional life contributed a great deal to your personal development?

H: No. It's brought me money. But I never went to school. I quit school to go to work in my first year of high school. I had gone to a school with one teacher and a single classroom where all eight grades were taught. I didn't learn much there. My first wife was a Jewish girl and an intellectual. She spoke three or four languages and knew about music. We'd been married for about eight or nine years when she came to me one day and said, "You're going to quit work and go to school and get an education or I'm leaving you." I was an assistant director at the time. I went to Paul Bern, the production executive who married Jean Harlow, and turned my heart inside out to him. Paul said, "Henry, I think the way for you to get the best education is to read for two hours every day." So I did that. I read two hours a day for ten years. But my wife divorced me anyway.

D: Did you read a great deal trying to find stories you thought would make interesting films?

H: Studios always had so much material that they'd bought that I didn't need to do that. The only thing I think I brought in from the outside was the picture [*Legend of the Lost*] with John Wayne and Sophia Loren. I was trying to branch out with that one, but the script never worked. I told the idea to Wayne, and he was fond of it. That was the only thing I started from scratch in all the pictures I've made. The rest were studio productions.

D: Do you think there's a "Henry Hathaway style" in your pictures?

H: I've done too many different kinds of pictures for that to be true. If I had only made one kind of picture, you could say that. But I've made every kind there is to be made. A good script is the important thing. I didn't care what the story was about—children, grownups, Chinamen—so long as the script was good and there were good relationships between the characters. It didn't matter what the background was.

D: Do you consider yourself primarily a storyteller?

H: That's all any director is. You tell the story in the most interesting fashion with the most interesting people you can find. If you can't tell the basic situation in one sentence, you haven't got a story.

Henry Hathaway's Feature Films

1932   *Heritage of the Desert*
          Wild Horse Mesa
1933   *Under the Tonto Rim*
          Sunset Pass
          Man of the Forest
          To the Last Man
          The Thundering Herd

1934   *The Last Round-Up*
            Come On Marines!
            The Witching Hour
            Now and Forever
1935   *The Lives of a Bengal Lancer*
            Peter Ibbetson
1936   *The Trail of the Lonesome Pine*
            Go West, Young Man
1937   *Souls at Sea*
1938   *Spawn of the North*
1939   *The Real Glory*
1940   *Johnny Apollo*
            Brigham Young—Frontiersman
1941   *The Shepherd of the Hills*
            Sundown
1942   *Ten Gentlemen from West Point*
1943   *China Girl*
1944   *Home in Indiana*
            Wing and a Prayer
1945   *Nob Hill*
            The House of 92nd Street
1946   *The Dark Corner*
1947   *13 Rue Madeleine*
            Kiss of Death
1948   *Call Northside 777*
1949   *Down to the Sea in Ships*
1950   *The Black Rose*
1951   *You're in the Navy Now*
            Fourteen Hours
            Rawhide
            The Desert Fox
1952   *Diplomatic Courier*
            O Henry's Full House ("The Clarion Call" episode)
1953   *Niagara*
            White Witch Doctor
1954   *Prince Valiant*
            Garden of Evil

1955   *The Racers*
1956   *The Bottom of the Bottle*
          23 Paces to Baker Street
1957   *Legend of the Lost*
1958   *From Hell to Texas*
1959   *Woman Obsessed*
1960   *Seven Thieves*
          North to Alaska
1962   *How the West Was Won* (three episodes)
1964   *Circus World*
1965   *The Sons of Katie Elder*
1966   *Nevada Smith*
1967   *The Last Safari*
1968   *5 Card Stud*
1969   *True Grit*
1971   *Raid on Rommel*
          Shootout
1974   *Hangup*

Joseph Newman (right) with film editor Fred Berger

JOSEPH NEWMAN

The Realization of a Boyhood Dream

Budget film director Joseph Newman was born in Logan, Utah, in 1909 but grew up in California. He became fascinated with the motion pictures business as a child and at age sixteen went to work for Metro-Goldwyn-Mayer. He directed his first feature film at that studio in 1942 and made more successful pictures at other studios after the Second World War, among them *711 Ocean Drive*, *Pony Soldier*, and *The Outcasts of Poker Flat*. He watched silent pictures being shot as a boy, experienced the advent of sound, worked at Twentieth Century-Fox during the introduction of CinemaScope, and made the transition to television production. Retired from filmmaking since the 1960s, Newman lives in Chatsworth, California.

The following interview with the director was taped at the Del Capri Hotel in Westwood, California, on July 23, 1984.

D: How did a Utah boy like yourself become interested in film work?
N: I'm really not a Utah boy, because my family moved to Los Angeles when I was eight years old. So I was really raised in Hollywood. We lived next door to Wallace Reid on a street called Morgan Place. Hollywood then was very rural. As a boy, I used to go up in the hills above Franklin Avenue and pick wild holly and sell it around Christmas time. Hollywood was named after the holly. I used to ride my bicycle on Hollywood Boulevard, which was two lanes then and not even asphalt, just oil and gravel. It was the days of the old silent pictures, before 1917, and they were filming all around Hollywood. Instead of following fire engines, I used to get on my

155

bicycle and go where they were making movies. They'd set up on a corner someplace or up in the hills, and watching them work was a great attraction for me. From the time I was eight years old my ambition was to make motion pictures. Movies really fascinated me.

D: Which studios were located in the Holllywood area in those days?

N: There was Famous Players-Lasky before the studio became Paramount, and that was located near Vine and Sunset. Then the Christie brothers had a studio where they made comedies. Fox, before it became Twentieth Century-Fox, was at Western and Sunset. Mack Sennett was out in Edendale. Charles Chaplin had a studio at LaBrea and Sunset. Charlie Ray built a studio, and that was just about at Vermont and Sunset. It later became Allied Artists and Monogram and now is the public television studio—KCET. Also where Hollywood and Sunset come together there was a large track of land where D. W. Griffith built this tremendous Roman city for *Intolerance,* and it stood there until into the 1920s. To a boy of nine years old, that was really fascinating. There was the Vitagraph Studio, too, at Sunset and Vermont. That is now a television studio—KABC. And there were numerous smaller studios all around.

I was a great fan of Douglas Fairbanks, as I guess every young boy was at that time. My family had a friend who was an actor and a makeup man. In those days makeup was not a profession yet. The actors mostly did their makeup themselves, but when they'd have a great number of people in a scene or if they had difficult makeup, then some of the actors would double as makeup men. My family's friend was a makeup man for Douglas Fairbanks, and he took me to the set. Fairbanks was making *Robin Hood* at the time. That was one of the great thrills of my early existence.

I was an avid reader. Every afternoon and evening I would read everything I could get my hands on. I was especially fond of drama, and I used to get collections of Broadway plays from the library. But my father died when I was eleven years old and didn't leave my mother in very good financial condition. So I really started to work when I was eleven years old. I still went to school until I was sixteen. Then I got a job at Metro-Goldwyn-Mayer.

D: What was your first position at Metro?

N: I became L. B. Mayer's office boy. That was in 1925. Mr. Mayer was awfully good to me, so advancement came pretty fast.

D: How would you describe the atmosphere around the MGM lot in 1925?

N: It was a family atmosphere. The people in the motion picture industry at that time were very generous and very outgoing. It was a relatively new industry and practically everyone was learning. Most of the people working in the business were young, and they were willing to let other people learn with them. The jealousies that came later hadn't developed. People were exceptionally good to me as a sixteen and seventeen-year-old. I hadn't had too much education, but I ended up getting a great education because of all the things I did and all the traveling I did later and all the different subjects I worked on and had to research. MGM was a small company in 1925; it had just been formed. There were very few executives. There was L. B. Mayer and Irving Thalberg, who was Mayer's right-hand man. In those days they didn't have producers. L. B. Mayer was the head of the whole production unit, and Irving Thalberg was essentially the producer of all the pictures. He had Harry Rapf, to whom he delegated some of the pictures, but there were really just the two men. There was a group of great directors there at the time, and some very innovative directors. Of course, when I started, it was still the days of silent pictures, and the first stages that were built at MGM were all glass. They had developed the klieg light by the time I got there, so they didn't have to depend on sunshine any longer. But the glass stages were still there, and they painted the glass black so they could use the lights. I think the silent days were the most interesting of all in my experience, because people were so inventive and innovative and eager to develop different techniques. Everybody was trying new things, and it was a great period.

King Vidor was at MGM then. As a matter of fact, the first set I ever worked on was his picture *The Big Parade*, which became a silent masterpiece. I worked on some of the mob scenes. I also worked on the silent *Ben-Hur*. They had a big track of land about four miles from the studio, which is now where Venice Boulevard and La Cienega meet. La Cienega didn't come through in those days, but the old Pacific Electric tracks did. They built the Circus Maximus there. The studio made most of the picture in Italy, and then they brought the whole company back to California and did the chariot races here. They had ten thousand extras. In those days people would work as extras for three dollars a day and a box lunch. So I was the forty-fifth assistant on *Ben-Hur*. I was hired to handle the mobs and give out the box lunches.

D: What kind of a man was L. B. Mayer in your experience?

N: Mayer in my experience was a very fine man. He was a very human man and a very kind man to me and very considerate. I remember one incident when I was working as his office boy. Mayer went to visit all the stages, even the ones that were way out on the back lot. He was expecting a call from New York from Nicholas Schenck, who was Mr. Loew's right-hand man at the time. Later, when Loew died, Nicholas Schenck became president of MGM. Mayer took me along on his visit to the sets on the back lot so that I could go to a nearby telephone to find out when this important call came in. Finally the call from New York came through. Mayer got in a car and started up the street, and I started to walk back to the office. Suddenly Mayer realized that I hadn't gotten in the car. So as important and expensive as that long-distance call was, he backed the car up, apologized, and had me drive back to the office. I know that in a lot of his dealings Mayer was ruthless, but I can only give my personal recollections of him. With me he was always considerate and gave me tremendous opportunities.

D: How about Thalberg?

N: Thalberg I didn't get as close to. I didn't really get to know Irving Thalberg until about a year before he died, about the time that he and Mayer had their misunderstandings and difficulties. Thalberg went on to produce his own pictures, and the first one he did was *The Merry Widow*, which Ernst Lubitsch directed. I was his assistant director. By that time Thalberg had moved away from the executives' offices and had his own little bungalow out on the back lot. I came to know him better then and continued working with him. We made a picture with Clark Gable, Jean Harlow, and Wallace Beery called *China Seas*. I also did a number of pictures with Norma Shearer, Thalberg's wife. On *Riptide* they didn't have a script. Eddie Goulding, who was British and a wonderful man but a very erratic man, liked to do his own writing as well as directing. So Goulding was writing the script. We only had four or five pages on yellow paper, and every night Goulding would write the scenes, and I'd take them down to Thalberg. He was living on the ocean front then. We had a lot of trouble on the picture, and I was constantly shuttling back and forth between the set and Thalberg's house. He wasn't feeling too well in those days. But I went on working with him.

I also worked with Thalberg on another picture that Goulding directed—*Maytime* that starred Jeanette MacDonald and Nelson Eddy. (Actually Goulding started the picture, and Robert Z. Leonard finished it.) By that time Thalberg was pretty ill, and it was a bad script. Goulding was trying to doctor it up. Sigmund Romberg, who had composed the original score, was there, and we were about one-third through the picture. Thalberg was failing and failing. I would go down with the rushes every morning, and Thalberg would look at them at his house. The picture wasn't going well at all, and Thalberg was failing more and more. He died right in the middle of the picture.

Thalberg was a brilliant man, but he was a little cold. It took a long time to know him, and he didn't have the personal warmth that I found in Mayer. Possibly it was because he was so preoccupied. Thalberg was a hard worker and had tremendous power. By 1926 or 1927 MGM had, through Thalberg's great leadership, become the leading maker of motion pictures in Hollywood. The big studio system really emerged from the fact that the theater chains controlled the producing companies, and the studios had outlets for their product.

D: Do you have vivid memories of Greta Garbo at MGM?

N: I remember the day Garbo arrived at the studio. She came with the man who had directed her pictures in Sweden, Mauritz Stiller. I was in the front office when in marched this tall, awkward, large-boned young girl. Garbo was only, I think, nineteen or so when she came to Hollywood. Someone had picked Stiller and her up at the railroad station in a car and brought them out to the studio, and I ushered them into Mr. Mayer's office. But then Garbo was really transformed. The first time I saw her on a set, which was about six months later, was on a picture called *The Torrent*. They were making it on one of the glass stages. I went over there, and under those lights she became a transformed person. I've never seen such a change. And it was the same all through her career. If you met her on the street, she wasn't the glamorous person she was on the screen. It seemed that the lights and the camera transformed her.

D: Did the arrival of sound really throw MGM into a panic?

N: It threw the whole industry into a panic. That was a very interesting time, yet it was a sad time because it changed the world for so many people. But it was one of the most exciting times I've ever lived through in the motion picture industry. The old silent cameras were very noisy. They sounded like a coffee grinder. So they had to build these great big chests, like butchers' ice chests, around the camera, with big doors that were padded. The cameraman and his assistant would get inside the chests, and they'd roast from the heat. This was before the days of air conditioning. Then there was all the trouble with the microphones. Nobody knew much about sound recording in those days. The studios brought a lot of people out from Victor and RCA, but it was all very chaotic. Getting quality in the recordings was difficult.

D: You mentioned that you were assistant director to Lubitsch on *The Merry Widow*. What would your duties entail?

N: Lubitsch wanted a lot of help from his assistants. So, for instance, in the great waltz scene, together with Albertina Rasch, who was the choreographer on the picture, we staged the whole waltz, where we had 400 people in this great ballroom. Assistant directors saw that all the actors were on the set on time, and we handled all of the mobs. An assistant rehearsed the mobs and the extra people and got them ready to shoot the scene. I was fortunate in the directors I assisted; in many cases they had me rehearse scenes for them. It was a great learning process for me. Lubitsch had the greatest sense of humor of any individual I've ever met, and that was reflected in his work. The famous "Lubitsch touch" was accented by human humor, not contrived humor. It was humor from the events that occur in life. Lubitsch had a very human quality about him. Actors loved him. It's a shame that *The Merry Widow* was made in the days of black and white; it would have been even better in color.

D: When did color come in?

N: The very first picture in color at MGM was called *The Mysterious Island*. Maurice Tourneur, who was a great director, made it, and that was about 1927 or 1928. There had been other color pictures earlier made elsewhere. But still there weren't very many pictures made in color until the late 1930s. Color cameras were cumbersome, and they used three different strips of color. Filming in color was difficult and expensive and sometimes the quality wasn't too good in those early days. They didn't perfect having all three colors on one film until the 1950s. The advancement of color wasn't as fast as the advancements in sound. The Depression really brought sound on much faster, because things were so bad in 1929 that the studios were looking for gimmicks to bring people into the theaters. So theaters were installing sound systems as quickly as they could.

D: Around 1937 MGM sent you to Great Britain. What were your duties there?

N: Studio executives had decided to make pictures in Britain and were forming a British company. The first picture MGM made there was *A Yank at Oxford*, which starred Robert Taylor. They sent me over to get the company ready and assist in any way I could. Jack Conway was the director of the picture, and we had a complete British crew. Jack Conway took ill in the middle of the picture, so Mr. Mayer said, "Let Newman go ahead." I shot about a week of the actual picture. Then I did all of the boat races, which was the major part of the picture. So *A Yank at Oxford* gave me great directorial experience.

I was directing my first short subject when the studio decided to send me to England. Previous to that I was assistant director to Robert Z. Leonard on *The Firefly*, which costarred Jeanette MacDonald and Allan Jones. We were up in Lone Pine, which is at the foot of the Sierra Nevada Mountains. Robert Leonard was a large man and very heavy. He had an enlarged heart and became very short of breath up there. So he had to be sent back to Los Angeles in an ambulance. Again they said, "Let Newman go head." I shot "The Donkey Serenade," and the number turned out to be a big hit. So Mayer already had begun thinking about making me a director. When I came back from England, I started directing a lot of short subjects. I did a tremendous number of the "Crime Does Not Pay" series. Those were very popular at the time and gave me great, great experience.

D: The first feature that you directed was *Northwest Rangers.*

N: Yes, at MGM. That was in 1942, right after the United States entered the war. It wasn't the greatest picture in the world, but it got me started. Before I made the picture I got patriotic, and although I was thirty-two years old at the time, I enlisted in the army. The minute that picture was finished I went into the Signal Corps and spent from 1942 until 1946 in the army. When I came back to MGM, the whole place had changed. I worked on some stories there for a year, did one short subject, and then the studio decided to cut out all low-budget pictures. The executives wanted me to stay on, but they wanted me to become an assistant producer. I had decided that I wanted to be a director, so I said goodbye to everybody and left MGM in 1947.

D: By then did you feel that you were prepared to direct big pictures.

N: Yes. I had done so much directing before the war that I didn't think I had to rely too much on the cameraman or anyone in the technical fields. The only area where I had to rely on somebody was in the writing of scripts. I'd always wanted to write, but I was never successful at it. The only thing I feel I hadn't had enough experience in was in the evaluation and preparation of scripts.

D: Did you go to Twentieth Century-Fox right after you left MGM?

N: No, I did independent pictures first. The army wanted me to make a picture for them as a civilian. During the war I had photographed all the rehearsals in Florida for the D-Day landing. Just as my outfit was getting ready to go overseas, I was transferred to Long Island, where I made propaganda and training films at a studio in Astoria, the old Paramount studio there. Right after I left MGM, the army asked me to come back to New York and make a training film on venereal disease, of all things. They paid me $1,000 a week, but after that I had tough going for a while. I worked on a lot of projects of my own, and finally I did an independent picture for Frank Seltzer, which Twentieth Century-Fox released. We made the picture in ten days for $150,000. It was a small picture but it got great critical acclaim.

D: What was the name of the picture?

N: The picture was called *Jungle Patrol*. That was the release title given to the picture by Twentieth Century-Fox, but the title of the play from which it came was *West of Tomorrow*. *Jungle Patrol* was a bad title, but that picture started me off again.

D: Soon after that you directed *The Great Dan Patch*.

N: I did *The Great Dan Patch*, which was a successful, money-making picture, but not a picture that I'm too proud of.

D: *The Great Dan Patch* I remember was filmed in sepia tone. What was the thinking behind the use of sepia.

N: They thought it was going to bring more people into the theaters than black and white would. The picture should have been made in color, but color was still in the three-strip process and costly. *The Great Dan Patch* was an independent venture, and the producers just couldn't afford color. The picture was especially successful in the middle west and all the places where harness racing was popular.

D: I know that you made another picture with Frank Seltzer.

N: Yes, we made a picture called *711 Ocean Drive*. That, too, we made for very little money, about $300,000, and it was a tremendously successful picture. It was a picture that got good reviews, and the studios all liked it. After that picture I was in great demand. Harry Cohn wanted to sign me up, and Howard Hughes was very interested in me. But I went with Twentieth Century-Fox, and I was with Twentieth Century-Fox for two years. I made six or seven pictures there—some of them very successful and some of them not too good.

D: How would you compare working conditions at Twentieth Century-Fox with what you had experienced at MGM?

N: Well, of course I'm biased, having grown up at MGM and having such warm feelings about the studio. There wasn't that warm feeling at Twentieth Century-Fox. They were wonderful people over there, but it wasn't that feeling of the place where I'd grown up. Darryl Zanuck was a very capable man. He was a tough taskmaster, but a good man to work for.

D: Did Zanuck have his hand in every production on the lot?

N: Every production. He watched everything and wrote notes to you. He looked at the rushes late at night. He didn't start until about eleven o'clock at night. Then he'd write you notes and give his criticisms and suggestions. He was a very able man and a hard worker. I hit Twentieth Century-Fox at a bad period. It was a period when the industry was in an in-between stage. They were just coming out with the wide screen, and that was another period of transition. They didn't know how much they wanted to spend on pictures, and they held budgets down.

I made the first test of Marilyn Monroe for Zanuck. It was made during preparation for a picture I did with Linda Darnell. Before they cast Linda Darnell, Zanuck said that he'd seen this young girl in a small part in a John Huston film called *Asphalt Jungle*. Her agent had been touting her to Zanuck, so we made a test of the girl. She wasn't quite right for this part and she didn't have the experience yet, but you could see the spark. Zanuck signed Monroe to a contract, and I later made a picture with her.

D: What was the first picture you directed for Zanuck?

N: My first film at Fox was a picture with Paul Douglas, Linda Darnell, and Joan Bennett called *The Guy Who Came Back*. Then the next one was *Love Nest* with Marilyn Monroe, June Haver, and Bill Lundigan. Monroe was still learning. She was a difficult person because she wasn't sure of herself. I don't think she ever got to be sure of herself. That was her major difficulty. She had exceptional ability and this childish charm coupled with great sexual attraction. She had a great natural talent, but I don't think she ever realized it. She was always insecure. Instead of just being satisfied with her native talent, she tried to develop into a great dramatic actress. But when I worked with her, she was basically a nice, naive girl. She was difficult to work with because it was hard to get through to her. She made things difficult for the rest of the cast, too.

D: How was June Haver to work with?

N: She was a delight. She had a great sense of humor and was full of life.

D: Did you enjoy making *Red Skies of Montana*?

N: Yes, although it was a challenge. We had tremendous physical problems doing the forest fire. The picture had a great cast. Richard Widmark is a fine actor and a great talent. And young Jeffrey Hunter was a fine actor. I'll say this with all humility: we had the best forest fire ever done on the screen. Fortunately that picture was made in color. Technically, as far as action goes, I think it stands up. I'm not talking about the dramatic values, but I think *Red Skies of Montana* was a great technical and mechanical achievement.

D: Do you think that your observation of silent filmmaking influenced your direction of sound pictures?

N: Yes, I do. I think that in silent pictures a filmmaker had to express in action and in gestures all of the necessary dramatic values. We didn't have the aid of sound to explain things, only an occasional title. I think the people who worked on silent pictures really perfected the great techniques of motion pictures. I think D. W. Griffith, King Vidor, and those people learned to tell the story with the camera. They didn't have the use of language to express things. I think the visual emphasis is the reason motion pictures have become whatever art form they are today. I learned a lot from those silent filmmakers.

D: How did you feel about *The Outcasts of Poker Flat*?

N: *The Outcasts of Poker Flat* is one of the pictures I'm most proud of. I have received praise for that one in places where you don't normally receive critical praise. It was a simple picture, based on Brett Harte's short story. It was a picture that involved human emotions. Unfortunately it wasn't a great box office success, but I think it's one of the best things I've done.

D: Was Anne Baxter good to work with.

N: Yes, very good. She was a great actress. In those days she was a little bit insecure. But she had great ability and was a joy to work with.

D: For the most part did you enjoy working with actors?

N: Yes, I did. I had great associations with actors and gained a lot from them.

D: What are your thoughts on *Pony Soldier*?

N: I don't think we had too strong a story. I must say that Tyrone Power was such a magnificent man and such a great person to work

with. He was very interested in acting and was a dedicated actor.
He improved with every picture. Power would have been one of
the top American actors if he hadn't died so young. He was developing fast.

D: Do you have vivid memories of *Dangerous Crossing*?

N: That was with Jeanne Crain and Michael Rennie. It was a very
low-budget picture. At that time Twentieth Century-Fox wanted to
cut down on costs. But I think it was a good mystery. Crain and
Rennie were both delightful people and pleasant to work with.

D: What was your attitude toward budget pictures? Did you look
upon them as a challenge?

N: Yes. I didn't mind having to work on short schedules. I don't
think that money and long schedules really are the answer to making
a good picture.

D: After the six pictures or so for Twentieth Century-Fox, you
began to freelance.

N: Yes. I did some pictures for Allied Artists and went back to Metro.
I made quite a few pictures in that period; some of them were very good.
But again, a lot of them were low-budget pictures, like *The Human
Jungle*, which was made for very little money but was a successful picture. I also started to develop projects of my own. Then together with
Vic Orsatti, who was an agent here in southern California, I formed a
company. I found a science fiction book, *This Island Earth*, got a script
written, and we went to Universal and made the picture. It was made
in 1954 and was a tremendously successful picture.

D: I know that you directed a couple of pictures with Joel McCrea.

N: Yes, I did those for the Mirisch brothers.

D: Did you enjoy making Westerns?

N: Yes, I liked Westerns. I like any good story. I don't care what the
locale is. I never specialized in any one kind of film. I'm thankful I
made a variety of pictures. I enjoyed working with any good script.

D: How did you feel about location work?

N: I liked location work. As a matter of fact, I like to work. On *711
Ocean Drive*, for instance, we actually went to all the places mentioned in the film. We were thrown out of Las Vegas. They told us to

get out and be out by midnight. We started to work in the casinos, and the powers in Las Vegas didn't care much for the type of picture we were making, which showed the wire tapping and so forth that was going on. But we had very few sets built for that picture. We went into a home in Malibu and shot interiors there. We shot scenes in offices. I did that on numerous pictures. Of course I had used actual locations when I made films for the army. I made a picture while I was in the army called *A Diary of a Sergeant*.

D: Oh, yes. The film that Harold Russell was in before he appeared in *The Best Years of Our Lives*.

N: That was why Willy Wyler and Sam Goldwyn signed Russell up for their picture. Wyler remembered him in *Diary of a Sergeant*. But making those films for the army we'd go into hospitals and we'd go into people's houses. We went all over the world and photographed wherever we were. So when I came back to Hollywood after being in the army, I tried to do the same in making features films. I was a great believer in reality in motion pictures.

D: Did you find Harold Russell, a double amputee, as secure a man with his handicap as he appears in *The Best Years of Our Lives*?

N: I've never seen a man who had no acting experience in his life before do such a magnificent job. Russell had worked in a butcher shop before he was drafted into the army. He lost both of his hands not in combat but in an accident during training. We made the story of his life, the transition he made after his accident. You would have thought this man had been acting for fifteen or twenty years. The only acting he'd done before winning an Academy Award for *The Best Years of Our Lives* was that picture I made with him for the army. He was just a natural.

D: Did you enjoy making *The Big Circus*?

N: Yes, I did. Again, we had difficulties, but it was a challenge and it turned out to be a money-making picture.

D: Did you work well with screenwriter Charles Bennett on that film? I know Bennett had written scripts for Alfred Hitchcock.

N: Yes, I liked Charlie Bennett very much. We had a great time on the picture. He's a real delight. *The Big Circus* had a good cast: Peter

Lorre, Vincent Price, Victor Mature, Rhonda Fleming, Kathy Grant. Peter Lorre played the clown, and Vincent Price was the ringmaster.

D: Did you sometimes feel that you had to be a psychiatrist on the set?

N: On any picture the director always has to be. Actors are sometimes like children. Any time you work with a group of people, I think you have to use psychology because we're all human beings, and we all have our doubts and our phobias.

D: Wasn't *The Lawbreakers* originally a pilot for a television series?

N: Yes, *The Lawbreakers* was a pilot for a series called *The Asphalt Jungle*. It didn't play for too long. That was made at MGM. The studio liked the pilot so much that they called me back, and we shot more scenes to make a feature out of it. The picture was never released in this country, but it did well in foreign countries.

D: How did MGM differ in those later days from what you remembered from your youth?

N: It was a different place. A lot of the old people were still there, but a great many new people had come in. There was a different feeling about the place. It had lost a little of the creative spirit.

D: Did you sense in the 1950s and early 1960s that the big studio system was coming to an end?

N: I sensed that after I came out of the army. I think the biggest thing I could sense was that picturemaking had become more of an assembly line operation instead of the individual thought that had gone into pictures by men such as Irving Thalberg and David Selznick and Hunt Stromberg. Picturemaking had become more of a committee approach. That wasn't just happening at MGM, it was happening almost industry-wide. More and more the authority of the heads of studios had become curbed so far as how much money could be spent and what type of pictures could be made. Things were run more by committee. The studio heads had to get more and more approvals. It had become an era where the agents were gaining increasing amounts of power. Up until the early 1930s there were only small agents. The agents would negotiate for the actors. A lot of the actors didn't even have an agent. But with the advent of Myron Selznick, David Selznick's brother, agents became powerhouses in the business. Myron Selznick cornered as much of the talent as he could get, until he could more or less dictate to the studios because the studios needed his clients for box office attractions. After he became successful, others entered the field. William Morris, who had primarily been in New York for stage and vaudeville, came out to Hollywood. So by the late 1940s, you could see that these agents were able to control the talent of the industry. Together with the constraints that were being put on the studio producers, you could sense that creativeness was being curbed or boxed in. Then, too, there were the government constraints with the theater chains being separated from the studios. That was about the time that I started to branch off on my own. I could sense that there was going to be a breakup of the old studios, and I tried to branch out. But I wasn't as successful as I should have been.

D: Why did you decide to leave filmmaking?

N: For two reasons. One reason was that I started directing television shows. There weren't too many feature film offers coming in, so I was doing television. I enjoyed some of the television, but I'm interested in good stories and good scripts and everything started to be so filled with action and sex. I just wasn't attuned to that, so I wouldn't have been successful had I continued. I started to write, and I had about finished a novel when there was a big fire out in Chatsworth, and it demolished our house and demolished everything that I'd spent a year working on. That set me back for a while. Then the traffic in the city got to be so heavy that I thought, "Well, working is just not worth it." My wife and I had some land that we could sell, so financially I didn't have to worry.

D: Did you develop an overall philosophy of filmmaking?

N: First of all, I think the basic thing is to make entertainment. If you don't entertain people, you haven't accomplished your purpose. Secondly, I think that you have to have a dramatic story. I feel now that there are not enough pictures being made with really good scripts. I think that is the major difference between today and filmmaking thirty years ago or, even more, fifty years ago. The writing has deteriorated. I think that's a great loss for the motion picture industry. Thirdly, I think a filmmaker must appeal to the better instincts of people. I think it's a mistake to appeal to the base instincts, and I have the feeling that that's being done today in the whole entertainment industry.

D: Do you feel that your professional life contributed to your personal growth?

N: Oh, definitely. I think I've been a very fortunate person. I've been without a formal education, yet I think I've achieved a knowledge that few people have been able to achieve. I'm very thankful and appreciative of all the people who have helped me. I've gone through a tremendous era. I've gone from the early days of silent pictures into the sound era, through the advent of color and wide screen, and into the television era. Now we'll see what comes next.

Joseph Newman's Feature Films

1942 *Northwest Rangers*
1945 *Diary of a Sergeant* (documentary)
1948 *Jungle Patrol*
1949 *The Great Dan Patch*
          Abandoned
1950 *711 Ocean Drive*
1951 *Lucky Nick Cain*
          The Guy Who Came Back
          Love Nest
1952 *Red Skies of Montana*
          Pony Soldier
          The Outcasts of Poker Flat
1953 *Dangerous Crossing*
1954 *The Human Jungle*
1955 *This Island Earth*
          Kiss of Fire
1957 *Flight to Hong Kong*
          Death in Small Doses
1958 *Fort Massacre*

1959 *The Gunfight at Dodge City*
The Big Circus
Tarzan the Ape Man
1961 *King of the Roaring Twenties*
The Story of Arnold Rothstein
A Thunder of Drums
Twenty Plus Two
The George Raft Story

ARTHUR LUBIN

Comedy and Camp

Screen-television director Arthur Lubin was born in Los Angeles in 1901 and began his career as an actor. He directed the early motion picture comedies of Bud Abbott and Lou Costello, the *Francis* movies, and such examples of high-camp as *Ali Baba and the Forty Thieves* and *The Spider Woman Strikes Back*. For television he directed the entire *Mr. Ed* series, a comedy show that paired Alan Young with a talking horse. Lubin died in California in 1995.

The following interview was taped in the kitchen of the director's home in Los Angeles on July 15, 1985.

L: I was looking over the pictures I've directed and the plays I've produced in New York, and I said, "My God, did I do all that?" I have directed sixty-three feature films and over 200 television shows. But sometimes I wonder if I had done less and done better work, maybe I would have been better off.

D: How did you first become interested in theater?

L: I think I inherited the desire from my mother. My father hated every moment of it. At a very young age I lived with my family on an Indian reservation in a ghost town called Jerome, Arizona. My mother was always giving musical entertainments and doing theatrics. I always felt that she was a frustrated actress, but she never did act professionally. Probably for that reason, my mother encouraged me to be on various church programs in this little town. There were only three churches—the Methodist, the Congregationalist, and the Catholic—and because we lived near the Methodist church we were called the "Methodist Jews." But at Christmas time when I played young Jesus for the Catholic church, I was a "young Catholic Jew."

So that started my interest in theater I guess, and when we moved to San Diego, I was immediately put into little class plays and seemed to like performing. What really fostered my interest more than anything else was playing the Vicar in *The Vicar of Wakefield*, a play my high school English teacher wrote. I was then fourteen years old, and the teacher encouraged my acting and being in the musical society and the dramatic society. In fact, she was responsible for my going to college at Carnegie Tech in Pittsburgh, which in those days was a fine acting school. At Carnegie Tech we had brilliant directors, among whom was B. Iden Payne, who had directed Helen Hayes on the stage. He brought other English directors over, and that's the exposure I had.

D: So you launched your career in New York as an actor.

L: I first acted in California in *Desire Under the Elms* with Walter Huston. A play had opened in New York called *Jealousy*, which starred Fay Bainter. John Halliday had gotten ill, and because I was under contract to Al Wood, they sent me back to New York to step into the part that Halliday had played. I was far too young to play opposite Miss Bainter, so they put a mustache on me. I've asked myself over and over, "What happened that I didn't continue acting from that time on?" I was offered a job with a New York producing firm, Crosby Gaige and the Selwyns, and from there I started directing. I think I would have made a better actor than I was a director. I felt that I was a damn fine actor. But I love the West, and I was puzzled by New York. Even now when I go there, I can't wait to get back to California.

D: Didn't you do some acting in films?

L: When I got out of college, in the silent picture days, I played the bad son of Rudolph Schildkraut, the famous actor. It was a small part. I did have a big role, opposite John Gilbert, in a film called *Bardelys the Magnificent*, which King Vidor directed. I would say that I appeared in five or six silent pictures after I finished college. Then I was in the first independent talking picture, called *Times Square*, with Alice Day. I was supposed to sing, but I think somebody else must have done that for me, because I had no voice. That film was made in Watertown, Connecticut, where they had the first sound studio for independent pictures.

D: I've long admired King Vidor, particularly for his silent pictures. What was Vidor's approach to direction?

L: Every director has his own special approach, but I think the reason King was so well liked was that he left the actors alone. I was playing King Louis XIII in *Bardelys the Magnificent*. Often Vidor would say to me, "Now, as Louis XIII, what would you do?" He had seen me in *Desire Under the Elms*, in which I played a country boy from Connecticut, but Vidor thought I'd be good as King Louis XIII, which came as a surprise to me.

Vidor was a kind man, he was gentle. I got to know him later because he liked to do card tricks and magic of all kinds. There was an organization in Hollywood called the Writers Club, and I was stage manager for the group and occasionally directed plays for them. King Vidor invariably had a magic act that he did there, and that's how we became friends.

D: What recollections do you have of John Gilbert?

L: Jack was a bad boy, really a bad boy, but he had a great photogenic personality, which was better than his acting. From any angle he was photographic. Everyone was crazy about him.

I knew Gilbert's wife, Leatrice Joy. I met Leatrice after I got out of high school in San Diego. She was the ingenue in the Virginia Brissac Stock Company, and I sometimes acted with the company. We did a new show every week. I used to usher when there was nothing for me to do as an actor. All of that was fine training, which I didn't realize at the time. During the three years I was with that company I got to be very close to Leatrice. That was her first stage job, and it was difficult for her to learn a new part every week. So I used to cue her for the following week's show in between rehearsals.

D: *Bardelys the Magnificent* was made at Metro-Goldwyn-Mayer. How would you describe MGM in the mid-1920s?

L: It was a tremendous studio. People either hated Louis B. Mayer or they loved him. My family knew Mayer quite well; he had been in the jewelry business originally in Boston. When he came to Los Angeles to make pictures, he was working down in the slum section of the city. I came to see him with a letter of introduction, and Mayer said, "Lubin, if you photograph well, that's all we ask of you. If you don't, get the hell out of the business." And I got the hell out of the business. In the early days of pictures they wanted handsome young men like Jack Gilbert and Wallace Reid. Nowadays films are great for character actors, and that's where I should have been. On the stage I had a personality that I never had in pictures. That's one of the reasons I got the hell out of acting.

D: Let's come to your directing career, which I understand started in New York.

L: Yes. I gave up acting after *Jealousy* and worked for the Crosby Gaige-Selwyn office. They wanted to try out summer shows in Greenwich, upper New York, and I directed two plays there. Then I came out to California, where I acted for a while in Pasadena, and then decided that I should stick with directing. I tried out two plays at the Pasadena Playhouse, which I later produced and directed in New York, with the financial help of Lee Shubert. One play was with Paul Muni, one was with Lenore Ulric, and I directed a third show with Pauline Frederick. After directing in New York, Paramount signed me, and I came back to California with great joy to be assistant to William LeBaron, a producer at Paramount Studios.

D: How was Paul Muni to work with?

L: Very difficult, like Claude Rains, whom I worked with later. They were such great artists that you had to listen to them. They were so imbued in the part, and they did things that you never would have thought of that enriched their role. Muni would get so mad that he would scream. He was a very temperamental actor; Claude Rains wasn't. Muni depended a great deal on Bella, his wife. She would stand in the back of the theater, and when he finished a scene, he would look for her reaction. She would make a negative gesture, and he would say, "Let's try it again." To me everything Muni did was wonderful. He was a great artist, as was Claude, but difficult.

D: As assistant to William LeBaron, how did you find the general atmosphere around the Paramoaunt lot?

L: Wonderful. LeBaron had once been the head of RKO. Why he left there to come to Paramount I don't know. He had a way of being able to pick new talent. LeBaron brought Cary Grant to the studio for his very first picture, *Hot Saturday*, with Nancy Carroll and Randy Scott. He also brought Mae West to Paramount. Then all of the associate producers, of which I was one, were fired. Suddenly the studio had a slump, and we were out. I went to Universal in 1934.

D: Did you find Universal a well-run studio?

L: In those days it was. My first exposure to Universal was as an actor, right after I got out of college. So it was interesting to come back as a director. Carl Laemmle, Universal's initial head, had sold the studio to an independent producer named Charles Rogers. Rogers had a secretary whose wife thought I was a good actor. She encouraged her husband to tell Mr. Rogers that I should be signed. So I was the first director signed under Rogers's administration. I made a picture for him called *Nobody's Fool* with Glenda Farrell and Eddie Horton.

Rogers didn't last very long as studio head. Nate Blumberg, a wonderful man, became the new head of Universal. He was a theater man, he ran theaters. He engaged the men who ran theaters to be his producers at Universal, but they didn't know much about story. All they knew was how to sell a picture, and that's all they were really interested in. So we directors were pretty much given a free hand.

Universal was like one big family in those days. The Hollywood studios will never be like that again. When I go to see some of the pictures now and hear some of the dialogue, I remember how I had to fight the Technicolor people and the censorship office over how much of the ladies' cleavage should show.

D: How would you describe the Universal lot physically?

L: It was small. There was one dining room where we all ate. Universal in those days had a studio school, which prepared young performers for stardom. Later I got Clint Eastwood started there. He was a discovery of mine, although he no longer talks to me.

D: You directed a number of the Bud Abbott and Lou Costello films at Universal.

L: I directed their first five. *Buck Privates* was their first at Universal. They were wonderful but crude. They were real burlesque comedians. Practically all of their material was based on gags which had strange names. They brought with them from New York their writer, who was a gag writer. The studio had a regular writer who wrote scripts, and then John Grant, their writer, would inject the gags. That worked out very well. I would read a script, and I would say, "What is 'spin the dragon'?" or "What is 'hit the bottle'?" All of these gags had weird names. And they would act it out for me. I would say, "Well, we'll put the camera here," and it was a cinch. They were sensational.

Abbott and Costello had done a picture at Metro before the first one I directed, but when we did *Buck Privates*, the studio wasn't sure how well they would go over with the public. After the preview, where the reaction was tremendous, I was called into the front office and told, "Lubin, we're going to have to ask you to start another Abbott and Costello picture right away. We'll give you a raise if you don't need a rest to do it." So they crowded the films in, one right after the other, until the boys got a little tired and started fighting among themselves. Bud drank a great deal and was shaking all the time, and the only way he could sleep at night was to drink himself into a stupor. Lou became ill when his little boy accidentally drowned in his swimming pool. That really killed Lou, and he started gambling. The team went to pieces. I left them after the fifth picture. It was a sad parting for me, I loved those guys very much.

They had a weird sense of humor and were always pulling tricks on me. They always remembered my birthday. I remember the last time, we were in the middle of a scene. Suddenly Lou said, "Hold it," and he threw a suitcase out and it was full of condoms. They were adorable boys, and I miss them very much. But they started repeating themselves in their films. I think John Grant finally said, "Well, let's go back to number one and see what we had there that was good."

D: I have a note here that Mike Frankovich, who later headed Columbia, was an actor in *Buck Privates*.

L: Yes, it was his first film. Mike was a radio commentator. He had ten lines in the movie. Later on I directed a fine picture for him in London.

D: Did you take to filmmaking easily?

L: Yes, I felt that motion pictures should have tempo. It was my feeling that actors should be kept moving, the camera should be kept moving. On my first directing job I had the help of a cutter, because I didn't know camera very well. I must have driven the cutter crazy because I kept moving the camera all the time. The pictures I was making early in my career were all second pictures, fill-ins. In those days there was a big feature of maybe an hour-and-three-quarters, then pictures which were a little over an hour. There were a lot of directors who made those second pictures in six or seven days until the Directors Guild stopped that. Making those quick movies gave me wonderful experience for the bigger pictures I made later.

D: Do you remember what the budgets on those Abbott and Costello films were?

L: I think the first one was about $250,000, and then they went up. I know that the John Wayne pictures I made cost practically nothing, because no one thought that Duke would ever amount to anything. But pictures weren't expensive then. When I made *Night in Paradise* and *Phantom of the Opera*, I think the budgets were both just under $1 million, and the studio screamed about the cost. In fact, when I was assigned to *Night in Paradise*, which was produced by Walter Wanger, the head of the studio said to me, "Can't you do something to cut the sets down? Wanger is killing us." Well, under $1 million is nothing in moviemaking today.

D: At Universal you also made several of Maria Montez's pictures.

L: They were very big hits. We always had a problem with Maria and the Hayes [censorship] office because she never wanted to wear clothes. We were always stuffing bits of tulle or flowers in places where she was hanging out. Montez was no actress, she was a great photogenic personality. She was from the Dominican Republic and was very lovely, very temperamental, and had a tendency to gain weight.

One day on the set she was terribly late, and we were behind in our schedule. Maria didn't know her lines. I got quite upset with her, which I hardly ever do. She said, "You, Lubin, are full of shit," and she walked off the set. I sent my assistant after her, and Montez went to the producer. My assistant came back laughing. I said, "What happened?" He said, "You won't believe this, but the producer said to her, 'Maria, don't worry, all directors are full of shit.'"

D: Do you have particular memories of making *White Savage* with Montez?

L: I don't think she and Jon Hall, her frequent costar, cared much for each other. They were always vying for closeups. Maria would say to me, "You gave Jon one, you didn't give me one." But Sabu, who often worked with them, was an angel. I think that most actors are anxious to please and anxious to do good work, but now and then you get those who have been very successful and made a lot of money and have become terribly demanding. I found out that yelling at actors is the worst thing you can do. You get much better results if you take them aside and say, "Do this or do that." A director needs to be something of a psychologist.

D: *Ali Baba and the Forty Thieves* with Montez and Hall was a huge success.

L: They run it all the time on television. For some reason it's become a fad.

D: What kind of budget did *Ali Baba* have?

L: Around $250,000, which was considered big in those days. One reason we could make it for that amount was that every set had already been built for other pictures. I think there was one location out at Red Rock, about 100 miles towards the desert. We'd go there early in the morning, shoot all day, and the minute the sun went down we'd rush back. So the studio didn't have to pay for hotels, only the expense of meals.

For the low-budget pictures that I and a lot of us were making in those days, if a set was standing, the studio would have a script written around that set. In *Buck Privates* there was a big staircase where all the principals came marching down with a band playing. That set had been used in many pictures ahead of us, but they put flags around and it looked different. That's the way the studio cut costs in those days.

D: Was shooting a picture in color much more difficult than making one in black and white?

L: It was only difficult because there were two supervisors for color checking things—Natalie Kalmus, the wife of the owner of

Technicolor, and her assistant. They would test the costumes for color. They would say, "No, there's too much red there," or "That's too bright," or "We shouldn't put this color against that color." They would work with the designers, so it wasn't a problem for the director. I left those things up to the art director and costumers.

D: You mentioned that the budget for your version of *The Phantom of the Opera* was under $1 million. Yet that was considered a big film by Universal standards.

L: Don't forget that the interior of the opera house itself had been standing since the Lon Chaney days, so there was a big reduction in cost there. All they did was repaint it where the gilt had faded. The biggest expense, I imagine, was building the sewer system underneath the opera house. That's one of my favorite pictures. I'm very proud of it. But afterward the studio ruined Susanna Foster, the leading lady, who had a magnificent voice. They put her in such horrible stories and just let her sing. They didn't seem to realize that all of this business depends on the script.

I feel that the writer is the least credited person in our business. If you haven't got a good script, you can put John Barrymore in the picture and audiences still won't like it. There are damn few fine writers. That's always been the great problem in the entertainment business.

D: Claude Rains was the star of your remake of *Phantom of the Opera*. Was part of his being difficult his desire for perfection?

L: Weeks and weeks before we started shooting the picture, Claude worked with the music department learning how to finger a piano and how to finger a violin. All fine artists in that period studied their parts and tried to figure out little nuances that would appeal and make their interpretation different. Claude spent days practicing how to play, and when we shot those scenes, he insisted on having somebody from the music department watch him to see that his fingering was right.

D: Do you feel that Universal gave you a chance to develop your talent?

L: Only in that they assigned me a great variety of stories. That's the only way contract personnel could develop. I would watch other directors to see what they did, and if I wasn't doing something their way, I would try what they did. Henry Koster always used to start a

shot on a bunch of flowers or something and then pan over to whoever was in the scene. I tried that once and said, "That's not for me."
People used to say to me, "Why do you go to see pictures twice?" And
I'd say, "If it's a good picture, how else am I going to learn?" Young
directors have a tendency to shoot through chairs or from imposing
angles. Instead of telling a straight story, they are more interested in
camera angles.

D: How did you feel about directing *The Spider Woman Strikes Back*?
L: I never saw it, but I hated it. I didn't want to make the picture,
but the studio said they would put me on suspension if I didn't. I had
just bought my home and needed the salary, so I did it.

D: How about *Impact*? Was that a good film for you?
L: *Impact* was an independent production. It was easy to make
because we went on location outside San Francisco. I had a brilliant
New York actor, Charles Coburn, in the cast, and the other actors,
Ella Raines and Brian Donlevy, were good. The script was written
by Mrs. Wallace Reid, but the producer never made another picture
after that.

D: Did you enjoy making the *Francis* films?
L: Very much. It was wonderful for me to see an audience come
out of a theater happy, laughing. Universal was very skeptical of the
idea of a talking mule, and the higher-ups at the studio didn't want to
make the original movie. At first I couldn't sell the idea to anyone. I
had an agent, Mike Levy, who was a very important man. I still have
a letter of his where he said, "Dear Arthur, if anyone buys this script
I'll eat it." Universal only made the picture because they had Donald
O'Connor under contract, and if they didn't have a picture for him
within a certain date, they were going to lose $30,000. The studio
needed the money in those days.

We didn't know how we were going to make the mule talk.
Certainly I didn't know. So the studio gave me $10,000 to see what
we could do. With the mule's trainer, we started out with chewing
gum, and that didn't work. Then we tried tobacco, and the mule got
sick. We tried all kinds of things. Actually we used three mules, but
don't ask me how we made Francis talk. I promised not to tell.

The studio didn't realize what a good comedy they had until the preview. And of course each sequel followed more or less the style of the first picture. The five of them were very successful. I don't think the first *Francis* cost more than $300,000. It was all made on the back lot, the war maneuvers and everything.

D: Why did you decide to use Chill Wills's voice for the mule?

L: We made tests of a lot of people. I felt that a mule, being a big animal, should have a rough voice. I thought the best kind of voice might be somebody like a cowboy, and it worked out that way. We didn't use Chill on *Mister Ed*, the television series that I directed; instead we used Rocky [Allan] Lane, who was a cowboy. Even with those deep voices, we always had to take the soundtrack into the lab and lower the voices to make them even more gravelly.

D: Was Donald O'Connor good to work with?

L: Most actors are wonderful when they start. After a while he got very difficult. He started drinking, and I think he had problems at home. He started swearing at me and being late on the set. Finally I gave up, the same as I did with Abbott and Costello. To be a good comedy actor, the person has to have a sense of timing. Donald knew exactly when to pause to get the laugh.

D: In that series of five *Francis* films, did you find it difficult to keep the shows fresh?

L: No, because the locations were all different. One was at a race track, one was at West Point, one was in New York, where we had Francis crossing Times Square in the middle of the noon rush. Those things added excitement. I never got bored, even doing 143 episodes of *Mister Ed*. Each one was new to me, and each one was a challenge. I tried to make them all a little different.

D: Clint Eastwood, whom you said you discovered, was in one of the *Francis* pictures.

L: I gave him his start. He was in *Francis in the Navy*, a bit part. Later, when I did *The First Traveling Saleslady* at RKO, Clint played his first big part as a Civil War soldier opposite Carol Channing. Then he was in *Escapade in Japan*. I had a contract with him when he began, but I haven't heard from him since.

D: You directed *It Grows on Trees*, Irene Dunne's last film. Was
Dunne pleasant to work with?

L: She was a doll. That whole picture was charming. It was made
during the 1952 election, and there was a lot of politics in the story
about money growing on trees. I think the front office sort of ruined
the comedy in it. There again, theater owners were making decisions
rather than producers.

D: Did you enjoy directing *South Sea Woman*?

L: Very much. I was a little timid about accepting the job because
I had heard that Burt Lancaster was not an easy man to work with. He
had gotten mad at his previous director, Michael Curtiz, and walked
off the set. But I had no problems with him. Everyone has their own
way of handling people. People sometimes say to me, "Why are you so
nice?" or "Why do you start a conversation by asking about someone's
baby before you get to the real subject?" I tell them, "Well, I've got to
knock down a few walls before I explain to people what I want." But
working with Burt was a cinch.

D: Why did your association with Universal come to an end?

L: The only reason I can think of is that I made a bad picture. That
was *Lady Godiva*. Nobody else wanted to do it, so the studio
assigned it to me. If I hadn't taken it, they would have put me on suspension. But that was my last job for Universal.

D: *Footsteps in the Fog* was the picture you made in London for
Mike Frankovich. Was that an interesting experience?

L: Yes. I made several pictures abroad, and I welcomed the opportunity. Everything was paid for. I was given first-class accommodations, I was given a chauffeur and a secretary, and the travel was lovely.
I worked only five days a week, so I had time off to see London. Mike
was a very nice person to work for. I had problems with the leading
man, Stewart Granger, who hated me. He didn't like anything. He
would go to Frankovich and say, "Mike, if Lubin doesn't stop annoying me, I'm going to be sick tomorrow." But miraculously, the picture turned out to be a good one.

The other English picture I made, *Star of India* with Cornel
Wilde, was a disaster. Wilde wrote the script, he wanted to act,
and he wanted to direct. We had a producer who had never made a

picture before, and I was stuck in the middle of Italy with a bad script. They had engaged an actor for the heavy named Herbert Lom. I hadn't met him during the readings we had in London, since he was working on another picture. When I arrived in Torino, the operator at the hotel said, "Mr. Lom would like to see you." Lom came up to my room, introduced himself, and said, "I didn't like the script at all, so I've rewritten my part." I was dumbfounded. I called the producer and said, "Mr. Stross, I won't ask for any money if you'll just let me go home." Ironically Herbert Lom and I have become fabulous friends since then. *Star of India*, however, I never saw. I didn't want to see it.

D: You also made *The Thief of Baghdad* in Italy. Was that an interesting project?

L: The location was interesting, but the picture was hard work. Again, the producer had never made a movie before, and the company was running out of money. I had a complete Italian crew and I don't speak the language. So the work was difficult. By the time I got to Tunis, I had wised up. I had two assistant directors—one who spoke French and one who spoke Tunisian. We were 100 miles into the desert and got up at five in the morning before the sun got too high for us to work.

D: When you were directing *Mr. Ed*, did you find that television work was appreciably different from making feature films?

L: In one respect, yes. You can't take the time to figure out setups. At night I would say to myself, "Now I have this many pages to shoot tomorrow," and I would write down where the camera had to be on each setup. The next day on the set the minute I said "Cut," I'd say, "Now the camera is over here." I knew I had to move fast. I had to shoot a script of thirty pages in three days. At five or six o'clock every afternoon I had to be through, because after that the company went into golden time and that cost extra money. I didn't have the luxury of rehearsing five or six times or doing five or six takes. Usually the first take was it. If a light blew or something happened mechanically, it was the director's fault.

D: In those 143 episodes that you directed of *Mr. Ed*, did you feel at times that the writers were running dry?

L: No, they were very good. We had five writers on *Mr. Ed*. If it hadn't been for George Burns, we would never have had a *Mr. Ed* show. George had a business accountant who was crazy about horses. When the accountant read the script, he went to George with it and said, "I think, because they made Francis talk, you'd be interested in investing in this." George Burns, out of his own pocket, put up $72,000 for the pilot of *Mr. Ed*.

D: Could you run through what an average week's work on *Mr. Ed* was like?

L: When we finished shooting on Monday, the script for the next show was given to everybody. On Tuesday morning at ten o'clock we all sat around a table with the writers and read the script through. Lines that were difficult for the actors were changed. Then we read it through a second time for timing. We had to be sure that we didn't overshoot or that we had enough film. That afternoon the ladies went with the wardrobe mistress to Orbachs to try on clothes, if the proper clothes weren't already in the studio. The men went with their costumer. The next morning we started shooting at eight o'clock sharp. I would be on the set with the crew at seven, give them the first setup, and by the time the actors got there the set was lit and ready to go. At twelve o'clock, because of union rules, we had to give the company an hour for lunch. By that time I had gotten any closeups I could possibly get of the leading ladies, because they were fresher in the morning. The horse we always shot last, because we didn't have to worry about his looks.

D: Where was *Mr. Ed* shot?

L: At the General Service Studio, which is where George Burns worked. No one wanted *Mr. Ed* even after we made the pilot. The executive producer, Al Simon, had a wonderful idea. An automobile company was looking for a television commercial, and Simon got the idea of doing a three-minute show with Ed, as a talking horse, selling the automobile. That's what sold the series. The show was so successful that CBS put it into network prime time.

D: Do you think your approach to filmmaking changed over the years?

L: No, I don't know how it could. I think I'm a good director, but I would never know how to do an automobile chase. I did a baseball picture once, and I went through hell on the day I had to shoot the baseball game. I'm no good at athletics, I was never athletically inclined. I'm not proud of all of my films—eight of them were flops. But my average isn't bad. I love to do comedy because I like making people happy.

D: Do you feel that your professional life contributed to your personal development?

L: I would reverse that. I think my personal life contributed more to the way I directed. I'm a gentle man. I love nice things and happen to be a very good cook. I have wonderful friends, and with the exception of Stewart Granger, who was a horse's ass, I've had few problems with the people I've worked with. A happy set depends largely on how the director treats people, and I preferred a mild approach.

Arthur Lubin's Feature Films

1934 *A Successful Failure*
1935 *Great God Gold*
       Honeymoon Limited
       Two Sinners
       Frisco Waterfront
1936 *The House of a Thousand Candles*
       Yellowstone
1937 *Mysterious Crossing*
       California Straight Ahead
       I Cover the War
       Idol of the Crowd
       Adventure's End
1938 *Midnight Intruder*
       Beloved Brat
       Prison Break
       Secrets of a Nurse

1939	Risky Business
	Big Town Czar
	Mickey the Kid
	Call a Messenger
1940	The Big Guy
	Black Friday
	Gangs of Chicago
	I'm Nobody's Sweetheart Now
	Meet the Wildcat
	Who Killed Aunt Maggie?
1941	San Francisco Docks
	Where Did You Get That Girl?
	Buck Privates
	In the Navy
	Hold That Ghost
	Keep 'Em Flying
1942	Ride 'Em Cowboy
	Eagle Squadron
1943	White Savage
	The Phantom of the Opera
1944	Ali Baba and the 40 Thieves
1945	Delightfully Dangerous
1946	The Spider Woman Strikes Back
	Night in Paradise
1947	New Orleans
1949	Impact
1950	Francis
1951	Queen for a Day
	Francis Goes to the Races
	Rhubarb
1952	Francis Goes to West Point
	It Grows on Trees
1953	South Sea Woman
	Francis Covers the Big Town
1954	Francis Joins the Wacs
1955	Francis in the Navy
	Footsteps in the Fog

Lady Godiva

1956   *Star of India*

The First Traveling Saleslady

1957   *Escapade in Japan*

1961   *The Thief of Baghdad* (in Italy)

1964   *The Incredible Mr. Limpet*

1966   *Hold On!*

1971   *Rain for a Dusty Summer*

Gordon Douglas (left) with Frank Sinatra

GORDON DOUGLAS

Short-Changed Filmmaking

Screen director Gordon Douglas was born in New York City on December 5, 1909. He moved to Hollywood in the late 1920s and eventually directed motion pictures at RKO, Columbia, Warner Bros., and Twentieth Century-Fox, specializing first in comedy and later in action and adventure films. His work in such movies as *The Iron Mistress*, *Young at Heart*, and *Santiago* is polished and technically efficient, yet seldom displays a strong personal style. After prolonged illness Douglas died in California in 1993.

The following interview was taped in the director's home in Los Angeles on July 23, 1987.

RD: As a boy growing up in New York, was theater an important part of your life?
GD: Yes. I was raised in Brooklyn. Across the street from where we lived was Maurice Costello's home. Maurice Costello was a big star. He had two daughters, Delores and Helen. There was a Vitagraph studio in Brooklyn, and anytime Costello made a picture with kids, he always wanted me there, along with his daughters. He was disappointed, I believe, that he didn't have a son. He paid more attention to me than to his daughters.
RD: What was the Vitagraph studio like?
GD: It was kind of crummy, in comparison with the studios on the West Coast. I came to California on a freighter. I worked for my passage, which was a real experience.
RD: I know that early in your career you went to work in the MGM offices.

GD: That was in New York. I worked as a clerk in advertising. That was a very dull job. In the summertime I used to work at Lunar Park, which was a famous, fun place in those days. When I analyze it, every dollar I've ever earned has come from show biz in one form or another.
RD: What was your first job in California?
GD: I went to work for Hal Roach, which I enjoyed. Roach was one of the greatest guys I've ever known. He was a pleasure to work for. He kind of took a liking to me. He said, "Look, I want you to work in a lot of different departments." So I worked as a prop man, I swept the stage, took over for a guy in the cutting room, and finally worked as an assistant director. I was also a gag writer for a while. We would sit around and make up gags, and half the guys were falling asleep. From there, Roach assigned me to assist on the *Our Gang* pictures. That was a real break. I loved the man I was working with, a guy named Gus Meins, and I got along great with the kids. When Hal Roach was ready to assign Gus Meins to direct a feature picture, he called me in and said, "Gus Meins is going to direct a feature, so I want you to start directing *Our Gang*." Boy, I was scared. I went on the set, and everybody was looking at me. I was at bat. I thought, "Oh, my God, what do I do?" But during the brief time I spent in the cutting room, I had learned quite a bit about coverage of scenes. Later you just naturally fall into that, but I had to study it a little bit in the beginning.
RD: Did the technical aspects of filmmaking interest you?
GD: Not too much. I enjoyed working with the kids and found myself using different approaches. Each kid was a problem, so there were all kinds of relationships. My relationship with the Gang was much friendlier that Gus Meins's had been. He would stand back, whereas I used to love playing with the kids. On Saturdays we used to play miniature golf. I got a lot of good breaks in the picture business. Things just kind of came together.
RD: Was there a great deal of improvisation on the *Our Gang* films?
GD: I wouldn't say a great deal, but there was always some. The printed word sometimes doesn't get on film. Sometimes you have to readjust and play loose. I had fun doing those pictures. I made about thirty of them. Each one in itself was a little different challenge. Then finally I directed Laurel and Hardy in a feature.
RD: That was *Saps at Sea*?
GD: Yes. The picture wasn't too good, but it got laughs. They used to clock laughs. You'd go to a preview and there was a clocker.

You'd get X number of ticks on the clock and that was either good or not so good.

RD: What was Stan Laurel like?

GD: Stan was a very hard-working guy, a very serious guy. He would work a lot on the stories. Babe [Oliver Hardy] was out playing golf. Stan had a lot of bad marriages. But he had a great gag mind. He could think of gags and really funny business. When you analyze their pictures, there was always a story thread in them. They played characters, people that we've all met—one that's stupid and thinks he's smart, a dopey guy who tops the supposedly brainy one. Stan and Ollie were two great guys, but they split up. There was some kind of argument between the two of them. Then Roach wanted to make a picture with Babe Hardy and Harry Langdon. I got involved with that.

RD: That was *Zenobia*?

GD: Yes. First it was called *So This Is Spring*. I don't know where the hell they got *Zenobia*. What a title!

RD: How would you describe the Hal Roach studio?

GD: I would describe it as a very healthy, warm family. We ground out pictures but it wasn't work, it was fun. There was no back stabbing, and everybody was on the same level as everybody else.

RD: What would you say was Hal Roach's special talent?

GD: He had a great funnybone, no question about it. He was a warm guy. I can't think of anything on the wrong side to say about Hal. To me he will always be the best in that field. I don't expect to see anybody top him.

RD: By "that field" you mean the comedy field?

GD: No, the whole business. The business has changed so much. Of course I've been out of it for quite a while.

RD: When you left Hal Roach, you went to RKO. How would you compare the situation at RKO with what you'd experienced at Hal Roach's studio?

GD: About 110 degrees different. There were a lot of guys at RKO that were good, but there were some real backbiters there. RKO didn't have the warmth that the Roach studio had, no way.

RD: Among other things, wasn't RKO in financial trouble?

GD: Yes, I think so. I think the lack of a team was the cause of that. People there couldn't seem to pull with each other, they pulled against. I enjoyed myself, but not as much as I did with Hal. It was like another business.

RD: I know that you made several *Gildersleeve* films at RKO. Were they fun?

GD: No. Hal Peary, with that crazy laugh of his, had a radio audience as Gildersleeve, and all of a sudden they were going to make him an actor. It was pretty tough. I liked Hal, he was a nice guy. But it was tough to write a script for this man and have an audience stay for sixty or seventy minutes.

RD: You also directed at least one of the *Dick Tracy* movies.

GD: Yes, *Dick Tracy vs. Cueball*. That was another one of those damned things. When we were under contract to a studio, if we turned a picture down, there was no check. We were suspended for the duration of that picture. Unfortunately, I had to get a check because I had my mother and father to take care of. I had been married for a short time, and I had a wife and her mother to take care of. I couldn't afford suspension.

RD: One director told me that being a director under contract was like having the morning newspaper thrown at your door; you shot whatever script they threw at you.

GD: Raoul Walsh told me when I first signed with Warner Bros., "Let me tell you something, Gordie, there'll be a script on your front lawn every morning." Raoul was a great action director and a wonderful man.

RD: How did you feel about working with Eddie Cantor on *If You Knew Susie?*

GD: Eddie Cantor never belonged on the screen in my opinion. He was a very selfish man. Joan Davis, his costar in the picture, was a talented person. It was tough to get anything out of them, because Joan would give but Eddie Cantor acted like he was playing on the stage. I kept telling him, "Tone it down, tone it down. You're working too hard, just talk." He'd try to get a laugh with every line. I didn't get along too well with Cantor.

RD: When you left RKO, you went to Columbia. How did you find conditions there?

GD: I didn't like Harry Cohn. I didn't like him at all. He pulled a fast boner on me. He and I didn't get along too well. He called me into his office and said, "You don't like me, do you?" I said, "Not too much." He said, "Well, I have a script here that I want you to make, and I want the picture to cost at least $3 million." In those days a $3 million picture was exceptional. Cohn said, "I want you to take the script home and read it." I took it home, and it was a good script. The next day I was having lunch with George Marshall, and he said to me, "What's your next assignment?" I said, "Cohn's just given me a script." He said, "What's the title." I told him, and Marshall said, "I'm going to make that picture!" I went back to see Cohn and said, "What's with telling me to read a script when you've already assigned the picture to somebody else?" Cohn made some lame-brained excuse, and we got into an argument. At one point he said to me, "You can't talk to me that way! If you say anything like that again, I'll come around this desk and beat you up." I said, "Come that way, it's a shorter walk. I'll knock you on your ass." And I walked out.

RD: While you were at Columbia, did you enjoy making *The Black Arrow*?

GD: Yes, I liked those swashbuckling pictures. I used to call them "clack-clack" pictures, because the swords were always going "clack, clack, clack" in fights.

RD: Was Louis Hayward good to work with?

GD: He was a very nice guy and had a beautiful accent. Louis always seemed to be on edge. He had trouble relaxing. The main thing for me as director was to relax my actors, get them comfortable. I don't think you can get a performance from a person who's all tied up in knots. I made about three pictures with Louis.

RD: Another of them was *Walk a Crooked Mile*.

GD: That was a good picture. Dennis O'Keefe was in it with Louis.

RD: Was *Mr. Soft Touch* a good picture?

GD: That was a fair picture. I got annoyed at one point and went to Cohn and said, "I'm stuck. This doesn't add up at all. The scene needs a complete rewrite." He argued with me and said, "There are a lot of ways you can handle that." When I asked him how, he thought for a while, then pressed the button on his intercom and told his secretary, "Send that goddamned writer in here!"

RD: Did you feel that the Rita Hayworth pictures at Columbia were the ones that got the big budgets while yours were sort of short-changed?

GD: Yes, sure. Rita was a very good friend of my first wife, the wife who died from cancer. Rita was a really nice girl, but so insecure. It's a shame how many people in this business are insecure. It's unbelievable.

RD: Did you like making Westerns?

GD: I liked all types of pictures.

RD: I had in mind the Westerns you made at Columbia with Randolph Scott: *The Doolins of Oklahoma* and *The Nevadan.*

GD: I enjoyed working with Randy. He was a fine gentleman and a good person.

RD: Did Harry Cohn have the final word on all of the pictures made at Columbia, or were the producers there also powerful? For example, on *The Doolins of Oklahoma* the producer was Harry Joe Brown.

GD: Cohn was on the throne; the rest of us were serfs.

RD: Another clack-clack picture, I guess, would have been *Rogues of Sherwood Forest.*

GD: Definitely clack-clack. It was fun. Our leading lady [Diana Lynn] had to squint her eyes when she was in the sunlight. When I saw the dailies, it looked like she had her eyes closed. I had to put her under an awning and do those scenes over. John Derek, the star of the picture, was prettier than the leading lady. He really was a gorgeous man. A closeup of John Derek was a beautiful thing to look at.

RD: Did you find Warner Bros. a different situation?

GD: Yes. I liked Jack Warner. He could be very cruel, but later he would kind of straighten things out in order not to feel quite as guilty as he really was. He loved to stand and talk to me, and he'd always maneuver himself so that I got the sun. But I had fun with Jack, he was a funny guy. One time I was walking across the lot coming from the private dining room, and I passed Jack's brother, Harry Warner. Harry said to me, "Is my dumb brother up there?" I didn't know what the hell to say. But Harry referred to Jack as his "dumb brother."

RD: Was Steve Trilling a force at Warners?

GD: Steve Trilling was Jack Warner's whipping boy, and Jack whipped Steve a lot. Steve was a fine man and a real gentleman. Some men are unlucky and don't deserve the position they wind up in. I guess that's the way it is in all businesses.

RD: Was Warners a relaxed lot?

GD: I'd say that Warners was more relaxed than RKO or Columbia. I was under contract there for about twelve years. I worked several times with Henry Blanke, whom I consider one of the finest producers. I worked on maybe four or five pictures that Blanke produced. He was a great little guy and used to walk around speaking with his German accent. He was probably a finer producer than anyone I've ever worked with.

RD: Do you have good recollections of *Only the Valiant*?

GD: No, not too good. They short-changed the picture. I enjoyed Gregory Peck a great deal—a fine, wonderful person. But that certainly wouldn't be a picture I would pay to see.

RD: By "short-changed" do you mean skimped on the budget?

GD: Yes, they did things on the picture that were beneath a man like Peck. They should have considered rewriting a little more, extending the schedule a little more. I used to fight about that. We ran into a lot of bad weather. The money kept going out, but nobody could work because of wind storms and hail storms. I don't think Mr. Peck thought much of the picture either. It wasn't a good picture.

RD: How was working with Errol Flynn on *Mara Maru*?

GD: Flynn was great up until three o'clock in the afternoon. Shooting a scene about 2:30 he'd be fine. I'd go into his dressing room and we'd talk, and he'd have what I thought was a glass of water. It was straight gin or vodka. Then he'd come on the set and he'd be stoned. He'd start hamming it up. I'd yell, "Cut," and tell him, "You're really eating scenery, man." He'd say, "No, I was fine." I'd have the shot printed early, and the next morning he'd be horrified when he saw the rushes. "Get rid of that film!" he'd say. Errol was a nice person, but unfortunately a terrible drinker. Believe me, he would have died at twenty-two if he'd done all the things he was given credit for doing. No man could take that.

RD: Did you enjoy making *The Iron Mistress*?

GD: Yes, I liked it. I liked it because there was one scene in the picture that I loved. That was the scene where Alan Ladd was to duel with this guy. Ladd laid out the conditions to the fellow he was supposed to fight. He said, "We'll fight in a dark room with Bowie knives." That reads well on paper, but how are you going to photograph a scene in an almost black room? So I had lightning flashes and big head closeups. It was storming, with lightning and thunder, and I liked that. But there were other things in the picture that were nice. I always liked Virginia Mayo, she was a wonderful gal. I made four or five pictures with her. I think Virginia Mayo got a dirty deal from the business. I think she was a far better actress than most people realized.

RD: Was Alan Ladd a secure performer?

GD: No, far from it. We did a picture called *The McConnell Story*, and we were on location. Alan and his family had one bungalow, and I had a bungalow twenty yards away. The morning the picture was to start shooting I heard somebody in Alan Ladd's bungalow throwing up and coughing and gagging. When Alan came on the set, I said. "Somebody was sick over at your place. Who was it?" Alan said, "Nobody was sick." I said, "Well, I heard somebody throwing up." He said, "Oh, I always do that when a picture starts." Alan was afraid of dialogue. He'd go behind the set and throw up. His was a sad story. He started hitting the jug, too. But Alan was basically a very lovable guy.

RD: Was he truly sensitive about being short?

GD: Definitely. I remember one day Alan said he was talking to Jimmy Stewart, and Alan's wife, Sue Carol, came by. She said to him, "Get up on the steps a little bit, Alan." Jimmy Stewart was over six feet tall, and Alan was about five feet six or seven inches. He used to wear lifts in his shoes, which threw him off-balance all the time. He'd have to have plank inclines three or four inches high to walk on, while whomever he was playing the scene with was on the stage floor.

RD: How did you feel about making *She's Back on Broadway* with Virginia Mayo?

GD: That was fun, but it was a cheater again. The script wasn't good. You've got to have it on paper before you can make a good picture. Virginia Mayo was under contract, and she didn't want to be put on suspension either. We talked it over and decided we didn't have much choice. Virginia was a beautiful lady.

RD: What was your attitude toward 3-D when you directed *The Charge at Feather River*?

GD: There was a scene where Frank Lovejoy couldn't move; he was hidden and he wanted to stay hidden from the Indians. All of a sudden a rattlesnake slithered over to him. He had to get that rattlesnake away, so he spit. One reviewer wrote, "Gordon Douglas makes use of 3-D by having actors spit into the camera."

RD: How did you feel about *So This Is Love*, which was the story of opera singer Grace Moore?

GD: I used to say, "So this is love—and the next time it's two dollars." I thought Kathryn Grayson was a wonderful gal. One time I was looking at her, and frankly I was thinking sex. She said, "Are you undressing me?" I said, "You're stripped." She worried about a crying scene she had in the picture. I told her not to worry. The line in the script was, "You'll never sing again, Grace Moore." When we got to the scene, I told her to think, "Kathryn Grayson, you'll never sing again." Apparently she did that, and tears started coming to her eyes.

RD: What do you remember most about making *Them!*

GD: I was working with James Whitmore, Edmund Gwenn, and James Arness, and the studio had concocted these giant ants. This was a science fiction picture. We were on location, and the cutter came out to see me. I said to him, a guy named Tommy Riley, "How are the dailies? Do the ants look real? Do they look honest?" And he said, "As honest as a twelve-foot ant can look." (Both laugh.)

RD: Did you work well with Frank Sinatra on *Young at Heart*?

GD: I liked Frank. Frank had high ups and low lows. The problem on that picture was that Doris Day liked a lot of rehearsal and Frank didn't. The more we rehearsed I realized that she was getting better and Frank was going down. So I had to kind of reach a happy medium. I would tell Frank, "Walk through a couple of rehearsals. Walk through it, and then when we get ready for the take, you can go all out." So that's the way we did it.

RD: How did you feel about *Sincerely Yours*, the picture you made with Liberace?

GD: We went up to San Francisco to preview that picture. The theater was jam-packed, and I was sitting in a little balcony. I looked down and everybody there, it seemed to me, was either in a wheelchair or about to go into one. I didn't see any young people at all. I was sitting next to Henry Blanke, who produced the picture, and I said, "Do you think there'll be anybody here tomorrow?" He said, "What do you mean?" I said, "The youth are not here, Henry." The next day the theater opened with this picture and by noon it was packed, but that afternoon attendance started dropping off. That night there was nobody in the damned theater. That happened every place this picture opened. It broke a lot of records the first day, but that was Liberace's audience.

RD: You worked with Virginia Mayo again on *Fort Dobbs*.

GD: Yes. Some of these pictures sort of run together in my mind. Sometimes I get a flash when I watch television, and it will remind me of something. The picture comes right at me, but I can't remember what it was or who was in it. It gets me mad as hell. I feel like I'm losing my marbles.

RD: Did you enjoy working with Elvis Presley on *Follow That Dream*?

GD: Elvis was a good actor and played some damned good scenes. He could do more than sing. I often wondered why they called that film *Follow That Dream*. It sounded like a Doris Day picture. The picture played pretty damned well, and Elvis was a wonderful person. He had a lot of guys hanging around him, parasites.

RD: How about Bob Hope? Was working with him on *Call Me Bwana* a good experience?

GD: Hope was a funny guy. He had two or three sets of writers. I didn't know about that. We would come in in the morning to shoot, and he'd say, "I've got some new material for you to look at. I got this from such-and-such a writer, and that's from such-and-such. I like this joke better. Which one do you like? Bob was a stand-up comic, and he liked those good joke lines. The audience accepted that. If you did something else with Hope, they wouldn't like it.

RD: You worked with Sinatra again on *Robin and the Seven Hoods*.

GD: Sinatra and Bing Crosby and Dean Martin and Sammy Davis, Jr. and Peter Falk. We were shooting a scene in a cemetery when we heard that President Kennedy had been shot. Several crew members were there with portable radios. I remember walking away, and the next thing I remember is coming face-to-face with Frank Sinatra among the gravestones. Frank had tears in his eyes. Mine were also quite moist. I looked over and Frank said, "What the hell are we going to do, Gordie?" Then later on during the making of the picture, Sinatra's son was kidnapped. Frank always came in on time, always knew his dialogue. I've heard so many crappy stories about Frank, and they're ridiculous. He's a very warm guy. I regard him as a real friend.

RD: Was making *Harlow* an interesting experience?

GD: Yes. Unfortunately, Carroll Baker was very sick, physically and also mentally, I think. She was going through bad times with her husband. But she did a hell of a good job on the picture.

RD: You were brave to do a remake of *Stagecoach*.

GD: That was a big mistake. I had a crazy producer, Marty Rackin. I said, "Why are we going to do this?" It was mad. Ann-Margret was playing a broken-down hooker who's run out of town. In those days Ann-Margret was a young and beautiful girl. I forget what ranch we were working on, but there was an altitude problem. I got dizzy and had a tough time breathing. At night I quit work, went to eat dinner at the cabin, and got ready for bed. Bing Crosby, who was in the cast, would come in, smoking his pipe, and we'd start talking. We'd sit there all evening. Sometimes there was conversation, sometimes there was no conversation. Bing was a real pro.

RD: In the remake you recreated the famous wagon stunt that Yakima Canutt had devised for the original *Stagecoach*.
GD: I love stunt men. They are a special breed. They're flirting with disaster all the time. When they weren't shooting a picture, they'd be working with their horses. Some of them had a couple of horses they were working with all the time.
RD: In the 1960s you made a number of pictures at Twentieth Century-Fox. Were you under contract there?
GD: It was a two-picture-a-year deal, for three years.
RD: What was the Fox lot like?
GD: I liked Fox very much, and I liked Dick Zanuck, Darryl's son. He was a fine producer.
RD: Did you find Sidney Poitier a talented actor when you directed him in *They Call Me Mr. Tibbs*?
GD: He was wonderful, a real gentleman. I've been lucky. There was only one actor, and I'll not mention his name, that I really disliked. Otherwise my relationships with actors were mostly pleasant. Some actors you have to more or less kick around a little bit; others you have to pet a little bit and baby them. But I worked on at least fifty pictures, and I had the pleasure to directing many talented people, some only in small roles.
RD: Why did you decide to leave filmmaking?
GD: Physically I ran into some problems. I've been operated on so many times. It seems to me I'd be operated on, recuperate, and it'd be time for another operation.
RD: Do you feel that your professional life contributed to your personal development?
GD: Yes. I wish I could go back and do some of the pictures I made over again. A studio or a director or a producer doesn't start out to make a bad picture. You try to make as good a picture as you can. If you get a really good script, that's money in the bank. A director can add a little something, put a couple of extra roses in, but it's got to be on paper first.
RD: As you look back, what is your assessment of the big studio system and the long-term contract arrangement?
GD: When we were under contract to a studio, we had security. For two years I had a little bit of my salary sliced off so that I would be paid for three years. That was better for tax purposes. But I ended up

broke anyway. I had a nice time during my career, but close the book on it and forget it.

Gordon Douglas's Feature Films

1936   *General Spanky* (co-directed with Fred Newmeyer)
1939   *Zenobia*
1940   *Saps at Sea*
1941   *Road Show* (co-directed with Hal Roach and Hal Roach, Jr.)
    Broadway Limited
    Niagara Falls
1942   *The Devil with Hitler*
    The Great Gildersleeve
1943   *Gildersleeve's Bad Day*
    Gildersleeve on Broadway
1944   *A Night of Adventure*
    Gildersleeve's Ghost
    Girl Rush
    The Falcon in Hollywood
1945   *Zombies on Broadway*
    First Yank in Tokyo
1946   *Dick Tracy vs. Cueball*
    San Quentin
1948   *If You Knew Susie*
    The Black Arrow
    Walk a Crooked Mile
1949   *Mr. Soft Touch* (co-directed with Henry Levin)
    The Doolins of Oklahoma
1950   *The Nevadan*
    The Fortunes of Captain Blood
    Rogues of Sherwood Forest
    Kiss Tomorrow Goodbye
    Between Midnight and Dawn
1951   *The Great Missouri Raid*
    Only the Valiant
    I Was a Communist for the FBI
    Come Fill the Cup

1952   *Mara Maru*
        The Iron Mistress
1953   *She's Back on Broadway*
        The Charge at Feather River
        So This Is Love
1954   *Them*
        Young at Heart
1955   *The McConnell Story*
        Sincerely Yours
1956   *Santiago*
1957   *The Big Land*
        Bombers B-52
1958   *Fort Dobbs*
        The Fiend Who Walked the West
1959   *Up Periscope*
        Yellowstone Kelly
1961   *Gold of the Seven Saints*
        The Sins of Rachel Cade
        Claudelle Inglish
1962   *Follow That Dream*
1963   *Call Me Bwana*
1964   *Robin and the 7 Hoods*
        Rio Conchos
1965   *Sylvia*
        Harlow
1966   *Stagecoach*
        Way . . . Way Out
1967   *In Like Flint*
        Chuka
        Tony Rome
1968   *The Detective*
        Lady in Cement
1970   *Skullduggery*
        Barquero
        They Call Me Mr. Tibbs
1973   *Slaughter's Big Rip-Off*
1977   *Viva Knievel!*

BUDD BOETTICHER

Struggling for Quality

Screen director Budd Boetticher was born Oscar Boetticher, Jr., on July 29, 1916, in Chicago. A varsity boxer and football player, he dropped out of Ohio State University and went to Mexico, where he became a professional matador. After serving as technical adviser on the classic bullfight film *Blood and Sand* (1941), Boetticher worked as assistant director on a number of Hollywood movies and made his debut as a film director in 1944. He worked mostly on low-budget pictures, but the semi-autobiographical *The Bullfighter and the Lady* earned him a contract with Universal, where he made such features as *Horizons West*, *The Man from the Alamo*, and *Wings of the Hawk*. Between 1956 and 1960 he directed a series of Westerns starring Randolph Scott that enhanced his reputation, particularly in Europe. An avid horseman, Boetticher died in southern California in November 2001.

The following interview was taped in the director's home in Ramona, California, on August 13, 1988.

D: As a boy in Chicago were you particularly interested in movies?
B: I was only a boy in Chicago for about two weeks. I was born in Chicago and raised in Evansville, Indiana, and I was always very interested in movies. That's what we did on Saturday afternoons when we were grade school kids, and what we did on Sunday afternoons when we were in high school.
D: You made a number of Westerns. Were you fascinated with the mythic West as a child?
B: I made ten Westerns. Western fans call me a Western director, whereas the bullfight fans call me the bullfight director. I made one

gangster picture, *Legs Diamond*, so I'm also a gangster director. I realized that every picture I made might be my last, and I really put out
to make each one worthwhile. I love the industry, but I knew that each
picture had to be a success. I think films are like the hundred meter
dash: it's all your fault if you lose, and it's all to your credit if you win.
Nobody is going to help you. There's too much "help" today. I was on
a set recently with a very well known, talented director, and every
time he would say "cut" they would have a meeting. That wasn't the
way I made pictures. The minute I said "cut, print," I knew where to
go next and was ready to continue.

D: Growing up in the Midwest, you must have heard a great deal
about the frontier West.

B: No, I didn't. I didn't know anything about it. I never saw a
western saddle until I came to California. I was raised on horseback
as a hunter and a jumper. But cowboys were a far cry from anything
I did. There were no cowboys in evidence in Indiana.

D: When you enrolled in Ohio State, what kind of career did you
envision for yourself?

B: I was interested in Ohio State because there was a well-known football coach there, and my high school team had been national champions.
I went to Ohio State specifically to play football. If Jesse Owens hadn't
been there as a senior, I would have gone there to run, but I didn't figure
I could compete with Owens. Before that I'd attended Culver Military
Institute for two years after high school. While I was at Ohio State a
football injury, I thought, ruined my life. That really was the beginning
of my career. I went to Mexico in 1939 on the way around South
America for a long vacation to heal my football injury. Fortunately my
family had money. Sometimes it's difficult to grow up with a silver
spoon in your mouth, and I had that trouble. I was disowned several
times because I went into the motion picture business. When I was
seventeen, my father said to me one day, "Oscar, I can't understand why
you don't want to take over the family's hardware concern." I wanted
to make it on my own. I wanted to go on to more exciting things.

D: In Mexico didn't you study bullfighting with Lorenzo Garza?

B: Yes. I was at a big party. It was the Sunday night after the first
bullfight I'd ever seen, and I was tremendously intrigued with what
I'd seen. Lorenzo Garza had fought that afternoon, and it was done so

beautifully and so gracefully and so bravely. I was thrilled. That night at the cocktail party I was up to my hairline in enthusiasm. I wanted to become a bullfighter. I met Lorenzo Garza the next day. I recreated our meeting in *The Bullfighter and the Lady*, my first really good picture, in which Robert Stack played me.

D: I know that your introduction to the movie industry was as a technical advisor on *Blood and Sand*.

B: Yes. That was a great experience, although I hated the director, Rouben Mamoulian. I was very young and very arrogant and a fine athlete. I wasn't used to being told what to do and where to stand. Mamoulian had a bell on the left side of his director's chair that he rang for Robert Webb, his assistant, and one on the right side of the chair that he rang for me. We stood in front of him and he told us what he wanted from us. I felt since I was technical director on bull-fighting he should ask me questions, and I would tell him what to do and he would do it. Later Mamoulian became a great friend of mine and I really learned to love and admire him. I realized that I had had a chip on my shoulder earlier. But I figured out working with him on *Blood and Sand* that I wanted to be a director. It was such a romantic picture, and it gave me a taste of Hollywood.

D: Did you go from Mexico to Hollywood?

B: Yes. Darryl Zanuck, who produced *Blood and Sand*, wanted to see me. I walked into his office and he said to me, "Young man, you have five minutes to tell me all you know about bullfighting." I had a cape, a muleta, a sword, and a bunch of pictures in my suitcase. I said, "Mr. Zanuck, that's like a bunch of atheists telling a Catholic that he's got five minutes to tell them all about Catholicism." He said, "Now you've got four-and-a-half minutes." Zanuck ended up running a chair playing the bull for me, while I made a few passes with my cape. Then he made a few passes and I played the bull. So I got the job on *Blood and Sand*.

D: Didn't you work for a while at the Hal Roach studio?

B: Yes, I worked for Hal Roach. Hal, Jr., was my very best friend. His father, even in old age, was also a dear friend. He was my real mentor, he was like my uncle. He was closer to me than my father and I ever were. I went to work for Roach as a messenger boy. It was wonderful, because Milton Bren, Frank Capra, Gordon Douglas, and

George Stevens were all on the lot at the time. I was making $46 a week. But as my career progressed, all of these men to whom I used to deliver letters helped me in the industry, especially George Stevens.

D: I know that you were assistant director to Stevens on *The More the Merrier*. What kind of person was he?

B: George was an absolute delight, besides being a great director. He hated Harry Cohn. He had a backboard made, and whenever Cohn came on the set, I would toss Stevens a tennis ball. He would play hand-ball with himself until Cohn left. Cohn looked a lot like Mussolini and was a tyrant. But he gave me my first directing job.

D: How would you describe the Columbia lot at that time?

B: It was a small studio, but Columbia was making wonderful pictures. They had Capra, they had Stevens, they had Bill Seiter, and they had a lot of good B directors. They had a B unit, the Briskin unit, where they gave people like me an opportunity to direct ten and twelve-day pictures and learn the business. Those pictures cost no more than $100,000. My first picture was a "Boston Blackie" picture. The reviewer for the *Hollywood Reporter* wrote, "This picture wasn't released, it escaped." So I figured after that I had only one way to go—up. I was once asked, "When did you realize that you were a full-fledged Hollywood director?" And I said, "After about ten pictures." If you watch your mistakes and don't make them again, you've got to learn something. Directing is like any art form or any athletic form: the more you're allowed to do, the better you get. The studio let us make $100,000 pictures and make terrible mistakes because they knew those pictures would be the second feature on a double bill. So we had an opportunity that young film directors don't have today. I was twenty-five when I became a director. Few people saw my early pictures, so they didn't know how bad I was for a long time.

D: Was the B picture wing at Columbia separate and apart from A pictures?

B: The B pictures that I made were D, E, and F pictures. They were little tiny pictures.

D: Was *One Mysterious Night* one of them?

B: That was the first one; it was a "Boston Blackie" picture. Chester Morris and Janis Carter played the leads, and Dorothy Malone, who was just a teenager, was in it. That was a learning period for me, although I was too cocky in those days to take suggestions from anybody. I figured they were probably right and if I listened to them everybody would start directing the picture. I didn't know what I was doing but I had a wonderful gimmick, and it really worked. I would make a suggestion, and the cameraman would look at me like, "You've got to be kidding." I would pat him on the shoulder and look into his eyes and say, "You really don't know what I'm doing, do you?" I'd walk away, and everybody would think, "My God, maybe this guy is another Orson Welles." So they left me alone.

D: A couple of your early films were made for Eagle-Lion.

B: Working at Eagle-Lion was a lot of fun. I had a two-picture deal there. One picture was with Gene Raymond, and the other was with Lucille Bremer, a delightful gal, who later married the son of the president of Mexico.

D: Then you went to Monogram.

B: Yes. I made five pictures at Monogram that Lindsley Parsons produced. They were inexpensive pictures, but I did have the pleasure of working three times with Roddy McDowall. Those were fun days, but they weren't artistic days.

D: How would you compare the Monograph setup with Columbia?

B: I made better pictures at Monogram than I made at Columbia, but there was no comparison between the two studios. Columbia was a bigger studio, but I wasn't in a position to make big pictures when I was there.

D: Do you have vivid recollections of filming *The Wolf Hunters* at Monogram?

B: *The Wolf Hunters* was wonderful. We were all out of work until that picture came along. Everybody in that picture was a close personal friend of mine. We had a great, wonderful time. We went up to Big Bear to make the picture in the snow. The star of the picture was a white German shepherd. Everybody got out of financial trouble, so it was a great experience.

D: How about *Killer Shark*?

B: *Killer Shark* we made in Ensenada. We had the same group of people in that. It was a better picture than *The Wolf Hunters*. Doug Fowley, who went on to become one of the great character actors in Hollywood and often played a gangster in George Raft's pictures, got seasick out beyond the twelve-mile limit and vomited up his false teeth. We didn't have the money to come back in for him to get another set. So all the way through the picture we shot him without his teeth.

D: Was *The Bullfighter and the Lady* your breakthrough into A pictures?

B: *Bullfighter and the Lady* was supposed to be a B picture. Without John Wayne we never could have made it. His company produced the picture. Duke and I fought a lot. He was a bastard on one side and a wonderful guy on the other. But that film was my breakthrough. It should have been, because by that time I knew what I was doing and it was the story of my life. John Ford saw the picture and recommended to Wayne that forty-two minutes be cut out of it. He did that because Wayne and his writer, James Edward Grant, thought that *Bullfighter and the Lady* was a fiasco. We made the picture for practically nothing. In the cast we had Robert Stack, who was the pride of the Bel-Air circuit, Katy Jurado, who had played nothing but prostitutes, and Gilbert Roland, who had been the Cisco Kid in B pictures. So nobody expected our picture to be very good. What Ford cut out was what he called "all that chi-chi crap." That was the relationship between the great bullfighter and his protégé. Ford figured that two men couldn't love one another unless the relationship was homosexual. Well, that's a lot of baloney. I think strong men don't have to worry about their virility.

D: Was Gilbert Roland good to work with?

B: There are very few people in the industry that I really dislike, but he was one of them. I cast Gilbert because he looked the part. I've never had problems with an actor in my life like I had with Roland. I absolutely loathed the man, but he was great in the picture.

D: Did Victor Young's score contribute a great deal to *Bullfighter and the Lady*?

B: Tremendously. Vic was just great, and he loved the picture. One of the great moments of my life was sitting there while the orchestra dubbed the music to *Bullfighter and the Lady*. The musicians knew

I was there. When the lights came up, the orchestra members all stood up and turned around and applauded. I thought, "Boy, this was worth it."

D: Soon after that film you went under contract to Universal.

B: I had a choice of Universal or Metro, and I went to Universal because I liked the people there. I made a mistake because I didn't like Universal. I thought it was a factory, and it's worse now. I think that any major studio whose prime desire is to make a lot of money out of their showcase, putting people on a bus and giving them a tour, has hurt the industry a great deal. Movies used to be glamorous. Now everybody knows about special effects. I really hated that studio. I had some nice experiences there, and there was one man at Universal that I really cared about. That was Aaron Rosenberg. He was a wonderful producer. I thought he was great.

D: I knew that you had worked with Rosenberg on several films. What was his strength as a producer?

B: He was an all-American football player, but instead of being brutal and tough, he was one of the most sensitive men I have ever known. We fought a lot and once came to a point where we damned near had a physical fight. But we ended up great friends. I thought he was honest, and I thought he cared about being a good producer. He was concerned about quality. Nobody else at Universal cared. I made nine pictures at the studio in two years, with only Sundays off. I got a call from Katy Jurado in Mexico, and she said, "Budd, you're going to ruin yourself. You're making pictures like tortillas." And I was. It was very difficult because I was hot then. Whether producers on the lot wanted me or not, they thought it was a good idea to take me as their director. I would read a script sitting on the set and finish one picture the week before I started the next one. That's not the way to make movies.

D: Physically, what was the Universal lot like?

B: It had everything. Lots of wide-open spaces. I kept one of my horses there at the stable, and after work I would go riding in the spring and summer. I could ride where we shot all those Western pictures. I couldn't see the freeway, I couldn't see a building. It isn't like that anymore.

D: Was *Red Ball Express* an interesting movie for you?

B: *Red Ball Express* was a lot of fun. Aaron Rosenberg produced that. It was really the first *Patton*, but we weren't allowed to use Patton's name, so we had to call our general something else. *Red Ball Express* was the story of a black company in the military. They were the boys at Fort Benning that were taught to drive trucks into combat. Patton got himself stuck behind the German lines, and these boys drove trucks into the war zone. A lot of them lost their lives. I wanted to tell the truth about the sacrifices, but of course Universal wouldn't let me. These boys were our kamikazi pilots during World War II, although we never admitted that. Part of the charm of that picture for me was that it was Sidney Poitier's first big picture, and he was a sensation. It was the first time Sidney had had a chance to really act. He did a scene with Jeff Chandler that was pure genius. There was a place called Nigger Town near Fort Eustace, Virginia, and the blacks in our company had to eat down there. This was 1951. I wasn't allowed down there, so I didn't see much of some people I really cared about.

D: Was *The Cimarron Kid* the first time you worked with Audie Murphy?

B: Yes. Audie was a lot better actor than people thought. We became very good friends, and like good friends do, we fought now and then. But when you win a Congressional Medal of Honor when you're eighteen years old, as Audie did, even Hollywood isn't terribly exciting. I think that's what killed him. He just never could relive his youth.

D: Do you have fond memories of making *Horizons West*?

B: Not really. Although that was Julie Adams's first picture with me. I think I cared more about Julie than any other actress I worked with. Personally, I mean. If Julie hadn't been married, I would have done my best to steal her. She is quite a lady. I went to Brazil to get away from that situation, and I'm not sure Julie even knew that. I was very much in love with her. But there were other good people in the picture. Robert Ryan was the best, and Rock Hudson was a delight. The studio at the time was trying to make a Western star out of Rock.

D: Was Rock Hudson serious about developing his craft?

B: He was very serious and very frustrated. I never had any indication that he was homosexual. He was a wonderful fellow to work with.

D: Do you have fond memories of *The Man from the Alamo*?

B: I don't have a lot of fond memories of any of the pictures I made at Universal, although *The Man from the Alamo* was a pretty good film. I'm sure the story wasn't true, but the picture was well done. Julie Adams was in that, and Glenn Ford was a pro. Any picture that Glenn was in, he made you feel that this was a legitimate show. He was so honest with what he did. The same was true of Van Heflin.

D: I was going to ask if you enjoyed working with Heflin on *Wings of the Hawk*.

B: Van was a pleasure to work with. He used to come up to me in the morning when we were on location and say, "Budd, is this a riding day or an acting day?" He would have the trunk of his car filled with beer and liquor. If I said, "It's a riding day," he'd go to his car and get a shot. If it was "an acting day," he'd never touch a drop until we finished work that evening.

D: Wasn't *Wings of the Hawk* released in 3-D?

B: Yes.

D: Did 3-D pose problems for you as director?

B: No, because I didn't shoot the picture in 3-D. And I got hell for it. After I left, the studio spent ten days on retakes, shooting 3-D stuff with another director to put into my picture. I didn't shoot the picture in 3-D because I saw Jack Warner stand in front of 250 or 300 producers and directors, hold a pair of 3-D glasses up in his hand, and say, "Ladies and gentlemen, I want to tell you that within one year every man, woman, and child in the United States will have his own personal pair of these glasses." I thought, "This is a lot of crap. Why do we have to have rocks fall on us and arrows shoot us in the eye and fire burn our noses to make good pictures?" So I shot the picture flat. I think that helped get me out of Universal more than anything else.

D: You made several films at Universal with Anthony Quinn. Was Quinn good to work with?

B: I made eight shows with Tony. He's one of my favorite friends and actors. I wrote what they eventually called *The Magnificent Matador*, a terrible title, for him. My title was *The Number One*, and Hollywood said it sounded like you had to go to the bathroom. I'd met Tony back when we were working on *Blood and Sand*.

D: Did you enjoy working with Maureen O'Hara on *The Magnificent Matador*?

B: Maureen O'Hara is the greatest lady I've ever directed. Now there's a big difference between Julie and Maureen. I was in love with Julie. Maureen is the most professional woman I've ever known. She knew everybody's dialogue. She could set the cameras if you wanted her to and change the lights. She got to the set and was ready to work right on the nose of the time she was supposed to be there. At six o'clock the chauffeur would drive up, she got in the car, and she went away and nobody knew where she went. She is a great lady, and I admire her tremendously.

D: You've said that Lucien Ballard was the best cameraman you ever worked with.

B: Lucien was one of the best ever. But Bill Clothier, Pev Marley, Russ Metty, and Charles Lawton were all great. I had a great relationship with them. If the director and the cameraman aren't in love with each other, it's going to cost the producer money and the production manager days. It has to be a romance, and there has to be a great understanding. I had that with Lucien and with my other cameramen.

D: Was it important to have your own supportive crew working with you?

B: You have to. You have to have people who are on your side, who really want to make a good movie. I had a crew of stuntmen at Universal and all through the pictures I made with Randolph Scott. There were about forty of us who could have won World War II by ourselves if they'd turned us loose. They were the most loyal bunch of guys. They would have died for me, and I for them. We really had a team. That was the problem at Universal. We fought to make better pictures, and nobody else cared. My nine pictures there were damned good, and they weren't supposed to be.

D: How would you describe the Budd Boetticher style?

B: Honest, tough. Perhaps unpredictable, because that's the point of telling the story.

D: Did you consider yourself primarily a storyteller?

B: I think I've always been a storyteller. I didn't get to tell a lot of the stories I wanted to tell.

D: How did you feel about *The Killer Is Loose*?

B: I made *The Killer Is Loose* for a very definite reason. The producers had an eighteen-day schedule, filming in black and white, and they had a pretty fair cast—Joseph Cotton, Wendell Corey, and Rhonda Fleming, an absolute delight and so beautiful. I read the script, and it was a good script. Lucien and I made the picture in fifteen days to stop the rumor that we were so concerned with artistry that we couldn't finish an assignment within the allotted schedule. It turned out to be a hell of a good picture!

D: Would you say that by 1956 Hollywood was beginning to change?

B: I wasn't aware of it. I wasn't aware of it for the reason that I never became a "big Hollywood director." I rode horses when other people played tennis or swam in Darryl Zanuck's pool. By 1956 I was doing pretty well and doing as I pleased.

D: How about the big studios? Were they declining?

B: That was never a problem for me. When I went to Warner Bros., people at the studio like Steve Trilling and Walter MacEwen, second and third in power, wondered why I got away with everything I did. They forgot that Jack Warner's stepdaughter was my leading lady in *Bullfighter and the Lady*. They forgot that *Seven Men from Now*, a Warner Bros. release, was considered in Europe maybe the best Western ever. And I was making a gangster picture, which Warners had built their reputation on with Cagney, Bogart, Raft, and the rest. So with Jack Warner I could do no wrong.

D: *Seven Men from Now* was the first of the pictures you directed with Randolph Scott.

B: Yes, it was. Duke Wayne called me. He was making a picture with Jack Ford, and I was doing *Killer Is Loose*. Wayne said, "I've got a script I bought that I want you to read. If you like it, you can direct it." I took the script to lunch with me, and I read thirty-five pages. I walked back on the set, and Wayne was sitting there with a bunch of fellows. I said, "Duke, this is brilliant. I want to do it. I'd certainly like to meet the author." Wayne turned to the young man seated next to him and said, "Burt Kennedy, meet Budd Boetticher." Burt and I have been close friends ever since. I've worked with him every time I could.

D: Did you like location work?

B: I liked that better than anything. It's a lot cleaner, and the people are a lot happier and healthier. We went to Lone Pine and somebody said, "Why didn't you ever go to Monument Valley?" I said, "Well, I think Jack Ford covered Monument Valley pretty well." In Lone Pine, California, on one side of the road we had those wonderful lava rock formations, and on the other side we had deserts, lakes, and rivers. It was unbelievable, like two different countries. We did *Seven Men* there, we did *The Tall T* there, we did *Ride Lonesome* there, and we did *Comanche Station* there.

D: Did location work pose technical problems for you?

B: None at all. In the opening of *Ride Lonesome*, Lucien Ballard and I wanted to show how infinitesimal a person was in the frontier West. I wanted Randy Scott to be a half-inch high on a horse in miles and miles and miles of the West. So Lucien and I got up at four o'clock, got a limousine, and rode out to where the pack mules were. Then we climbed to the top of this mountain where we could see all of Lone Pine down below. I could see where the sun was going to come up in about another half-an-hour, but it was just beginning to glow. I looked at my watch and I said, "Lucien, quarter-to-seven tomorrow morning, right here, with a thirty-five lens." He said, "Wait a minute." He walked over about ten feet, he dug, and there was a spike. He said, "Come over here and take a look and see if maybe you like this angle better. Raoul Walsh and I made this shot twelve years ago." I said, with my usual arrogance, "I like mine better." Mine was only ten feet way, so it would have been the same shot.

D: Did you find Randolph Scott a rewarding actor?

B: I found him a rewarding friend. Randy and Burt Kennedy and I usually had dinner together when we were on location. If we had a young actor in the picture worth his salt, Randy would say, "He's a nice young fella. Let's give him some more dialogue." We did that time and again. Randy was one of the wealthiest men in Hollywood. He came into the business as a millionaire in the 1920s, and he was an absolute delight.

D: Did you work well with producer Harry Joe Brown?

B: He was great. Harry Joe had in the contract that he could come on the set and tell me what he thought about yesterday's rushes. But he never bothered me. He was a delightful, wonderful man. As a young person, just starting in the movie business, I found that my two best friends, the producer and the writer, with whom I had lunch every day and cocktails in the evening before filming started, disappeared the first day of shooting. Suddenly they were my deadly enemies. I was "destroying the writer's pearls" with my directing and spending the producer's money. That why I'm not making pictures any longer.

D: Did you enjoy working with Virginia Mayo on *Westbound*?

B: Not at all. She was a pain in the neck. Virginia Mayo, who was married to actor Michael O'Shea, decided that she wouldn't come to work one day. She'd been a star, and she had a right to be a prima donna. Maybe she was the most beautiful girl that Warner Bros. ever had under contract. But she didn't report to work one day, knowing that we had nothing else to shoot. Karen Steele was in the picture, and Karen had probably the greatest figure of anybody in Hollywood. In five minutes we devised a sequence where she ran out of the house to help her husband in a cotton nightgown and not much underneath. You couldn't see through it, but it was rather exciting. Then she played a touching scene with the husband. I rushed into the cutting room that night and cut the whole sequence for the picture. Miss Mayo came in the next morning and said, "Oh, I'm so sorry that you didn't have anything to shoot." I said, "Oh, no, we had a good day's work. What we shot wasn't in the script. Do you want to see it?" She saw the footage and was never absent again. I felt she thought that it was degrading to be in a Randolph Scott picture with Budd Boetticher directing and didn't owe us her support.

D: Was *The Rise and Fall of Legs Diamond* a favorite project of yours?

B: God, no! Again I had Karen Steele, the only person in the world I've really learned to hate, and Ray Danton, who at one time was married to Julie Adams and was no friend of mine. It was the most difficult picture I've ever been on in my life. *Legs Diamond* was produced by Milton Sperling, and it was a big hit. Somehow I worked harder when I didn't like the people.

D: How did you feel about directing for television?

B: I think television is not a director's medium, you don't have the time. I made the *Maverick* pilot. I liked Jim Garner so much that after the first *Maverick* I did three others on a six-day schedule. Besides having so little time, there really isn't enough money to do quality work in television.

D: It's interesting to me that the film directors who seemed to make an easy transition to television had been B directors in movies.

B: Yes, because they never got success, and they'd put up with a lot of crap. A star of a television series isn't going to let a director, who comes in to direct every third show, tell him what to do. Television directors are hired by the star's company to do the job, and they do the best they can.

D: You directed three or four episodes of *The Dick Powell Show*.

B: Yes, for one specific reason. I got a call one day from Dick Powell. I was married to Debra Paget at the time. She was in Europe and I was pretty miserable. Powell said, "I'm really not well and I have to make five Westerns this year to keep my series alive." He asked me to direct them and I was flattered. Dick Powell was something! So was Aaron Spelling, the producer.

D: How did you feel about the film *A Time for Dying*?

B: *A Time for Dying* was made specifically to get Audie Murphy out of a lot of trouble financially. I made it, and we never thought it would be released. The picture paid off some gambling debts Audie had. I had two real schmucks—the leading man and the leading lady—in the picture because they were cheap. I had Victor Jory, whom I liked and who did a hell of a good job as Judge Roy Bean, and Robert Random, who played Billy the Kid about as well as anyone could. We made the picture in eighteen days. It was discovered in Europe and got great reviews. It wasn't one of my favorite pictures, but it did what I wanted it to do for Audie. Audie didn't drink and he didn't smoke, but he gambled. If you and Audie and I were driving in an open car through Texas, he'd stop with two birds on a fence and bet you a hundred to one that the bird on the left would fly off first. He had to have action.

D: You wrote the original story for *Two Mules for Sister Sara*. Did you view that as a special project?

B: I thought it was going to be a great picture. It had a disaster for a producer, and neither he nor the director understood the story.

Clint Eastwood was wrong for the part. I think Clint is a better direc-tor than he is an actor. I'm a little tired of that bravado. I wrote the part for Bob Mitchum. *Two Mules for Sister Sara* could have been a wonderful picture. It was a sweet story. Shirley MacLaine, who is one of my favorite actresses, was not a believable nun. She wasn't the nun I wrote. Shirley's nun was smoking cigars and drinking liquor. Mine was a credible nun until the last two minutes of the picture.

D: Do you think that your approach to filmmaking changed over the years?

B: I think it vastly improved. I think I've been a very good director on a lot of pictures. I don't think I ever had the opportunity to be a great director. I went to Mexico again because I honestly felt that I had failed. Nothing was happening with my career. I was indignant about that. I went to Mexico to make *Arruza* and I expected to be gone six months. I was gone seven years. I knew that this was a sub-ject nobody could do better than I could, because I'd been a torero and owned bullfight horses.

D: Do you feel that your professional life contributed to your personal development?

B: I was married four times before I met Mary, my present wife. If I'd married Mary the first time that would have been my first divorce, because she wouldn't have put up with the fellow I was then. By the time I got to Mary, thank God, I'd grown up. Maybe my business helped, certainly the difficulties I had did. I learned to be tender as well as tough. And I think there's a lot of tenderness in my pictures. I think everything in your life contributes to your personal growth, but I don't think you grow up until you have the intelligence to realize that you *need* to grow up.

D: What's your attitude on the *auteur* theory of filmmaking? Do you think the director is the ultimate author of a film?

B: Yes, I think so. The writer has to contribute a great deal, but if the director doesn't improve a perfect script, he or she is no director. If you destroy a script, then you should never direct again.

D: What is your assessment of Hollywood today?

B: The art has gone out of the industry I think. It's hard today to be nice in Hollywood. The only people with whom I fought were producers and heads of studios that could fire me. Once you've been fired, and we all have, you discover that it isn't so bad. You'll live through it if you have any talent. But I think fear is the big problem in Hollywood, always has been. Maybe if I'd been smarter, I wouldn't have been so brave.

Budd Boetticher's Feature Films

1944   *One Mysterious Night*
       The Missing Juror
1945   *Youth on Trial*
       A Guy, a Gal and a Pal
       Escape in the Fog
1948   *The Fleet That Came to Stay*
       Assigned to Danger
       Behind Locked Doors
1949   *Black Midnight*
       Wolf Hunters
1950   *Killer Shark*
1951   *The Bullfighter and the Lady*
       The Sword of D'Artagnan
       The Cimarron Kid
1952   *Bronco Buster*
       Red Ball Express
       Horizons West
1953   *City Beneath the Sea*
       Seminole
       The Man from the Alamo
       Wings of the Hawk
       East of Sumatra
1955   *The Magnificent Matador*
1956   *The Killer Is Loose*
       Seven Men from Now

1957   *The Tall T*
       Decision at Sundown
1958   *Buchanan Rides Alone*
1959   *Ride Lonesome*
       Westbound
1960   *Comanche Station*
       The Rise and Fall of Legs Diamond
1971   *A Time for Dying*
       Arruza (documentary)

INDEX

223